THE
POLITICAL
INFLUENCE
OF THE
BRITISH
MONARCHY
1868–1952

By the same author
THE POLITICAL INFLUENCE OF QUEEN VICTORIA 1861–1901

THE POLITICAL INFLUENCE OF THE BRITISH MONARCHY

1868–1952

FRANK HARDIE

HARPER & ROW, PUBLISHERS
New York and Evanston

To Sir John Masterman

Contents

Contents

Acknowledgments

My thanks are in the first place due to Her Majesty the Queen for gracious permission to use information obtained from the Royal Archives. In the second place I should like to thank Mr R. W. Mackworth-Young, Librarian at Windsor Castle, and his staff, for their constant patience and painstaking trouble in solving problems, both large and small. My typescript was also read by Mrs Miriam Alman, Miss M. K. Ashby, Professor Max Beloff, Mr Roger Fulford, Sir Alan Lascelles and Dr Paul Smith. I am very grateful for their criticisms, which led to many changes. Professor Fred Leventhal in a Harvard thesis made criticisms of my previous monograph on Queen Victoria which were stimulating and acceptable. For all errors of fact or judgment I, however, of course remain entirely responsible.

Through the kindness of Mary Lady Trevelyan some of the writing was done at Wallington. The shades of Macaulay and George Otto Trevelyan were over-mighty competitors, but I did my best. As a former Harmsworth Scholar I enjoyed the privilege of two spells of work at Merton College. For this, and for much friendliness, hospitality and mental stimulation, I express my gratitude to the Warden and Fellows. I am grateful to Mrs P. Hannay for compiling the Index.

F.H.

18 Kensington Gate,   *19 August 1969*
London, w8

...although the admirable arrangements of the Constitution have now completely shielded the Sovereign from personal responsibility, they have left ample scope for the exercise of a direct and personal responsibility in the whole work of government. The amount of that influence must vary greatly, according to character, to capacity, to experience in affairs, to tact in the application of a pressure which never is to be carried to extremes, to patience in keeping up the continuity of a multitudinous supervision.... Subject to the range of these variations, the Sovereign, as compared with her Ministers, has...the advantages of long experience, wide survey, elevated position, and entire disconnection from the bias of party...there is not a doubt that the aggregate of direct influence normally exercised by the Sovereign upon the counsels and proceedings of her Ministers is considerable in amount, tends to permanence and solidity of action, and confers much benefit on the country, without in the smallest degree relieving the advisers of the Crown from their undivided responsibility.

W. E. Gladstone
(*in The Contemporary Review, June 1875*)

I

Introduction

SUBJECT AND SOURCES

The political role of the reigning Sovereign is, of all the processes of the British Constitution, that least known to contemporaries. This is true of our present Queen and has been true of the five preceding reigns. The innermost arcana of defence and foreign policy are not more closely guarded. The darkness in which the subject is enveloped is generally lightened only by death—by the posthumous publication, that is to say, of the biographies or memoirs of those concerned or of the rawer material of their papers. There is never enough information about it to enable a contemporary (unless in a special coign of vantage, such as, most obviously, the Prime Minister) to make a reasoned assessment of the position. Indeed the gap between the appearance of royal politics to the multitude and their reality, known at the time to a few people only, may, as will be seen in the case of Queen Victoria, be huge. There can seldom have been a bigger political secret than this, or one so well kept. Indeed, the full extent of her political influence could only for the first time be properly appreciated, 31 years after her death, with the completion in 1932 of the publication of *The Letters of Queen Victoria*. The *éminence grise* of the Victorian Constitution was Victoria herself.

As a political animal one may, and for good reasons, be content with this secrecy about the political role of the reigning Sovereign. For a historical animal, however, the case is altered. It is right that the political roles of past Sovereigns should be known, whether or not morals are to be drawn for the present and future.

For our knowledge of this subject gratitude must be expressed and credit mainly go to successive Sovereigns. They have been most liberal about the use allowed to be made of their archives; the '50 years rule' (now a 30 years one[1]) was never applied by them. Indeed A. J. P. Taylor cautions us against allowing this loophole in the rule to magnify the royal role.[2]

Edward VII decided, on Lord Esher's advice,[3] that there should not be an official biography of his mother. Probably there never will be one.* As an alternative, however, an extensive selection of her letters and of entries from her journal was published between 1907 and, as we have just seen, 1932. This series was importantly supplemented the next year by two volumes of correspondence between the Queen and Gladstone, edited by Philip Guedalla. The four volumes of correspondence between Gladstone and Granville, covering the years 1868–86, so splendidly edited by Agatha Ramm, supply much confirmatory detail. The Queen spoke, or rather, wrote her mind about politics more freely to Sir Henry Ponsonby (her Private Secretary from 1870 to 1895) than to anyone else, and the many quotations from these uninhibited letters give great importance to Arthur Ponsonby's life of his father.

The Victorian period was the great age of political letter-writing. Politicians then carefully explained their attitudes and actions in writing, and as carefully kept copies of what they wrote. This is a main reason for the vast mass of original material published on our subject. For the Edwardian and later periods there has not been the same amount of correspondence to publish. Not only did the instinct to write and pre-

* The most up-to-date, fullest, authoritative and very readable biography is Lady Longford's *Victoria, R.I.* The literary quality and much of the psychology of Lytton Stracheys *Queen Victoria* have more than stood the test of time

serve diminish, but the telephone entered politics. At 10.15 p.m. on 17 June 1895, the Prime Minister telephoned the Chief Whip to ask what was going on in the House of Commons;[4] maybe earlier instances are known of what formerly would have been written being spoken along a wire.

So far as this study is concerned, however, just when correspondence begins to diminish biographical evidence becomes more authoritative. An official *Life of Edward VII* was published in two volumes between 1925 and 1927. Sir Philip Magnus' brilliant biography is a more than worthy successor to it. Sir Harold Nicolson's superlatively good official biography of George V appeared in 1952. In the nature of the case colouring as dramatic would have been inappropriate in depicting George VI, but Sir John Wheeler-Bennett's official biography of him, appearing in 1958, is invaluable. The Duke of Windsor has told his own story. Of other biographical sources high and special praise must be given to the revised versions of Asquith, Disraeli, Gladstone and Rosebery recently given us by Roy Jenkins, Robert Blake, Sir Philip Magnus and Robert Rhodes James respectively.

On the subject of sources, I cannot resist making one penultimate point. The correspondence of Queen Victoria may at first sight seem a huge quarry of a rather rough stone; in fact it is a diamond mine. Her memorable remarks are scarce ('He speaks to me as if I was a public meeting' is not authenticated), her epigrams non-existent, but the revelation of her character and the highly personal style make her letters preeminently readable. Indeed the taste of this particular literary dish is notably 'moreish' and, once acquired, can never be completely satisfied. Indications of this truth appear, I hope, in the quotations from the Queen's writings in the ensuing chapters. Meanwhile, just as a good tutor seeks to encourage his pupil to read more widely by discriminating recommendations, I make (for the benefit of the uninitiated) this one, specially strong, recommendation of the same kind.

On sources it should finally be said that the published material becomes thinner the nearer one gets to the present. This is always true of the recent past, as one waits for biographies, autobiographies and diaries to be published. On the other hand, as the past becomes more remote, so does the published material about it normally tend to increase. In the case of this particular subject, however, this is not the normal process, for as the political influence of the Monarchy has declined, material about that subject can only be, *pro tanto*, smaller at the source. All in all, however, enough information is now available to enable us to see in perspective the political roles of Victoria, Edward VII, George V, Edward VIII and George VI; to trace the story from the reign of Elizabeth II's great-great-grandmother to that of her father. It is the availability of this information which has stimulated me to attempt the synthesis which follows.

It is only right, however, that its limits should be defined as clearly as possible. The painter's paper, or canvas, defines the area of his picture. The title of my picture shows that my canvas can hardly be other than large, but I must explain the principles on which I have decided the precise size to which it is to be cut.

The most important of these principles is to distinguish as sharply as possible between royal influence and royal power and describe the operation of the former and not of the latter. For this decision there are two reasons. In the first place the political power of the Monarchy had virtually disappeared before my starting date. In the second, the use of what remained of that power is clearly set out in other books. My aim is not a book which could be an extract on the Monarchy from a constitutional history of England. Such a book would be concerned primarily with the vestigial remains of the Prerogative and in such a book it would be right to dwell on such matters as, for example, the abolition of Army Purchase by Royal Warrant in 1871, the decision to appoint Rosebery as Prime Minister in 1894, the choice of Baldwin rather than Curzon for that position in 1923, and so on. In fact it will be seen that about these and similar matters I have said little or nothing. This is because my aim is to direct more light on the parts of the iceberg normally submerged rather than on a surface which already glitters in the sun. In other words, my exact subject is the day-to-day role of the British Monarchy in politics. This subject is subtle, but my handling of it will, I hope, say something useful and fresh to the reader.

Other parts of my self-imposed terms of reference can be more briefly set out. I have interpreted 'politics' narrowly, that is to say I have wholly excluded consideration of the Monarchy's influence in Church affairs, whilst finding it impossible wholly to exclude consideration of its influence in Army and Navy affairs. The role of the Crown as Fountain of Honour has its political side, but that too has been excluded. I have also drawn a line against any discussion of the relations between successive Sovereigns and Dominion Prime Ministers. An understanding of the role of successive Private Secretaries is an aid to understanding the role of their employers, but the Private Secretaryship is a subject in itself and I hope we will soon have a first-class book on it. The same is true of the role of what Lord Palmerston called 'unofficial advisers'. Another separate and excluded subject is that of public opinion about the Monarchy. It is relevant to my theme in the sense that the more popular the Monarchy the greater can be its political influence. Here, however, its popularity and unpopularity are only fleetingly discussed. The subject of the social role of the Monarchy is plainly of the utmost importance and the more its political influence declines the greater becomes the importance of that role. Plainly too, however, that again is a separate subject for a separate volume. Let me lastly say that I have resisted temptations to point, in various places, or in an epilogue, some morals for the present day which might be drawn from this account of the past. Here I let the historical facts to the best of my ability speak for themselves.

CHOICE OF DATES

The ending date for any serious study of the political role of the British Monarchy always settles itself. It is bound to be that up to which information adequate for the purpose is available. That is now the date, 6 February 1952, of the death of George VI, and that, therefore, is the date up to which this study is carried.

The choice of the date from which to start such a study is, on the other hand, difficult. Any choice is bound to be in a sense arbitrary.

When I wrote about the subject previously, I chose 1861 as a starting-point for a number of reasons.[5] The principal one, the fact of much fresh information having just become available on the period from 1861 to 1901, no longer holds good. The information which is now fresh is, for the most part, about the period from 1901 to 1952. None the less, having done my best to explore and map the 1861–1901 territory, I have decided to start my new journey by travelling the same road again, though starting a little further along it, in the year 1868, for reasons shortly to be explained. The principal features to be seen from this road seem unchanged. Indeed, that was only to be expected unless my mapping had been much at fault. But the interval between the two expeditions has been used for adding to the material brought back from the first one and for the sorting of the material as a whole. It seems a pity that this revisory work should be wasted. In short, a journey further up the road and the consequential mapping of a larger area is being used to redraw the old map on a new scale. On the one hand, much detail can be omitted; on the other the principal features, however unchanged in essence, can be depicted in truer colours and more exact proportions. Sometimes I draw my reader's attention in a footnote to the fuller material in the earlier book.

There are strong reasons for choosing 1868 rather than 1861 as a starting date. In 1861 Lord Palmerston was Prime Minister, for the second time. He died in office four years later at the age of 80. He had formed his Government in 1859. In a sense it was the first Liberal Government and, as such, not altogether welcome to the Queen and the Prince.[6] But the Conservative Leader, Lord Derby (the 14th Earl) shrewdly described him as 'a Conservative Minister working with Radical tools and keeping up a show of Liberalism in his foreign policy'.[7] So far as home affairs were concerned, Palmerston did nothing in particular and did it very well. The Queen's Speech of 1863 did not announce any legislation. The Election of 1865 was fought on the cry of 'Palmerston and no principles'. The State's slumbers were only disturbed by the reforming zeal of the Chancellor of the Exchequer, W. E. Gladstone. In foreign affairs these years of Palmerston's second Premiership were marked by the Schleswig-Holstein crisis of 1863–4. The matter was one about which the Queen held strong views, and they prevailed. They did so, however, not so much because they were her views as because they were shared by a powerful party in the Cabinet, headed by Gladstone.[8] His role on this occasion delighted the Queen.[9] There is no special significance, therefore, in the history of this episode in foreign policy considered as one in the history of the political influence of Queen Victoria.

Palmerston was succeeded, briefly, by Lord John Russell (the first Earl Russell), aged 78, the last Whig Prime Minister.

(He lived until 1878, but never held office again.) Lord Derby was Prime Minister from June 1866 until February 1868, when, because of ill-health, he gave way to Disraeli. In other words, there was at this time one of those 'changes of generation' in political life which Bagehot rightly thought important.[10] The entire generation of pre-1832 statesmen had left the stage: Wellington, Melbourne, Peel, Aberdeen, Palmerston were dead; Russell and Derby retired. The latter had been born in 1799 and first entered the Cabinet in 1831. After 1868 there were no statesmen to whose opinions the Queen needed to defer on the grounds of greater age or experience. Disraeli and Gladstone were both older than Victoria, but her accession had preceded their entry into the Cabinet. Gladstone indeed had first held office under William IV, but he was far from feeling any sense of seniority over the Queen. By his own account he dreaded his first personal introduction to her as much as he had dreaded his first meeting with his Headmaster.[11] General Grey, a bolder Private Secretary than his successor, Sir Henry Ponsonby, died in 1870. Of the entire pre-1868 circle of the Queen's advisers only the Dean of Windsor, Wellesley, continued in office for any appreciable length of time thereafter, until 1882.

By 1868, too, the Party kaleidoscope had reset in the traditional pattern of a two-party system; a period of loose and shifting Party groupings dating back to 1846 had ended. Before 1868 it was not true, as after that date for a long time it was, as Sir Llewellyn Woodward reminds us:[12]

> *That every boy and every gal*
> *That's born into the world alive*
> *Is either a little Liberal*
> *Or else a little Conservative.*

In other words there began in 1868 the regular rhythm of government alternating, basically, between Liberal and Conservative Parties, which (with the exception of the Coalition

Governments of 1915–22) prevailed until the first Labour Government in 1924, the subsequent alternation being (with the exception of the 1940–45 Coalition) basically between the Labour and Conservative Parties. An incidental consequence of the return to a two-party system was an enhancement of the power of the House of Lords in which the Tories had had a majority since the turn of the century. Thus a Liberal majority in the House of Commons was always faced by a Conservative majority in the House of Lords, and a constitutional crisis between the two Houses, involving the Crown, was in those circumstances always a possibility. On the other hand the return to a two-party system of itself diminished the power of the Crown to the extent that it had less room for manoeuvre on a change of Government in picking and choosing between parties and persons.

More important, however, in this context, than the change in the Party system, was the passing of the second Reform Bill in 1867. Each Party thereafter was based on a vast popular electorate. In 1867 the Crown and what was then called 'American democracy' confronted each other for the first time.

By a fortuitous but, for author and reader, a fortunate coincidence, 1867 was the year not only of the second Reform Act but also of the publication of Bagehot's *English Constitution*. Thus, as we stand on the threshold of the period to be studied, we stand also in the most favourable possible position for seeing what was at that time supposed to be the political role of the Queen.[13] Bagehot's guidebook in hand, theory and practice can easily be checked against each other at the start of the journey to be made. We do not know whether the Queen read this book; we do know that the Duke of York made careful notes of what the author had to say about the Monarchy,[14] and, as George v, quoted him to his Prime Minister.[15] When the Queen one day found her grandson reading Bagehot's 'economic

essays' she was quite displeased that he should be studying
such a radical writer.[16]

A minor constitutional innovation recognised the new constitutional realities brought into being by the Reform Act. Disraeli resigned as Prime Minister on 1 December 1868, not
because he had been beaten by a vote of the House of Commons but because he had been beaten by the popular vote in
the Election held in November. He was the first Prime Minister to resign because of a defeat at the polls. By the end of the
century the rarity was for a Prime Minister to surrender office
to his opponents for any other reason.[17]

The new Prime Minister was Gladstone. He had begun his
political career as a Tory. He had been Member for a most
Conservative constituency, the University of Oxford, from
1847 to 1865. Palmerston had thought him a 'dangerous man'.
'Keep him in Oxford', he said, 'and he is partially muzzled;
but send him elsewhere and he will run wild.'[18] Did these
words, one wonders, come to Gladstone's ears? He no more
cared for Palmerston than Palmerston did for him. The day
after his electoral defeat at Oxford (18 July 1865) he spoke at
the Free Trade Hall at Manchester and said: 'At last, my
friends, I am come amongst you. And I am come... un-
muzzled.'[19] ('Muzzling' was in the political air, Lord Derby
having compared Roman Catholics to dogs that ought to be
muzzled.[20]) Now Member for Greenwich, Leader of the Liberal
Party, and with a Parliamentary majority of 112, the first clear-
cut majority since 1841, Gladstone had his first audience with
Queen Victoria as Prime Minister at Windsor Castle on
3 December 1868.

2

Victoria

POLITICAL ATTITUDES

The Queen whose hand Gladstone kissed on first becoming
Prime Minister in 1868 was, for all practical purposes, a Conservative. She had begun as a Whig; he, as we have seen, as
a Tory. In the Prince Consort's time both had been Peelites.
By now, however, they were moving apart in their political
views, he to the Left and she to the Right—not that that
nomenclature was then used. He was a Peelite turned Liberal,*
she a Peelite turned Palmerstonian, and Palmerston, be it remembered, was, *pace* Mr Blake, 'A Whig who was in many
ways more Tory than the Tories. . . .'[1] Queen and commoner,
as they got older, became not more mellow but more partisan.
She, indeed, had always been hot-tempered.[2] As late as December 1870, however, he saw her as 'a kind of high impartial
counsellor to the Cabinet . . .'.[3] From Disraeli's death in 1881†
until Gladstone's final retirement in 1894 he and the Queen
became 'the fell incensed points' of the 'mighty opposites' of
Conservatism and Liberalism. The beginning of the war between them, fought in private, cannot be precisely dated. But
it lasted longer and was more dramatic than even the great
public conflict between Gladstone and Disraeli.

The barometer was not exactly set 'fair' in 1868, but it was

---

* He described himself, in *Dod's Parliamentary Companion*, as a Liberal
Conservative as late as 1870

† He became Earl of Beaconsfield on 12 August 1876, but I follow Robert
Blake in calling him Disraeli throughout

not set 'stormy'. The storms came, however; a small one in
1871, a great one in 1872. The sad paradox is that, both times,
what made the wind begin to roll was Gladstone's intense
royalism. The Queen's seclusion had made her unpopular and
he, therefore, pressed her to be seen to be doing her duty. In
1871 it was only a question of her postponing her departure
for Balmoral for a few days because Parliament was still sitting. She took extreme umbrage at this request and refused it
absolutely.* When, later, the Prime Minister visited the Queen
at Balmoral he felt himself on 'a new and different footing with
her. . . . The repellent power which she so well knows how to
use, has been put in action towards me on this occasion for the
first time since the formation of the Government'.[5] He remained, however, deeply concerned by what he called 'the
royalty question'. He told his sister, on New Year's Day 1872,
that it was only to solve it that he stayed in public life.[6] Judging
that he could not solve it through the Queen, he tried to do so
through the Prince of Wales. He proposed the abolition of the
Lord Lieutenancy of Ireland and the residence of the Prince
in Dublin for four or five months every year as the Queen's
representative. This was a major, far-sighted, and most states-
manlike proposal. Its adoption would have increased the popularity of the royal family, provided employment for the Prince
of Wales, and perhaps also have made a contribution to the
pacification of Ireland. The Queen firmly closed her mind to
this proposal of her Prime Minister and the Prince was too
stupid or lazy or cowardly to back him up.

The decisive break between Victoria and Gladstone came in

* By contrast Disraeli in 1874 persuaded the Queen to postpone her departure for Balmoral by two days so that she could meet the Tsar: 'My head
is still on my shoulders. The great lady has absolutely postponed her departure! Everybody had failed, even the Prince of Wales; but she averted
her head from me... at the drawing room to-day, and I have no doubt
I am not in favour. I can't help it. Salisbury says I have saved an Afghan
War, and Derby complimented me on my unrivalled triumph. . . .'[4]

1876. The Queen was not rabidly anti-Russian when the Eastern
crisis broke, but she soon became so. Critical as she was of
Disraeli's insufficient bellicosity, Gladstone's emergence from
retirement and his first Midlothian campaign were for her a
treacherous stab in the back, not only of her Prime Minister,
but of herself and of the country.[7] Country and Queen, moreover, tended to be one and the same for her.* Disraeli did not
denigrate his rival to her; there was no need for him to do so.
As against Gladstone she identified herself completely with
the Government. It was not just *a* Government or *the* Government but *her* Government which Gladstone attacked. This
revolutionised her attitude to him; for this she never forgave
him. She had been a Conservative partisan before 1876; after
that date she was a ferocious one. One may guess that her
attitudes were hardened by Disraeli's death in 1881. It is certain that what specially incensed her was that it was over
foreign affairs that her Government was attacked:

> The Queen has never made any secret of her disapproval
> and indignation at Mr Gladstone's conduct and that of his
> followers and General Ponsonby may repeat it to anyone—
> as it is totally different to Home affairs and thus future
> interests of this country are imperilled by his conduct.[9]

When, therefore, Gladstone became Prime Minister for the
second time in 1880, the barometer was at its lowest point. It
was a year earlier that Sir Charles Dilke wrote quite bluntly
of her (was anyone else as blunt?): 'She is a Conservative.'[10]
When, in 1886, Gladstone espoused the cause of Irish Home
Rule, so many fires were already blazing that this fresh and
potent fuel could hardly make the flames leap higher. Home
Rule for Ireland was a new issue in British politics. It broke up

---

* 'Windsor Castle, April 18, 1880. I saw Lord Beaconsfield at ½ pt. 12.
After remarks on the sad and startling result of the elections... I asked him
what he advised me to do for the real good of the country, which we both
agreed was inseparable from my own....'[8]

the previous Party pattern. If the Queen had changed her attitude to Gladstone and Liberalism because of this seismic disturbance, that change would have been understandable. In
fact, as we have seen, the Queen's utter detestation of Gladstone and all that he stood for ante-dated his raising of the
Home Rule banner by a decade. One cannot make allowances
for the Queen's ferocious partisanship by holding it to be the
product of a sudden and sharp dissent from a major change of
policy suddenly presented.

It might be objected that evidence of the Queen's love of
Disraeli and hatred, and jealousy, of Gladstone (the terms are
by no means too strong) is not evidence of Conservatism, only
of politics seen as a conflict between politicians, and two in
particular, rather than policies. But her likes and dislikes
among the politicians of her reign were not limited to these
two men; they were almost as strong in other cases. The personal element in these feelings was, in a way to her credit,
fused with the political. Statistically, in other words, she liked
more Conservative than Liberal politicians. And her likes and
dislikes waxed and waned in relation to the political views and
actions of their objects. Thus Joseph Chamberlain was Gladstone's 'evil genius'[11] in 1882 and 'a dreadful socialist'[12] in 1885
but came into high favour after his break with Gladstone.[13]
Thus, too, Granville, whom she and the Prince would have
liked to have had as Prime Minister in 1859,[14] and who was in
favour throughout Gladstone's first Ministry,[15] was completely
out of favour as Gladstone's Foreign Secretary and principal
political ally in 1882. To Ponsonby she complained 'bitterly'
of 'the want of respect and consideration for her views' of Ministers, '... especially Ld Granville who she has known *so long*
and who lately *ignores* all her remarks! She feels *hurt* & *indignant*, as he is the *only* friend (tho' he has never *really*
proved to be that) or at least the only *person* she has been in
the habit of speaking out to in the Cabinet.'[16] Both Granville

and Hartington committed the crime of opposing the Royal Titles Bill in the House of Lords, but as her opinion of Granville went down, so her opinion of Hartington went up. By December 1882 he was singled out among Ministers as 'the most straightforward and reliable and far less radical'.[17] In 1885 the Queen 'very properly vetoed'[18] the return of Granville to the Foreign Office. By then his powers were failing. Hartington joined Chamberlain as one of the leaders of Liberal Unionism. The Queen told Hartington that she regretted his decision not to join Lord Salisbury's Ministry in August 1886.[19]

A third example of the dominance of political over personal considerations in royal relationships with politicians can be clearly seen in Victoria's relations with Rosebery. She had a considerable affection for him as a person, but became markedly cold to him after the Midlothian campaign.[20] It was largely on her insistence that he was made Foreign Secretary in Gladstone's third Cabinet in 1886, and he was her personal choice as Prime Minister when Gladstone finally resigned in 1894. As Foreign Secretary Rosebery strove for 'continuity of policy'[21] and his work was highly approved of by the Queen. (It was a signal mark of royal favour at that time that, asking her to open an exhibition 'with all pomp' she replied: 'With all the pomp you like—as long as I don't have to wear a low dress.'[22] All the same she would not wear a crown, but only a bonnet.[23]) As Prime Minister, however, as he had foreseen,[24] Rosebery and the Queen fell to quarrelling, especially about the role of the House of Lords, in much the same way as she and Gladstone had done.[25] After Gladstone's resignation 'in spite of the Queen's special liking for Lord Rosebery, her language, as far as we see it in her communications to her Private Secretary, was as violent as ever'.[26] It was not fundamentally to Liberal men that the Queen objected, but to Liberal measures, Liberal policies and Liberal attitudes.[27] It is extraordinary that Gladstone should so ceaselessly have pondered his bad relations with his Sovereign without, apparently, perceiving this basic truth: a rare instance, perhaps—to invert his own language—of his being so eager upon persons as to forget what was due to things.[28]

We have seen Gladstone entering Windsor Castle on 3 December 1868, for his first audience as Prime Minister. On the 1st he had been in the grounds of his country house, Hawarden Castle in Flintshire, when he was handed a telegram announcing the impending arrival of the Queen's Private Secretary. 'Very significant', said Gladstone. Plainly General Grey's mission was to ask him, rather than Russell, to become Prime Minister. 'My mission', he said next, 'is to pacify Ireland.' It was the prime occupation of the rest of his life. For a time, however, he thought the 'royalty question' even more important than the Irish one.[29]

He was already committed to the disestablishment of the Irish Church. This measure was distasteful to the Queen, but she gave her new Prime Minister invaluable help in the role of mediator with the Anglican hierarchy and the House of Lords, so much so that at the end of the day he wrote, in a letter to Granville:

> Pray combine my thanks with your own for the powerful and valuable aid which she imparted through the Dean [of Windsor]: always of course within the limits of the constitution.[30]

In this political transaction the Queen, in short, showed to great advantage. Once thereafter did she show to similar advantage, as a mediator, in 1884, between the two Parties and the two Houses, over the Franchise Bill. We shall return[31] to this second act of mediation on a major issue (an 'eruption into politics... on the grand scale and entirely beneficial in its results'[32]) in due course. Meanwhile, however, one has to note the appalling contrast between the Queen's mediation over the third Reform Bill and her violent opposition to the first Home Rule Bill. In 1885, with a Conservative Prime Minister, Salisbury, at that moment prepared at any rate to consider Home Rule, she had a magnificent opportunity to use her influence to settle the Irish question once and for all. In fact, she was so anti-Irish that the Prime Minister held it 'to be inexpedient' to tell her of his negotiation, through his Home Rule Viceroy in Dublin (Lord Carnarvon) with Parnell.[33] But if this vital item of information was kept from her, she knew well enough in a general way what was going on. Carnarvon wrote from Windsor to Lord Salisbury on 25 November 1885:

> I found H.M. very much alive to the whole subject, and desirous both of knowing the state of affairs and my own opinion.... I find Beach [Chancellor of the Exchequer] has spoken very strongly to the Queen in the direction of great concessions to Irish sentiment, and the Queen is, I think, quite aware of the different modes of treatment of which the subject is susceptible.[34]

Ponsonby, in January 1886, pressed on her the idea of an agreed Salisbury–Gladstone–Parnell Irish settlement, but she took that idea lamentably lightly.[35] She opened Parliament in person in January 1886, by way of demonstrating her support for Lord Salisbury who had by then come down against Home Rule. The Queen's Speech she read on that occasion contains an anti-Home Rule passage couched in strong and personal terms.[36]

Thus the Queen missed a unique chance of exercising her influence on the grandest possible scale. It was an important turning-point. All the terrible Anglo-Irish troubles of the next 50 years might have been averted.

Not only did she not seek to mediate, she actively opposed the Home Rule Bill. She was indeed in opposition to Gladstone's third Government.[37] She wrote to Hartington praising and thanking him for a speech against the first Home Rule Bill.[38] As the climax to the Home Rule debate came nearer, she showed Salisbury copies of all Gladstone's important letters to her and many of her answers.[39] On 10 May she wrote to Salisbury:

> There is one *vital point* which she hopes Lord Salisbury, Lord Hartington and Mr Goschen will *fully consider* and which must *not* be *tolerated*. It is the withdrawal of the Bill, for Mr Gladstone to bring it forward again next year. . . . Pray advise me how to protest against such a fearful danger and *possibility* and consult *together* how this contingency can be stopped.[40]

For the Sovereign to ask the Leader of the Opposition for such advice is truly, as Lady Longford comments, 'a strange thing'.[41] When the defeat of the Bill seemed inevitable she asked Salisbury whether she should grant a request from Gladstone for a dissolution.[42] Six years later, when the second round was fought, her attitude was as firmly anti-Home Rule as ever; she refused to have the second Bill described in the Queen's Speech as a measure for the 'better government' of Ireland.[43]

'Poor Ireland. It holds but a small place in her heart.' So wrote Gladstone on resigning office in August 1886.[44] If it had held the same place as Scotland, the history of Anglo-Irish relations would have been substantially different.[45] As it was, the Irish were for her what the Americans had been to her grandfather, George III.[46] Failure to draw on the fund of loyalty she initially held in Ireland* was, according to G. M. Young, the gravest error of her life.[49] In 1893 she vetoed a proposal for an Irish visit by the Duke and Duchess of York (the future King George v and Queen Mary), telling Ponsonby 'in so many words that no member of the Royal Family should visit Ire-

---

* In 1849 as a young mother she had charmed a largely hostile Dublin,[47] as her son charmed a largely hostile Paris in 1903[48]

land so long as a Home Rule Government was in office ...'.[50] Her grandson, we shall see,[51] more than made up for his grandmother's sins of omission over Ireland.

This summary of the Queen's role in Irish affairs opened with the Disestablishment Bill of 1869. From time to time thereafter the idea was mooted of disestablishing the Church of Scotland. The Queen made clear her position about this as early as possible: 'I would never give way about *the Scottish Church*, which is the real and true stronghold of Protestantism'.[52] She was as vehemently opposed to Welsh Disestablishment. No sooner had Rosebery become Prime Minister than there was a sharp difference of opinion between him and the Queen about the proposed mention in the Queen's Speech of Bills for the Disestablishment of the Scottish and Welsh Churches. To Ponsonby he threatened resignation,[53] but the difference was patched up by a change in the wording.

The Queen was much more interested in the Army than in the Navy.[54] She considered the Navy a 'most distasteful profession ... the worst for morals and everything that can be imagined'.[55] She told Lord Rosebery that '... not caring about being on the sea, I have always had a special feeling for the Army'.[56] It was, however, noted as late as 1900, with the Boer War raging, that a new Secretary of State for War's 'main trouble will be with the older generation of soldiers and with the Crown. The Navy is a constitutional force. Every commission is signed by the Board. The Army is a royal force and, while the Queen never interferes with the Navy, she interferes* very much with the Army. As she listens to soldiers rather than to Ministers, the task of the Secretary of State for War is never easy.'[58] The Queen herself admitted that she listened to soldiers rather than to War Secretaries. She spoke out clearly in that sense to a Maid of Honour, who was much embarrassed

---

* The same verb had been used by Dilke in a larger context[57]

by this confidence. Her Ministers, she said, 'do not take my
advice or the advice of experts about the Army and civilians
cannot understand military matters; General Peel was by far
the best and strongest Minister of War we ever had and the
present Lord Derby the worst'.[59]

The Prince Consort had been an Army reformer, but the
Queen's 'interference' consisted largely of opposition to reforms. She was reluctant to sign, in June 1870, an Order in
Council subordinating the Commander-in-Chief to the Secretary of State. Since 1856 the Commander-in-Chief had been
her cousin, the second Duke of Cambridge, a consistently obstructive force. The Prince had objected to his appointment on
the ground that it would damage the Crown[60] and by the time
—39 years later!—when the Duke was, with immense difficulty, made to resign, he had been more than proved right.
The greatest War Secretary of the Queen's reign, great precisely because he was a great reformer, was not General Peel
but Cardwell. Him she wanted to 'kick upstairs':

> The Queen hears that the Speaker is to resign. Would not
> that be an excellent opening for Mr Cardwell? It is all
> very well saying the Duke is satisfied. It *never* will work
> well, and Mr C. is much disliked by the Army, who know
> he understands nothing of military matters. . . .[61]

She continuously opposed the abolition of the office of Commander-in-Chief, a proposal which she saw as an infringement
of the royal prerogative. When the Hartington Committee recommended it in 1890 she told Sir Henry Ponsonby that it
was a 'really abominable report, which she beyond measure is
shocked should have emanated from a Conservative Government'.[62] Because of her opposition, the recommendation was
not carried out.[63] In 1881 a proposal that Sir Garnet Wolseley
should be given a peerage so as to advance the cause of Army

reform in the Lords was crushed by the Queen.[64] He had to wait four years for his peerage.

In 1895 she was 'horrified at the motion for payment of M.P.s being carried'.[65] She was always an ardent upholder of the rights of the House of Lords, seeing proposals to diminish them as an attack on the Monarchy. ('The House of Lords cannot be totally set aside or a republic with *one* House had better be proposed.')[66] In 1894 she was much alarmed by a proposal of Rosebery's[67] to bring before the House of Commons a motion enunciating the 'impossibility of the elected representatives of the people allowing their measures to be summarily mutilated and rejected by the House of Lords'. She took the view that she should insist on a General Election before such a motion was put forward,[68] and asked Lord Salisbury: '... is the Unionist party fit for a dissolution now?'[69] In 1878 two 'very bad Members' proposed that all treaties should be put to Parliament before ratification: 'Even Mr Gladstone', she noted, 'spoke most strongly against so monstrous an idea.'[70]

She was opposed to Death Duties, first introduced on a serious scale by Sir William Harcourt in 1894.[71] On the other hand, she had, in 1871, criticised a proposed match tax because its burden would 'in fact be only severely felt by the poor, which would be very wrong and most impolitic...'.[72] Again, in 1899, she expressed the hope that the increased taxation necessitated by the Boer War would not fall upon the working class, and the fear that they would be most affected by the extra sixpence on beer.[73] She was mildly interested in working-class housing.[74] In general, however, in common with most of her contemporaries of high rank, she was not interested in what came to be called 'the Social Question'. She was not interested in Disraeli's social legislation, sometimes thought to be his greatest achievement. Her interest in public education was limited to deprecating the 'too high a standard' to which it was carried.[75] On the other hand she told the Prince of Wales that there was no danger 'in the *power given to the Lower Orders*, who are daily becoming more well-informed and more intelligent, and who will *deservedly* work themselves up to the top by their own merit ...'; by contrast 'the REAL danger of the *present* time ...' was to be found 'in the conduct of the Higher Classes and the Aristocracy'.[76] She sought to apply the principle of 'equality of opportunity' to Court appointments:

> That division of classes is the *one thing* which is most dangerous and reprehensible, never intended by the law of nature and which the Queen is always labouring to alter. ...'[77]

A Scottish land-owner on a large scale, she was 'rather afraid' of Bryce's 'Access to Mountains Bill', which she thought would ruin the deer-stalking.[78] She was a passionate opponent of Women's Rights. On one occasion at any rate she deemed 'her *own* position' an anomaly,[79] but on another nonetheless wrote: 'The Queen is most anxious to enlist everyone who can speak or write to join in checking this mad, wicked folly of "Women's Rights" with all its attendant horrors. ... Lady — ought to get a *good* whipping.'[80] The Prince Consort had helped to abolish duelling, but as late as 1890 the Queen had her reservations about that.[81]

Somehow, in the light of all these opinions, it seems not altogether in character that Queen Victoria was a strong anti-vivisectionist.[82] She protested vehemently against orders for muzzling dogs.[83] She also had a liberal attitude to colour. She objected strongly to Indians being called 'niggers'.[84] In the last year of her life she exhorted Lord Salisbury to 'put his foot down' on the prejudice against allowing Indian troops to fight alongside white ones in South Africa.[85]

It will have been noticed that in the foregoing paragraphs there has been only one mention of a disagreement with a Conservative Government, that about the Beer Tax in 1899. Her

political role from 1868 to 1901 was, in short, distinctly similar to that of the House of Lords at the same time, 'a vigilant
and destructive opposition to the programmes of all Liberal
Governments',[86] alternating with happy periods, on the whole
without history, when Conservative Governments were in
power. As Dilke put it:[87]

> The Queen does interfere constantly; more, however,
> when Liberal Ministers are in power than when she has a
> Conservative Cabinet, because on the whole the Conserva-
> tives do what she likes, as she is a Conservative; whereas
> the Liberals are continually doing, and indeed exist for the
> purpose of doing, the things she does not like.[88]

There were, however, two disagreements with a Conservative
Government, both significantly about overseas questions. During the Eastern crisis of 1876–8 the Queen was far more bellicose than her Ministers. Lady Salisbury reported that she 'had
lost control of herself, badgers her ministers and pushes them
towards war'.[89] On five occasions during the crisis she threatened abdication.[90]* Angry, however, as she was with the Government, and particularly with Lord Derby (the 15th Earl),
Foreign Secretary until March 1878, she was, as will be seen,[93]
far more angry with those who thought it too bellicose rather
than too pacific.

The second disagreement arose out of the Zulu War. After a
British defeat at Isandhlwana there was a cry for the recall of

---

* Edward VII talked a lot about abdication during the winter of 1909–10,
but this was an expression of his feeling unwell and depressed and was not
meant to be taken seriously. Knollys' view was that 'however much Sovereigns may threaten to abdicate, they rarely . . . carry their threat into execution. In this respect they are like people who say they are going to commit
suicide.'[91] Probably Disraeli took this view of the Queen's threats of
abdication; Gladstone would have been considerably disturbed. He once
told Ponsonby that the 'threat of abdication was the greatest power the Sovereign possessed—nothing could stand against it, for the position of a Minister
who forced it on would be untenable'.[92] Plainly by the time of Edward VIII
this had entirely ceased to be the case

the two 'men on the spot', Sir Bartle Frere, the High Commissioner, and Lord Chelmsford, the Commander-in-Chief. Beaconsfield, by no means consistently a statesman of firm decisions, shilly-shallied and proposed to reinforce Frere and Chelmsford by Sir Garnet Wolseley. The Queen opposed this. She wrote that she would sanction this proposal 'if her warnings are disregarded, but she would *not* approve it'.[94] Blake is emphatic that the Prime Minister 'pushed the Cabinet into a double-faced treatment of both the High Commissioner and the Commander-in-Chief, which seems on any view indefensible. He should either have sacked them or backed them. On this rare occasion of divergence from her favourite Prime Minister the Queen was in the right.'[95] One may note here that the Prime Minister and the majority of the Cabinet had been in favour of Frere's recall at an earlier stage, but this having been strongly opposed by the Queen and the Colonial Secretary (Hicks-Beach), 'the Prime Minister', as Lord Salisbury told his nephew, 'was unable to resist his Sovereign and the Colonial Secretary together'.[96]

The decisive breach between Queen Victoria and the Liberal Party came, as we have seen, over a foreign-policy question in 1876, and she was more at loggerheads with Liberal Governments over foreign, and imperial, than over home affairs. These disagreements can be related to particular incidents, but they sprang from fundamental differences of attitude. The Queen's attitudes can be summarised under three heads. In the first place she believed that it was a paramount duty of all British Governments at all times to keep up national defences. With Gladstone as Prime Minister in 1870 she was 'uneasy about military reductions',[97] having previously expressed strong objections to economies which would reduce England to the state of a second-rate Power.[98] Even to Disraeli a decade later she felt she had to point out:

One great lesson is again taught us, but it is never followed: NEVER *let* the *Army* and *Navy* DOWN *so low* as *to be obliged* to go to *great expense* in a hurry.

This was the case in the Crimean war. We were *not* prepared. . . . If *we are* to *maintain* our position as a *first rate* Power . . . we must, with our Indian Empire and large Colonies, be *prepared* for *attacks* and *wars*, somewhere or other, CONTINUOUSLY. And the *true economy* will be *to be always ready.*[99]

The Queen in the second place believed that what Britain had it should hold.[100] At first, however, she was not in favour of increasing the size of the holding. She was alarmed at the idea, in 1874, of annexing Fiji[101] and, when the deed was done, wrote to the German Crown Princess: 'I have such a horror (unlike what is felt by many in Germany now) of the love of acquisition and conquest.'[102] Later, however, the words of A. C. Benson, although not written until the next reign (at the King's suggestion),[103] 'wider still and wider, may thy bounds be set', expressed her sentiments admirably. William Blake's pre-Imperialist idea of building Jerusalem in 'England's green and pleasant land' would have seemed to her high-flown. It was one of the many obstacles to a good relationship with Gladstone that he was a great 'European', but a highly reluctant Imperialist. A Maid of Honour recorded as late as 1896:

> I read the Queen *The Times'* leader on Lord Salisbury's speech last night. She is so tenacious of Egypt, says it is a great mistake we ever promised to go and that we owe all this European enmity to Mr Gladstone.[104]

The Queen, in the third place, believed that Britain should make its might felt in the affairs of the world, believed, that is to say, in a 'spirited foreign policy'. She was, in short, in spite of her frequent and acute differences with Palmerston on the particular European questions of his day, basically a Palmer-

stonian, as much in foreign as in home affairs.[105] To Palmerston's doctrines she added the newer, imperialist ones which
Disraeli did so much to make fashionable. She read J. R.
Seeley's *Expansion of England*, which was published in
1883.[106] Arthur Ponsonby, once her Page, and later a Labour
Minister, rightly calls her a Conservative Imperialist.[107] Fulford
accepts her own evaluation of herself as a Liberal, but adds
that 'where she parted with the Liberals was in her ideas of
Empire. Although she would not have liked the label she was
a Chamberlainite, a Kiplingite. . . .'[108]

As an imperialist the Queen had, if she had but known it,
much in common with Dilke, author of *Greater Britain*, published in 1868. She did indeed write to Gladstone in 1882:
'The Queen would far rather see Sir C. Dilke in the Cabinet
than Lord Derby, for the former *has right* views on foreign
politics.'[109] Her detestation of Lord Derby was so great that this
was not saying very much.[110] In the same year she momentarily
found she had something in common with Joseph Chamberlain, whose Radicalism she detested, writing in her journal:
'Found Mr Chamberlain very sensible and reasonable about
the question of Egypt. . . .'[111]

When in 1879 she was trying to face the, for her, grim prospect of another Liberal Government and formulating '*certain*
things which I *never can* consent to' she put first on her list:

> Any lowering of the position of this country by letting
> Russia have her way in the East, or by letting down our
> Empire in India and in the Colonies. This *was* done
> under Mr Gladstone quite *contrary* to Lord Palmerston's
> policy. . . .[112]*

Again, we find her, in a letter to Lord Granville, after she had
had more than three years' experience of the second Gladstone

---

* She put second never giving way about the Scottish Church, 'the real
and true stronghold of Protestantism'[113]

Ministry, setting out her attitudes explicitly and with a direct and unfavourable comparison between Gladstone on the one hand and Palmerston and Disraeli on the other:

> She has no doubt that Lord Granville feels as Lord Palmerston did; who with all his many faults, had the honour and power of his country strongly at heart, and so had Lord Beaconsfield. *But* she does *not* feel that Mr Gladstone has. Or at least he puts the House of Commons and party *first*; thinking *no doubt* that he *is* doing what is best by keeping this country out of everything and swallowing offences like the conduct of the French at Madagascar.[114]

Their conduct was basically that of seizing an island to which, if Africa was to be partitioned amongst European Powers, we had more right than they.[115] But this particular episode in the general history of European expansion overseas does not concern us here. What concerns us is only the statement of Queen Victoria's general principles provoked by it. To Gladstone himself the Queen wrote:

> As regards Madagascar ... the Queen has telegraphed what she meant. What she fears is a growing tendency to swallow insults and affronts and not taking them up in that high tone which they used formerly to be. . . .[116]

Another direct comparison (there are not many) between Gladstone and Disraeli was provoked by the latter's purchase of the Suez Canal shares in 1875, precisely the sort of dazzling stroke she admired. He announced it to her in secret and in just the sort of Disraelian language that appealed to her:

> It is just settled: you have it, Madam. The French Government has been out-generalled. . . . Four Millions sterling! and almost immediately. There was only one firm that could do it—Rothschilds.[117]

She wrote to Sir Theodore Martin:

> It is *entirely* the doing of Mr Disraeli.... His mind is so much greater, larger, and his apprehension of things great and small so much quicker than that of Mr Gladstone.[118]

Gladstone's final resignation, in 1894, though given out as due to old age, was in fact in protest against an increase in the Navy estimates. Thirty years earlier, when a project of his as Chancellor for reducing military expenditure was opposed by the Prime Minister, the Queen expressed 'her cordial and unqualified approval of every word said by Lord Palmerston'.[119]

From her point of view Gladstone had been right about Germany in 1863–4.[120] But to her he seemed invariably wrong about Russia. 'The Queen', noted Sir Henry Ponsonby, 'looks at foreign affairs always as a struggle for supremacy against Russia...'.[121] J. A. Farrer (a neglected writer) speculates on 'a certain affinity of spirit between the Prince Consort and Lord Beaconsfield.... An anti-Russian policy, vigorous to the point of risk, and leaning to absolutist government, were the leading ideas of both.'[122] In his discussion of the breach between the Queen and Gladstone, Farrer suggests that:

> The difference began when Mr Gladstone and other Peelites forsook Lord Palmerston's Ministry in 1855, in the middle of the Crimean War, and, much to the offence of the Court, threw the weight of their influence on the side that wished to stop the war.[123]

Be that as it may, it is certain that Gladstone's emergence from his retirement in 1876 (he had resigned the leadership of the Liberal Party in January 1875) to conduct an anti-Turkish campaign, in opposition to the Beaconsfield Government's policy, caused the Queen more indignation—which is saying a lot—than any previous action of his.[124] She called his attitude unfortunate and disloyal;[125] to the Duke of Argyll (the 8th

Duke) she stated '*solemnly*, that I know that this war . . . would have been prevented, had Russia not been *encouraged* in the strongest manner by the extraordinary, and, to me, *utterly* incomprehensible, agitation carried on by some Members, and especially by one, of my late Government . . .'.[126] Among those tarred in the Queen's eyes with the Gladstonian brush were the Duke himself,[127] Burne-Jones, Carlyle, Froude and Ruskin. She thought 'the Attorney-General ought to be set at' them for their part in a meeting of protest.[128] She seemed unable to understand why the Opposition had attacked the Government during the Eastern crisis; she thought it must have been 'simply for party reasons. . . . Lord Granville and the Whigs believe . . . that they have a just cause of grievance if any other party but their own is in office.'[129]

Two years after the Eastern crisis had been ended by the Treaty of Berlin, struggling to avoid taking Gladstone as Prime Minister for the second time, she was saying to Sir Henry Ponsonby:

> Mr Gladstone *she* could have nothing to do with, for she considers his whole conduct since '76 to have been one series of violent, passionate invective against and abuse of Lord Beaconsfield, and that he *caused* the Russian War. . . .[130]

She added, however, on the assumption that Lord Hartington or Lord Granville would be the new Prime Minister, that she wished to show the new Government confidence, 'as she has hitherto done all her Governments but that *this must entirely depend* on their conduct'. What was required in this respect again gives a good indication of her general views:

> There must be no democratic leaning, no attempt to change the foreign policy (and the Continent are terribly alarmed), no change in India, no hasty retreat from Afghanistan, and *no* cutting down of estimates. In short,

no lowering of the *high position* this country holds, and *ought always* to hold.

It is scarcely surprising that, after all this, and unable to avoid the return of Gladstone to the highest office, the Queen's relations with the Liberal Government over foreign affairs reached their nadir between 1880 and 1885. They were better in 1886 and again between 1892 and 1894, with Lord Rosebery as Foreign Secretary.[131] She told the Prince of Wales in 1886:

> The only really good appointment, (and that is *my* doing, for I asked for him and insisted on having him) is Lord Rosebery.[132]

In 1880 she had warned against a 'hasty retreat from Afghanistan', but Gladstone's Cabinet decided to reverse the 'forward policy' of their predecessors and evacuate it. This decision was immensely distasteful to the Queen on every ground (yielding what we held, reversing Disraeli's policy, making Russian intervention easier) and a remarkable sequel occurred at Osborne House on 5 January 1881, which came to be known, at Court at any rate, as 'the Memorable Day'.[133] The Cabinet proposed to announce withdrawal from Candahar in the Queen's Speech from the Throne. The Queen objected strongly to something she disapproved of being announced in her name and a Council summoned to approve the Speech* was postponed from 10 a.m. to 4 p.m. while the Queen and the Prime Minister exchanged telegrams on the subject. She had in the end to give in but only after being told 'that to disapprove was to eject the

---

* The practice of the King's Speech being approved in Council was discontinued in July 1921. A memorandum from the Clerk to the Lord President written at that time states:

> There is nothing to show that any constitutional sanction attaches to the approval of a King's Speech after a Council. It is certain on the other hand that such approval is no part of the business of the King in Council, and it appears probable that the practice is the result of convenience hardening into custom[134]

Ministry and that . . . was revolution'.[135] Sir Henry Ponsonby said that he had never seen her so angry.[136] Queen Victoria was always against withdrawals, holding, says Lady Longford, 'that they always led to hasty improvised returns at enormous cost'.[137]

But the climax came over the death of Gordon. His orders, to evacuate the Sudan, were unpalatable to the Queen. As things fell out he was cut off at Khartoum in May 1884. To what extent this was his own fault, to what that of the Government at home can still be argued. But it then became their plain duty to organise a military expedition to rescue him, and their hesitation and delays over this are unquestionably blameworthy. Even so, the expedition eventually sanctioned came near to success. It reached Khartoum on 28 January 1885, only to find that the place had been stormed and Gordon killed on the 26th. The news reached Lady Ponsonby in a dramatic way. She was sitting after breakfast in her house near Osborne, when the door opened and in came the Queen, unattended and unannounced. She stood, and without any preliminaries said: 'Khartoum has fallen, Gordon is dead.'[138]

On 5 February the Queen wired Gladstone, Granville and Hartington *en clair*, (quite deliberately),[139] 'these news from Khartoum are frightful, and to think that all this might have been prevented and many precious lives saved by earlier action is too frightful'.[140]* There can be little doubt that this was the point of view of the majority of the nation. It must too be said

* Another telegram sent *en clair*, which leaked and caused a lot of trouble, was one sent on 9 September 1899, à propos of the second conviction of Dreyfus, to the Secretary of our Paris Embassy:

Thanks for your telegram with news of this monstrous verdict against this poor martyr. I trust he will appeal against this dreadful sentence.[141]

It is possible that William II of Germany, the Queen's grandson, had let her know that it was not Dreyfus who had sold French military secrets to his Government[142]

that the Queen had been warning her Ministers of the danger
to Gordon incessantly for the previous 12 months.[143]

Perhaps the best way to grasp the growth of the Queen's
Conservatism is through her comments on successive Elections.
Thus in 1874 she wrote to a confidant:

> What an important turn the elections have taken! It shows
> that the country is not *Radical*. What a triumph, too, Mr
> Disraeli has obtained, and what a good sign this large Con-
> servative majority is of the state of the country, which
> really required (as formerly) a strong Conservative party.[144]

When the results of the 1880 Election were known, she wrote
to the Prime Minister, Disraeli:

> My great hope and belief is, that this shamefully hetero-
> geneous union—out of mere folly—will separate into
> many parts very soon, and that the Conservatives will
> come in stronger than ever in a short time ... possibly a
> coalition first. . . . I do not care for the trouble of changes
> of Government, if it is to have a secure and safe one,
> which the new one cannot be. I am shocked and ashamed
> at what has happened. It is really disgraceful.[145]

When the result of the 1885 Election was known, she wrote to
Lord Salisbury, the Prime Minister:

> The Queen has been much distressed, she must say, at the
> unsatisfactory turn the Election has taken. But it must be
> observed that the extreme Radicals have not succeeded ...
> the Conservatives have gained many seats since '80. The
> feeling of the country is therefore very healthy in that
> respect.[146]

When Lord Salisbury's Government was defeated at the polls
in 1892 she wrote to Lord Lansdowne, Viceroy of India at the
time:

By an incomprehensible, reckless vote, the result of most unfair and abominable misrepresentations at the elections, one of the best and most useful Governments have been defeated....[147]

To her Journal she confided:

These are trying moments and it seems to me a defect in our famed Constitution, to have to part with an admirable Government like Lord Salisbury's for no question of any importance, or any particular reason, merely on account of the number of votes.[148]

By contrast the Election of 1895 produced for Lord Salisbury a 'wonderful majority'.[149] Strachey was right to point out that Victoria did not really understand the Constitution over which she presided.[150]

Such, briefly, is the evidence for the Conservatism of Queen Victoria, but she did not see herself as a Conservative. Thus in 1874 she told Forster that:

No one can be more *truly* liberal at heart than the Queen is, but she also thinks, that the great *principles* of the *Constitution* of this *great country* ought to be maintained, and that too many alterations (and there have been so many) should be avoided....[151]

That last sentiment is echoed in March 1880, when a Liberal Government was impending: 'Improvements and progress in the right direction and with prudence will ever meet with the Queen's support but not constant change for change's sake.'[152]

In April 1880, commenting to Ponsonby on the results of the Elections, she wrote:[153]

The Queen cannot deny she (Liberal as she has ever been, but never Radical or democratic) thinks it a great calamity for the country.[154]

After four years of Liberal rule the start is the same but the note shriller. A draft letter to Gladstone reads, in part:

> No one is more truly Liberal in her heart than the Queen, but she has always strongly deprecated the great tendency of the present Government to encourage . . . the stream of destructive democracy which has become so alarming. This it is that, she may say justly, alarms the House of Lords and all moderate people. And to threaten the House of Lords that they will bring destruction on themselves is, in fact, to threaten the Monarchy itself. Another Sovereign but herself must acquiesce in any alteration of the House of Lords. She will not be the Sovereign of a Democratic Monarchy.[155]

A letter that actually went to Gladstone a little later makes a similar point as sharply and vehemently:

> According to Mr Gladstone's observations there ought to be a Radical House of Lords . . . as well as the House of Commons, so that any radical measure should pass! The Monarchy would be utterly untenable were *there no balance* of power left, no *restraining* power. The Queen will yield to no one in TRUE LIBERAL FEELING, but not to destructive. . . .[156]

The Queen's avowals of her own Liberalism scarcely carry conviction. What is true is that she disliked the extremists of both parties, though those on the Liberal rather more than those on the Conservative side, and preferred a Coalition Government, based on the Right, to a straight Party Government on the Left. Thus, in 1869, when Lords and Commons were in disagreement about the Irish Church Bill, she urged Lord Granville to do all he could 'to enable the moderate Conservatives to *prevail*'.[157] In 1884, when the Houses were again in disagreement, over the Third Reform Bill, she formulated her position as follows:

The Lords are *not* in disharmony with the people, but unfortunately Mr Gladstone's Government leans so much to the extreme Radical side, instead of to the sound and moderate position of his following, that measures are presented to the House of Lords which the Conservatives and moderate Liberals do not feel they can with safety agree to.[158]

Later in the year she wrote to the Duke of Argyll, a close personal friend whose son (later the 9th Duke) had married Princess Louise, her fourth daughter:

I long for the moderates of both sides to form a third party which would be a check to both the others and prevent this mischief the violents are making. This might eventually lead to the formation of a third Party in the House of Lords, and is what Mr Goschen was very eager for, under possibly your Leadership.... We must save the country and the Constitution.[159]

It will be remembered that, after the Election of 1880, she expressed a hope that the 'shamefully heterogeneous union' which had won it would break up and the Conservatives 'come in stronger than ever.... Possibly a coalition first.'[160] In other words she wanted the break-up of what she saw as a coalition on the Left and the creation of one on the Right. After the Election of November 1885, when Irish Home Rule was becoming practical politics and when the Party kaleidoscope was visibly shifting, her mind reverted to that idea and to the idea of Goschen, Lord Hartington, and others, 'saving the country and the Constitution' by supporting Lord Salisbury, Conservative Prime Minister since June.

There was no doubt in her mind that the question was one of putting country before Party. She hoped that 'the moderate constitutional Liberals', i.e., the anti-Home Rulers, were 'patriots before they are party men.... Patriotism *must now* be the *one aim* of *all* who love their country and are loyal to their Sovereign.'[161] Week in, week out, she conducted an epistolary, anti-Gladstonian recruiting campaign.

She wrote to Goschen in December:

> I appeal to *you* and to all moderate, loyal and *really patriotic* men, who have the safety and well-being of the Empire and the Throne at heart, and who wish to save them from destruction, with which, if the Government again fell into the reckless hands of Mr Gladstone, they would be threatened, to rise above party and to be true patriots! You must convince Lord Hartington of what is at last his *duty* and of what he owes to his Queen and country, which really goes before allegiance to Mr Gladstone. . . .
>
> Let me urge and implore you . . . to do all you can to gather around you all the moderate Liberals, who indeed ought to be called *Constitutionalists*, to prevent Mr Gladstone recklessly upsetting the Government. . . .
>
> I am sure that you with Lord Hartington and many other moderate Liberals would save the country by standing aloof from Mr Gladstone, who is utterly reckless, and whose conduct at this moment, in proposing what would be *Home Rule*, is most mischievous and incomprehensible.
>
> Out of this might grow a Coalition in time.[162]

On the Queen's behalf Lady Ely made the same plea to W. E. Forster, who had been an independent Liberal since resigning from the second Gladstone Cabinet as Chief Secretary for Ireland, in protest against the 'Kilmainham Treaty' (an informal agreement under which in 1882 Parnell had been released from gaol):

> The Queen desires me to say her Majesty hopes that you are prepared to stand by the moderate patriotic and loyal men, who will not agree with the wild plans of Mr G.,

and that you will not join in trying to drive out the present Government to let Mr G. come in again. . . .[163]*

The Queen's campaign was a failure. Gladstone became Prime Minister for the third time in February 1886, and the Queen was left sadly reflecting to Goschen:

> It is sad, and I cannot help saying *not* creditable or pleasant fact that the Liberals do not *wish* to *unite* with the Conservatives at such a *supreme* moment of *danger* to the best interests of my great Empire. However, we must not mind this narrow party view (which is, moreover, NOT shared by the Conservatives!).[165]

Some of these attitudes could be classified as royal, others as implicitly rather than explicitly Conservative. By 'royal attitudes' I mean those one would expect a constitutional monarch to take, hoping, for example, that in times of major Party disagreements moderate men on both sides would combine to contrive an agreement; fearing that extremists would prevent its acceptance; hoping that a Centre Party would keep them in check; carrying such ideas to the point of favouring a Coalition of major parties when the unity of the State was endangered by Party strife. By 'implicitly Conservative' attitudes I mean distinguishing between good and bad Liberals—i.e., the moderate and sound on the one hand and the perversely Radical on the other; thinking that to support a Conservative Government is rising above Party, not wanting to do so a narrow Party view, and attacking it a mere Party attack.[166]

The young Queen Victoria, Melbourne's pupil, was a Whig, according to Lady Longford 'a rabid Whig with little comprehension of what Liberalism stood for'.[167] By 1880, however, as

---

* Shortly afterwards 'moderate, loyal, and patriotic' men are described, in another letter to Goschen, as Whigs: 'Why can you, moderate, loyal and patriotic Whigs not join and declare you will not follow Mr Gladstone, and not support him?'[164]

we have seen,[168] she wrote of herself that 'Liberal she has ever been, but never Radical or democratic . . .'. After two years of the second Gladstone Administration she was telling Sir Henry Ponsonby:

> Unfortunately the Government are *not liberal* but radical to the extreme.[169]

And for her extreme Radicalism verged on Communism. Thus when in 1892 Lord Rosebery, whom she already had in mind as a Liberal Prime Minister, and one to be preferred to Gladstone, made a public speech in favour of Irish Home Rule she was 'dreadfully disappointed and shocked' at a 'speech which is radical to a degree to be almost communistic'.[170] Two years later, the Liberals again in power, she wrote:

> It is degrading to be the so called Sovereign when such desperate Radicals are in power. Lord Clarendon used to say the Liberals' creed is Party 1st, then the country and the Sovereign and so it is always she grieves to say.[171]

The pen flew over the paper, somewhat illegibly, and the adjectives descriptive of Party allegiances were scarcely scientific. But it is true that the Queen never described herself as a Conservative, not even in the years of Peel's second Premiership. Later, in the last years of her marriage, she attained her highest point of political neutrality, but that was, in any case, a time of exceptional placidity in the Party system. The years between 1876 and 1880 were the decisive ones in the formation of her mature political opinions. Thereafter she entirely ceased to be open-minded.

If the Queen, with her views, had been a private person she might well have asserted from time to time that she had always been a Liberal at heart and never a Conservative. Indeed she would not have been a 'hack' Conservative Party supporter. She would have criticised Party policy from time to time, and even the Party leader. But she would have been basically a partisan, though she would have denied this, writing to Ponsonby in 1880:

> The Queen is *no* partisan and *never has* been since the first 3 or 4 years of her reign when she *was* so from her inexperience and g^t friendship with Lord Melbourne.[172]

She did not have the mentality of a thoughtful 'floating voter' or a 'cross-Bench mind'. In the absence of female suffrage, to which, as we have seen, she was opposed, she would not have been able to vote, but one can hardly doubt that at each successive Election she would have ardently hoped for a Conservative victory and done all she could to ensure it. This is the full meaning of the statement at the beginning of this Chapter, that the Queen was from 1868 onwards (whatever she was before) 'for all practical purposes, a Conservative'. More practical purposes were, of course, available to the Sovereign than to a private person. It must be emphasised, however, that although the Queen's partisan views were out of part in the case of a constitutional monarch, many of them were perfectly sensible. Her native commonsense was massive; on it she built a massive wisdom.

It is a comforting reflection that at the end of her life the Queen did get her way about a 'Right Coalition', fifteen years after she had first adumbrated the idea. Lord Salisbury's third Cabinet, formed in June 1895, was a Coalition of Conservatives and Liberal-Unionists. This Government was still in power when the Queen died in January 1901. The 'golden evening'[173] of her reign was clouded by the Boer War, but domestic politics during that period were altogether to Queen Victoria's taste.

3

Victoria

POLITICAL ACTIONS

Bagehot was wrong then, in holding in his time that the Crown was no Party.[1] Queen Victoria was a Conservative,* in however carefully qualified a sense, sympathetic (as might be expected of a Conservative) to Liberal-Unionism, but with little or no sympathy for Liberalism and none whatever for 'democracy', Radicalism or Socialism. It is to her credit that she read Henry George's *Progress and Poverty* and not to her discredit that she found it 'difficult'.[3]

It is important not to draw the wrong conclusion from these facts. Nothing fails like failure and historians too frequently assume that whatever succeeded was right. It does not follow that, because so many of the reforms she opposed came to pass, they were right. True, it now requires an effort to see, for example, what was 'England's case against Home Rule'. But the Queen, in sharing it, was in good intellectual company and in very large company just as her great-grandson was in large company, some of it good, in approving the Munich Agreement and in making Halifax rather than Churchill his first choice for the succession to Neville Chamberlain as Prime Minister.[4] Public opinion was overwhelmingly with the Queen in lauding Disraeli for buying the Suez Canal shares, in blaming Gladstone for the death of Gordon. For all her political

---

* Norman St John Stevas, the great authority on Bagehot and a Conservative M.P., has written: 'From 1876 until 1901, in domestic affairs, the Queen was virtually a supporter of the Conservative Party.' There is plainly a strong case against his qualification, 'in domestic affairs'[2]

and social isolation, she knew the feelings of 'the man in the street', especially the middle-class one. Lord Salisbury emphasised this in paying his obituary tribute to her in Parliament.[5] Queen Victoria can no more be called stupid just for being a Conservative than could all or any of the Conservatives of the Victorian age.

Moreover, she was, as has already been indicated, very far from being stupid personally. A superlative memory and exceptional commonsense are not perhaps the highest but are considerable intellectual gifts. Her latest biographer's assessment is that 'she lacked spontaneous intellectual curiosity. Without that gift, neither her immense industry nor taste for intelligent discussion could greatly extend her mental range. Within these limits her mind was alert and her understanding well above the average. No one has emerged from old letters more alive; no one without talent could have produced her journal.'[6] She had no bent, in other words, to be an 'intellectual'—not that her position would have allowed her the time to be one. But the combination of her particular sort of intelligence and her experience developed into wisdom.

The evidence of this is most plain in respect of defence and foreign policy. The drift, ill-prepared, into two World Wars, has surely convinced all, except absolute pacifists, that (pending effective international agreements) armaments must be always maintained and diplomacy be resolute in defending the vital interests of the nation. Whatever her errors of judgment on lesser matters, the 'judgment of history' has confirmed her judgment on these two supreme ones, to which she herself attached supreme importance.[7]

Credit must be given to her, not only for fastening on them, but for keeping them constantly and firmly in the front of her own mind and before the eyes of contemporary politicians, whatever the changes of circumstances and doctrines which seemed to call them in question from time to time. Politicians

are apt to resent reminders of awkward truths, which are none
the less true however unexpected the quarter from which they
come. The question in fact is not whether, in being Conservative, the Queen was as a person wise or foolish but right or
wrong as a Queen to be so partisan. It must in this connection
be recorded that neither the Queen herself nor the leading
statesmen of the time held that the Crown should be neutral
in politics, only that it should appear to be so. In other words,
the constitutional doctrine of the day was that the actions of
the Crown should be on the advice of Ministers, not that the
Sovereign was disentitled in private to express opinions quite
different from theirs.

Palmerston, for example, in 1864, addressing to the Queen
one of his sharpest rebukes, sent her a copy of a newspaper
and wrote:

> This paper, and others, which have been mentioned to
> Viscount Palmerston, tend to show, that an impression is
> beginning to be created that your Majesty has expressed
> personal opinions on the affairs of Denmark and Germany
> which have embarrassed the course of the Government. . . .
> It would be a great evil if public opinion were to divest
> your Majesty of that proper and essential protection which
> the Constitution secures for the Sovereign by making the
> responsible Ministers answerable for all that is done or not
> done; and if your Majesty's personal opinions and views
> were to become the objects of criticism and attack.[8]

Two days later the Queen told her Uncle Leopold, the King
of the Belgians, that 'Pilgerstein is gouty and extremely imper-
tinent . . .'.[9] But at the same time and in the same context, that
of the Schleswig-Holstein crisis, she wrote to her eldest daughter: 'I hope that my opinions and my actions will not be quoted
in opposition to my Government. . . .' The reprehensibility of
that had for her the highest sanction; it had never been per-
mitted by 'Beloved Papa'.[10]

Two generations later, substantially the same doctrine as Palmerston's was put forward in turn by a Conservative Leader of the Opposition (an ex-Prime Minister) and by a Liberal Prime Minister. In 1893 the Queen asked Lord Salisbury whether, if the House of Lords petitioned her for a Dissolution, she should grant one. He replied:

A Dissolution by the Queen, against the advice of her Ministers, would, of course, involve their resignation. Their party could hardly help going to the country as the opponents of the royal authority; or at least, as the severe critics of the mode in which it had been exerted. . . . There must be some hazard that, in the end, such a step would injure the authority of the Queen.[11]

The next year Lord Rosebery in a public speech[12] contemplated the moving of a resolution hostile to the House of Lords in the House of Commons. He explained to the Queen that it would declare 'the impossibility of the elected representatives of the people allowing their measures to be summarily mutilated and rejected by the House of Lords'.[13] No such motion was in fact moved because Rosebery could not get the backing of the Cabinet for it.[14] Meanwhile, however, the Queen was deeply disturbed. She asked Lord Salisbury whether she would be in order in insisting on a Dissolution before such a motion was moved and whether the Unionist Party was ready for one.[15] He answered 'Yes' to both questions,[16] and Sir Henry Ponsonby was in fact instructed to tell the Prime Minister that she would insist on one.[17] She had already told Rosebery that he should not make any such proposal without her knowledge and consent, and it was this which led him to state his view of the constitutional issues:

. . . he would never dream of proposing a constitutional resolution to the House of Commons without submitting it, after mature consideration by the Cabinet, to your

Majesty. But he would humbly deprecate the view that it is necessary for a Minister, before laying a question of policy before a popular audience, to receive the approval of the Crown. Such a principle would tend to make the Sovereign a party in all controversies of the hour, and would hazardously compromise the neutrality of the Sovereign.[18]

Referring to the incident two years later the Queen explained that, because of it, she 'was not sorry when he was turned out'.[19]

Palmerston, in one generation, Rosebery and Salisbury in another, all saw the same hazard, of the Crown being known not to be acting on the advice of the Ministry of the day and so becoming embroiled in Party controversies. In the intervening period, however, Disraeli had seen more deeply into the heart of the matter. In his first letter as Prime Minister in 1868 he wrote to her:

> Your Majesty's life has been passed in constant communion with great men, and the knowledge and management of important transactions. Even if your Majesty were not gifted with those great abilities, which all must now acknowledge, this rare and choice experience must give your Majesty an advantage in judgement, which few living persons, and probably no living Prince, can rival. . . .[20]

This was hyperbolical, but substantially true. He made the same point to her after his retirement.[21] In a public speech at Manchester, in 1872, one of his major pronouncements, he said:

> I know it will be said that . . . the personal influence of the Sovereign is now merged in the responsibility of the Minister. I think you will find a great fallacy in this view. The principles of the English Constitution do not contemplate the absence of personal influence on the part of the Sove-

reign; and if they did, the principles of human nature would prevent the fulfillment of such a theory.[22]

For this percipience on Disraeli's part one should probably give credit not so much to his 'leaning to absolutist government'[23] as to his innate acumen and his personal experience of the Queen's political activities. The speech in question was made after his first term of office as Prime Minister, in 1868; his second term, from 1874 to 1880, can only have confirmed him in the view that he had earlier expressed. One cannot help wondering, however, having regard to the turn of the particular phrase ('The principles of the English Constitution do not contemplate the absence of personal influence on the part of the Sovereign'), whether he, a great lover of phrases, had read or knew of the famous phrase, in Bagehot's *English Constitution*, the second edition of which had appeared earlier in the same year (1872). 'To state the matter shortly', Bagehot had written,[24] 'the Sovereign has, under a constitutional monarchy, such as ours, three rights—the right to be consulted, the right to encourage, the right to warn.'* The exercise of these three rights amounts precisely to 'personal influence'.

The constitutional theory of the time was therefore that the Sovereign acted on the advice of the Minister but retained a right to 'personal influence'. Bagehot, asserting that the Crown was of no Party,[26] would no doubt have asserted also that the three rights he ascribed to it should not have been exercised in a consistently partisan manner. The statesmen,

---

* Bagehot was writing strictly in the context of relations between the Monarch and Ministers. Queen Victoria gave them on balance more warnings than encouragement. But she gave much encouragement to men outside the Ministerial ranks, particularly soldiers and pro-Consuls. In this context a letter written from Cairo by Lord Cromer is revealing: 'I can never cease to remember with the utmost gratitude the personal support I received from Her Majesty in the dark Gladstonian days. . . . Her Majesty has, I dare say, forgotten a few words of kindly encouragement sent to me a few years ago when things looked very black. But I can assure you that at the time they were like Manna in the Egyptian wilderness'[25]

however, who had direct experience of the Queen's personal
influence did not take that view. Sir Charles Dilke, the 'brain'
of Liberalism,[27] said bluntly that she was a Conservative[28] and
emphasised how constantly, because she was one, she interfered when Liberal Ministers were in power:[29]

> The Queen is a woman of great ability.... She writes to
> the Prime Minister about anything she does not like,
> which, when he is a Liberal, means almost everything that
> he says or does. She complains of his colleagues' speeches,
> she complains, with less violence, of his own. She protests
> against Bills. She insists that administrative acts should
> not be done without delay, for the purpose of consulting
> with regard to them persons whose opinions she knows
> will be unfavourable.

But Dilke went on to say that 'her action, to my mind, is
strictly speaking constitutional...'.[30]

The ideas, and still more the customs, of the time thus
allowed the Queen great latitude as to the manner in which
she 'interfered' in politics. Was no line drawn beyond which
it was thought wrong to step? Gladstone, during his second
Ministry, although exasperated by many of her interventions,
seems to have thought only three of them incorrect.

The first, a small matter, was an appointment to junior
office. When the Ministry was formed she objected strongly
to the appointment of Leonard Courtney to the Under-Secretaryship at the Home Office because he was a Radical. Gladstone patiently explained that the appointment was not his
but, according to the correct constitutional usage, that of the
Secretary of State.[31] The Queen did not contest that point, but
none the less had the last word ('The Queen hopes the next
appointment to a place in your Government will be made from
the party of the moderate Liberals')[32] and objected next year to
Courtney being transferred to the Under-Secretaryship at the

Colonial Office. On this letter (it was nominally Ponsonby's) the Prime Minister minuted Lord Granville, Sir William Harcourt and Lord Kimberley:

> I think this intolerable. It is by courtesy only that these appointments are made known to HM. W.E.G.[33]

Significantly the other two occasions arose out of Egyptian affairs. In 1882 he penned to Hartington about the strongest condemnation of the Queen he ever allowed himself to put down:

> I must own that I think the Queen's resolute attempts to disturb and impede the reduction of the army in Egypt are (to use a plain word) intolerable. It is my firm intention not to give in ... to proceedings almost as unconstitutional as they are irrational. ...[34]

When he received the telegram about the death of Gordon,[35] he asked Ponsonby 'if the message had been made known by the telegraph clerks to others' and Ponsonby thought 'he evidently wishes to bring the matter forward again as a question of whether he could remain in office if publicly condemned by the Queen'.[36] Gladstone was so angry on that occasion that he told Morley that 'He had resolved never to set foot in Windsor Castle again. ...'[37] Three years earlier a letter from the Queen to Lord Granville about the murder of Lord Frederick Cavendish was such, in its recipient's opinion, 'as would almost require our resignation if I was to show the letter to my colleagues'.[38]

The sending of the telegram on Gordon's death *en clair* was, as we have seen, a quite deliberate act on the Queen's part. (Fortunately the discretion of the telegraph clerks concealed her indiscretion.) A little later, however, the Queen again acted improperly when she wrote to Lady Wolseley, whose husband was in command of our army in Egypt:

> In strict confidence I must tell you I think the Govern-
> ment are more incorrigible than ever, and I do think that
> your husband should hold strong language to them, and
> even THREATEN to resign if he does not receive strong
> support and liberty of action. I have written very strongly
> to the Prime Minister and others, and I tell you this; but
> it must never appear, or Lord Wolseley ever let out the
> hint I give you. But I really think they must be fright-
> ened. . . . Pray either destroy this, or lock it up. . . .[39]

If it was wrong thus to intrigue against the Government in
being, it was also wrong to intrigue against one at the moment
of its formation. When Gladstone became Prime Minister for
the third time in February 1886, the Duchess of Roxburghe refused the appointment of Mistress of the Robes, and the Queen
wrote to the Dowager Duchess:

> I think your son might put it into the papers that the post
> had been offered to Anne, and, tho' she was greatly
> honoured and would willingly have accepted it, the Duke
> felt he could not support Mr Gladstone's Irish policy, and
> she had therefore declined it. Something of this kind I
> should like to appear.[40]

An important modern writer sees in the Queen's discussion
with Salisbury, during the third Gladstone Ministry, of the desirability of granting Gladstone a Dissolution,[41] her 'departures
from accepted practices' reaching 'their most extreme
form . . .'.[42] But Salisbury is surely more to be blamed for giving
his advice from a strictly Tory point of view than the Queen
for asking him for it. In her times the idea of the Ministry of
the day having a duty to be loyal to the Crown had not been
replaced by the idea of the Crown owing a duty of loyalty to
the Ministry. If, by our standards, many of Victoria's actions
were unconstitutional, by contemporary standards she was a
model constitutional monarch in comparison with her predecessors. Can we not place ourselves alongside Bagehot in

1867 in saying: 'If we look at history, we shall find that it is only during the period of the present reign that in England the duties of a constitutional sovereign have ever been well performed.'[43] In any case the fundamental question is not when and to what extent Victoria acted unconstitutionally, but how great was her political influence.

In answering this question it is important in the first place to be clear that the old days of royal power as distinct from influence had gone. It seems to have been Gladstone who first drew this distinction publicly, in 1875.[44] Three years later, however, alarmed by an inside report of the relationship between the Queen and Beaconsfield's Cabinet, he said that the position she had adopted recalled James II, was 'much more advanced than that of George III', and was, in short, 'an outrage... due to Lord Beaconsfield...'.[45] From Gladstone's own point of view, therefore, he was being moderate when in 1880, after five months in office, he had felt for the first time the full force of the Queen's hostility to him, in saying that 'he would never be surprised to see her turn the Government out, after the manner of her uncles'.[46] This was a considered view. He expressed it quite deliberately in what he called the 'quasi-Cabinet' and repeated it in a letter to his closest confidant, Lord Granville.[47]

The last precedent for the action feared by Gladstone dated back to 1834 when William IV dismissed Melbourne and replaced him by Peel. There was no subsequent precedent because the ensuing Election, while costing the Reform Party 100 seats, did not give Peel a majority in the House of Commons. In fact, no Prime Minister could, after the passing of the Reform Act, remain in office with the confidence of the Crown but without the confidence of the House of Commons. Up to 1832 the King could, one way or another, by the manipulation of groups in the House of Commons or by manipulation of Elections, obtain a majority in that House for the Minister of his choice. After 1832 the majority in it was determined by popular suffrage, of ever-increasing extent;[48] a Minister staying in office without a majority would have been engaged in an impossible attempt to reverse the whole course of British constitutional history for centuries; to put, so to speak, Charles 1's head back on his shoulders, to depose William III and reinstate James II. Outvoted six times in six weeks in the new Parliament, Peel resigned in April 1835. That Ministry was the '100 days' of a lost cause.[49]

The matter was, understandably, not seen as clearly as that at the time. Melbourne, though it was he whom the events of 1834–5 brought back to office, did not completely grasp their significance. Arguing against a dissolution in 1841 he told the Queen:

> We know that Charles 1 and Charles II, and even Cromwell, appealed to the country, and had a Parliament returned into their very teeth ... since then the Crown had always had a majority returned in favour of it. Even Queen Anne, who removed Marlborough in the midst of his most glorious victories and dissolved Parliament, had an immense majority. ... William IV, even though he had a majority against him which prevented him from keeping his Ministers, had a much stronger feeling for him in that Parliament than he ever had before. But I am afraid that for the first time the Crown would have an Opposition returned smack against it. ...[50]

But the election had to come and, despite a royal progress round the chief Whig houses,[51] so did the 'smack'. Reflecting on the event five years later, the Queen still adhered to Melbourne's view:

> She considers the power of dissolving Parliament a most valuable and powerful instrument in the hands of the Crown, but which ought not to be used except in extreme cases and with a certainty of success. To use this instru-

ment and be defeated is a thing most lowering to the Crown and hurtful to the country. The Queen strongly feels that she made a mistake in allowing the Dissolution in 1841; the result has been a majority returned against her of nearly one hundred votes. . . .[52]

The Queen and her mentor thus viewed the Constitution through spectacles with a pre-1832 focus. To some extent she continued to do so. In the latter part of her reign, for example, she continued to entertain the idea of a Dissolution as a means of effecting her own purposes. Clearing her mind during the battle between the two Houses of Parliament over the third Reform Bill, she wrote, on a draft letter to Gladstone, in 1884:

> Mr Gladstone must be prepared for the Queen to hold him responsible for the agitation and danger which may be got up by the extreme Liberals and for her . . . insisting on a dissolution as the only safe means of putting a stop to it.[53]

Again, as we have seen,[54] as late as 1894, faced once more by what she thought a dangerous threat (which, in the end, did not materialise) to the House of Lords she seems definitely to have decided to insist on an Election.*

The prerogative of Dissolution had, in fact, ceased to be a personal one, i.e. it could now only be exercised on the advice of Ministers. The Queen could not, in practice, turn them out after the manner of her uncles and their ancestors. Of this particular prerogative, the power to appoint and dismiss Ministers, all that remained as personal, i.e., action which the Queen could take of her own volition, was the power to pick as Prime Minister *a* leader of a Party when it was undecided who was *the* leader, or to pick a Prime Minister when no one Party had

---

* Lord Salisbury assured her that she would have been entirely within her constitutional rights in doing so.[55] But he had been wiser, the year before, to emphasise the risk of a step of that kind injuring her authority[56]

a majority in the House of Commons. Thus in 1852 it was
really her decision which installed Lord Aberdeen as Prime
Minister at the head of a Whig-Peelite Coalition: in 1859 she
had freedom of choice between Palmerston and Russell, though
her first choice was Granville; in February 1868, she could
have sent for the Duke of Richmond or Lord Stanley in preference to Disraeli, in December for Russell in preference to Gladstone; in 1880, though she had in the end to take Gladstone,
she chose to send first for Hartington rather than, possibly in-
correctly, Granville. In 1885 Northcote had as much right to
be summoned as Salisbury; in 1894 she asked Rosebery to become the new Prime Minister without even asking the advice of
the retiring one about the succession. Incidentally there can be
little doubt that her choice of Rosebery rather than Harcourt
was a decisive factor in the ensuing enfeeblement of the Liberal
Party which lasted till 1906; it was not the case, however, that
this was her intention.

On at least two occasions the Queen went even further than
making a personal election of a Prime Minister and selected,
or sought to select, the Leader of the Opposition. Thus in 1875
she told Granville that she looked 'on *him* as the real leader of
the Liberal Party, and whosoever is chosen as leader of the
Liberal Party in the House of Commons as under him'.[57] Similarly, after Disraeli's death, she told Sir Stafford Northcote that
she would look on him 'as the leader of the great Conservative
Party, though it may not be necessary to *announce* this
now...'.[58] In March 1901, Edward VII contemplated asking
Rosebery 'to resume public life and the leadership of the Opposition'.[59] He was dissuaded from doing so, but it can be seen
that for such a step a kind of precedent could have been found.

The obverse of all this, and the most signal demonstration
of the fact that by this time the Crown had very little political
power left, was the fact that in 1880 the Queen had to name
Gladstone as her Prime Minister, because he was the popular

choice. No appointment she ever made can have been more distasteful to her. She tried again, in 1886[60] and in 1892,[61] but less hard, to find another Liberal Prime Minister.

In general, the Queen contested every inch of ground when it came to giving up any of her prerogatives;[62] indeed she thought she had preserved the position as she had found it.[63] For the Crown, as for Britain itself,[64] or any individual property-owner, her rooted belief was that what one had, so far as possible, one held. E. F. Benson records that she strongly recommended his father, her last Archbishop of Canterbury but one, to oppose the idea of Cuddesdon being given up as the home of the Bishop of Oxford: 'If you begin giving up, they will go on grabbing till they get everything.'[65] When Lord Salisbury proposed the cession of Heligoland in 1890, she was very uneasy: 'Giving up what one has is always a bad thing.'[66]

We have already seen how the Queen resisted any encroachments on her special position in relation to the Army.[67] She was not prepared wholly to delegate the prerogative of mercy to the Home Secretary, who threatened resignation when she objected to the commutation of a sentence of execution.[68] (Her great-grandson, George VI, twice differed from Herbert Morrison, when Home Secretary, about death sentences. The King accepted his Minister's decision 'with every good grace'.[69]) She strenuously maintained that she was 'the Head of the Church and also of the Scottish Church, but still more so of the English'.[70] At the end of her reign she was vigorously maintaining that she was the Head of the Welsh Church. Moreover, she saw attacks on the House of Lords as indirect attacks on the Crown, as attempts to pierce the outer defences of the royal stronghold, to take it by gradual infiltration rather than by any frontal assault: '. . . to threaten the House of Lords is, in fact, to threaten the Monarchy itself. Another Sovereign but herself must acquiesce in any alteration of the House of Lords. She will not be the sovereign of a Democratic Monarchy.' So she drafted a letter to Gladstone in 1884.[71] It was a great failure not to see that the best way to preserve the Monarchy was to increase its popularity rather than cling to its prerogatives.

Maitland described the Crown as 'a chattel entailed upon the Hanoverian dynasty'. Victoria saw it in a similar light, a family heirloom to be bequeathed, with all its appurtenances, to her successors in exactly the same condition as that in which she had received it. *'Son métier était d'être Reine'* and she held it a professional responsibility to preserve the institution of monarchy in general (she frequently deplored Republicanism in France) and the British Monarchy, with its surrounding institutions, in particular. Her conservatism about the Crown was a consequence of her personal conservatism,[72] a cause of her political Conservatism. 'Mr G.', she wrote, 'will find the Queen very determined and firm in all that concerns the *honour, dignity*, and *safety of the Vast Empire* confided to her care and which she wishes to hand down unimpaired to her children and their children's children.'[73]

Queen Victoria, then, did not see her role as limited to the exercise of personal influence; she saw herself as retaining much of the power of her predecessors. But it was another failure not to see how very great such an influence could be. Bagehot, having stated the three rights of a constitutional sovereign, as he saw them, added, rightly: 'And a king of great sense and sagacity would want no others.'[74] Let us put it another way. A permanent official with the right to gather information from any quarter, to read any State paper, to meet any person, to express any opinion and, withal, the right to be treated always with deference, and no other legal powers whatsoever, would be a very powerful official. If such an official were also able, conscientious, industrious and long-lived, his influence would be immense. That was the reality of Victoria's position. In comparison the last vestiges of the prerogative were unimportant.

Before proceeding, however, to an evaluation of how she used her position one should add a word or two about her relevant personal qualities. Two in particular deserve comment. Dilke described her as 'a woman of great ability'.[75] The many quotations already made from her letters should have gone a long way to convince the reader of this truth. Certainly she had the ability, and it is an important part of ability in general, to make her meaning clear. The Duke of Wellington, in the previous reign, had complained of the necessity of having to write long answers to letters from the King, 'respectfully telling him what an old fool he was'. William IV's niece was far from a fool even as a girl. The letters she wrote as a mature ruler required respectful answers, and very often long ones, not merely because of her position but on the merits of the opinions she expressed. Granville, who knew her well and for a long time, said that 'it was impossible to treat the Queen as a great statesman because she was such a child, but equally impossible to treat her as a child because she had the *aperçus* of a great statesman in some things'.[76]

Next, industry. Again the reader is bound already to have formed the impression that the Queen was industrious. But it is impossible to over-emphasise the immense extent of her industry.[77] The more one learns of her, the more one wonders how she found time to do anything but write. She did find it, but one cannot but be amazed at the vast daily output of letters and telegrams, to Ministers, to relatives, to Court officials,[78] and all this is in addition to the regular keeping of a detailed diary. One is reminded of Florence Nightingale, lying on her sofa in South Street, often, it is true, interviewing people, but mainly engaged on the writing of an unceasing series of papers on British Army administration.

Sir Howard Elphinstone, Governor to the Duke of Connaught, received six letters from the Queen in 48 hours. But this score was bettered many times. At the height of the

Eastern crisis Disraeli confided to a friend that the Queen, 'almost literally', wrote every day and telegraphed every hour.[79] At the time of the Egyptian campaign in 1882, one day alone brought 17 letters from the Queen or her Private Secretary to the Secretary of State for War (H. C. E. Childers).[80] In the same year Sir William Harcourt, à propos of his piloting an Irish Coercion Bill through the House of Commons, wrote:

> I got letter after letter from Balmoral as if I was an incompetent sluggard. This spurring of a willing horse ... is a very disheartening sort of treatment. ...[81]

In the Gladstone papers are 577 letters and 241 telegrams from the Queen, and this is apart from letters from Sir Henry Ponsonby.[82] The Queen, with the aid of a Private Secretary and virtually no one else, made herself one of the great Departments of State.

If the degree of the Sovereign's industry is to be reckoned in terms of the number of public functions presided at and the number of 'audiences' given, Queen Victoria was not, especially allowing for her annual withdrawals to the Scottish Highlands, notably industrious.* If, on the other hand, a Sovereign's industry is to be reckoned in terms of desk work, no British Sovereign could have been or, with the possible exception of George III, ever had been more industrious than his granddaughter. Bagehot was mistaken in describing her as 'a retired widow'.[85]

Hard work of this kind is bound to have its effect, even in a short run. In Victoria's case the run was a very long one. In

---

* 'I suppose', wrote the first Lord Redesdale[83]—and he was in the Diplomatic Service for 15 years and at the head of the Board of Works for another 12—'that few sovereigns have been less in contact with her Ministers, with the single exception of Lord Beaconsfield, than Queen Victoria was after the defeat of Lord Melbourne. ... Of the permanent officials she personally made no use. She never sent for them or consulted them, and I much doubt whether she knew the heads of even the Foreign Office or Treasury by sight.' Edward VII by contrast gave Civil Service dinners and knew 'all the men of mark' in it 'as he did those in the Army and Navy ...'[84]

assessing her political influence one must therefore add to the factors of ability and industry those of longevity and a first-class memory. Thus she could, and did, draw on increasing stores of experience. On that account her influence tended to increase rather than decrease with old age. In 1898 she was saying, à propos of her relations with Ministers, 'I cannot any longer argue',[86] but a year later Lord Esher, conducting her over Kensington Palace, found her memory and knowledge 'quite wonderful'.[87] At Balmoral in the autumn of 1899, after a long drive and a late dinner (it only began at 9.15 p.m.),* she twice, to his consternation, went to sleep while talking with Lord Balfour of Burleigh. But on waking up she condemned Sir William Harcourt's speeches as unpatriotic with 'great animation'.[89] In October 1900, she played an active part in the reshaping of Lord Salisbury's Cabinet. Only in November do the first tell-tale references to loss of appetite, sleeplessness, feeling 'poorly and wretched' appear in her diary;[90] only, in short, as her body began to wear out did her close and constant interest in public affairs begin to slacken.

As early as 1871 Disraeli said, in a public speech:

> No person likely to administer the affairs of this country would treat the suggestions of Her Majesty with indifference, for at this moment there is probably no person living in this country who has such complete control over the political traditions of England as the Sovereign herself. The last generation of statesmen have all, or almost all, disappeared; the Sir Robert Peels, the Lord Derbys, the Lord Palmerstons have gone; there is no person who can advise Her Majesty . . . who can have such a complete mastery of what has occurred in this country, and of all the great and important affairs of State, foreign and domestic, for the last thirty-four years, as the Queen herself. He, therefore,

* This seems to have become her regular dinner time; the meal lasted only half an hour[88]

would not be a wise man who would not profit by Her Majesty's judgment and experience. . . .[91]

One of Her Majesty's complaints against the second Gladstone Government was the want of respect and consideration for her views, based on an experience of 45 years.[92] Queen Victoria told Gladstone what Wellington had told her about Pitt.[93] Sir Henry Campbell-Bannerman said she made him feel like a little boy talking to his grandmother. The occasion was one when he was trying to persuade her to withdraw her opposition to some Liberal measure and she said: 'I remember Lord Melbourne using the same argument many years ago, but it was not true then and it is not true now.'[94]

The 18-year-old girl of 1837 who was Melbourne's pupil, the wife who leaned so much on her husband, was during the period with which we are concerned, replaced by an intelligent, able, self-confident, indefatigably industrious ruler, with a long and rich memory.* To be Queen of England from 18 to 82 is, to say the least, character-forming; the 'Widow at Windsor' was a formidable personage. Even Bismarck was 'almost nervous' when about to be shown into her presence.[96] Of course she was not in Bismarck's class as a statesman, nor in that of Gladstone, Disraeli or Salisbury.[97] She had not the same ability—or power—as any one of them, and her political experience was of a different kind. On the other hand, what ability and power she did have she exercised over a far longer period. How should that equation be resolved?

The Queen's political influence was further increased by her sex. As a woman she was treated by her Ministers with even greater deference than a male Sovereign would have been; as a widow, with even greater deference than a wife. Lord Rose-

---

*In 1873 when the Queen proposed one policy and the Foreign Secretary another—on the ground that it had been Palmerston's—she instantly found the relevant paper, which showed that her proposal was the same as Palmerston's[95]

bery once remarked: 'She is an old lady with all the foibles and strength of one. ...'[98] It was an advantage for her to be able to 'come the grandmother' over him, Sir Henry Campbell-Bannerman (as we have just seen), and doubtless many others.

Paradoxically, the Queen's position was in a way a disadvantage to her as a politician. The point involved has been well put by Viscount Gladstone, writing out of the experience of long years in the House of Commons and in office, followed by the Governor-Generalship of South Africa:

> ... continuity on the heights ... relieved her from the necessity of ever going to the roots of big questions by reason and argument. Politicians had to fight these things out in principle and detail on the platform, in the press, and in the House of Commons. ... Discussion and inquiry produced stages in their minds ... which were steps to progress. ... Those who are neither responsible actors nor students never undergo the grinding toil essential to the real understanding of difficult questions. ... So of necessity was it in the case of the Queen ... whose lofty isolation kept her apart from all the essential dynamics of politics.[99]

These are important truths. Against them must be set the fact that the Sovereign can—not necessarily will—take more detached and longer views of political questions than practising politicians. Moreover, the Sovereign can also hold, and press, those views for longer—usually—than most politicians. Again, one asks: how can that equation be resolved.

The Queen's influence as a political mediator, over the Irish Church Bill in 1869 and again over the Third Reform Bill in 1884, has already been mentioned.[100] Fortunately the tangled story of her role in 1884 has been most admirably disentangled by an American historian, Corinne Comstock Weston.

The Government's Franchise Bill of that year was intended to extend the 1867 franchise from the Boroughs to the

Counties; in other words, to give votes to agricultural labourers. It was generally agreed, however, that such a Bill must be rapidly followed by a Seats Bill to re-distribute and, as near as possible, equalise constituencies. To the Conservatives in particular it was plain that if an Election were to be held on the new franchise, but on the old distribution, the result would be disastrous for them. But when the Franchise Bill reached the Lords no Seats Bill had been put before the Commons. On 8 July, therefore, the Lords, with their large and permanent Conservative majority, passed an amendment to the Franchise Bill which was tantamount to a rejection of it. A major Constitutional crisis over the relationship between the two Houses therefore impended and many inflammatory speeches were made. On the other hand, manifold possibilities of compromise obviously existed. In fact, a compromise was announced on 17 November by which an agreed Seats Bill was to receive its Second Reading in the Commons simultaneously with the Franchise Bill starting its Committee Stage in the Lords. An inter-Party conference was then held which in 10 days settled the basic principles of the Seats Bill.

In the intervening drama, played behind the scenes, there were five principal actors, the Queen (supported by Ponsonby and C. L. Peel, the Clerk to the Privy Council), Gladstone (Prime Minister), Salisbury (Leader of the Opposition in the House of Lords), the Duke of Richmond and Lord Cairns (two leading Conservative Peers, who were also great Scottish landowners). The Queen was anxious for a compromise from the start; Gladstone was reasonably conciliatory throughout; Salisbury played by far the most partisan role, angling for a Dissolution rather than any concession to the Government. In these circumstances the roles of the Duke of Richmond and Lord Cairns, whose teamwork could not have been closer knit, became all-important. The Duke, invited to Balmoral, was delighted to find himself treated more as a friend than a subject.

Protracted and complicated negotiations followed, but the essence of the matter was that the Queen, the Duke and Lord Cairns (who had moved the Lords' amendment to the Franchise Bill in July) came to realise that it was the intransigence of Lord Salisbury which was the real obstacle to compromise. In her journal on 29 October 1884, the Queen noted: 'Something must be done, and if Lord Salisbury won't do what is right, then someone else must take the lead.'[101] The someone else was to be 'Richmond-Cairns' and, to Salisbury's chagrin, their view of the necessity of meeting a conciliatory statement by the Government with a conciliatory reply prevailed at a meeting at the Carlton Club. The crisis was over.

But how far was its ending due to the Queen's hard work? Salisbury and his nephew-secretary, A. J. Balfour, took the line that the Government could be met in conference because it had, for the first time since July, put forward in public terms which were both specific and reasonable. On that basis it was not the Queen's intervention which was decisive:

> A distinction is possible between the substance of the conflict, which Queen Victoria could not influence, and the manoeuvres to bring about an agreement when it was wanted, which she could influence.... The offer of previous consultation on the details of the Seats Bill, which Salisbury had indicated was a vital factor in the decision for conference, came from Gladstone and cannot be described as Queen Victoria's personal policy.[102]

But it was natural that Salisbury and Balfour should be silent in public on the Conservative disaffection which had manifested itself in private. There is, moreover, evidence that Salisbury was swayed by the difficulty of maintaining his majority in the Lords in the absence of an inter-Party agreement. On this basis one cannot underestimate the importance of 'the royal role in a quiet revolt within the Conservative ranks'[103] which made it virtually certain that the Government's compromise terms would be accepted by the Opposition; on this basis, in short, the Queen's mediation was decisive. Granted that that is the balance of the argument, one must also note that in 1884, as in 1869, the success of her intervention was due to the pressure put on the Opposition, not just to the waving of a magic, because royal, sceptre. This has its relevance, as we shall see,[104] to our consideration of later instances of unsuccessful royal mediation. What the Queen did in 1869 and in 1884 enabled 'the moderate Conservatives to *prevail*'.[105]

Anyone at the head of an organisation is necessarily almost as much concerned with appointments as with policy. And who is to say that in the long run good or bad appointments do not have as much, or more, influence on the course of events as right or wrong decisions about policy? We have seen[106] that in certain circumstances the Queen had the power to make an appointment to the highest political office of all, that of Prime Minister. In no circumstances had she any such power in respect of any other political appointment, but she could, and freely did, express her opinions about who was or was not suitable for what positions, even, as already seen,[107] relatively minor ones. In other words, in this particular part of the political field, as in the field in general, her personal influence was constantly and vigorously brought to bear.

The subject deserves a monograph. Here one can only summarise and say that sometimes, as in the case of Lowe in 1880, she announced that she would not accept some person as a Cabinet Minister,[108] and that person's name was never submitted to her. Sometimes, as in the case of the Chief Irish Secretaryship in 1887, she intended to put forward a name (in this case that of Balfour) when the Prime Minister put forward the same name first.[109] Sometimes, as in the case of Derby in 1882,[110] or Granville in 1886, she was able to secure that someone went to one office rather than another. Sometimes, as in the case of Lord Clarendon in 1868, or Lord Ripon in 1880,[111] she had to agree to an appointment to which she had objected. Sometimes the reverse was the case, Lord Salisbury, for example, telling her Private Secretary in 1895: 'Her Majesty was very anxious that Mr Matthews should not again be Home Secretary; and I have obeyed Her Majesty's wish.'[112]* Sometimes she succeeded where a Prime Minister had failed in making a man take a particular position, as in the case of Northcote becoming a Peer and Foreign Secretary in 1885.[114] Sometimes she was able to secure the appointment of her candidate to an important office, e.g., Lord Rosebery's Foreign Secretaryship in 1886.[115] Gladstone's candidate had been Lord Kimberley,[116] but the Queen had made up her mind, in advance even of the resignation of the previous Government, that the office should be Rosebery's.[117] Sometimes she was simultaneously successful in keeping one man out and putting another in, Gladstone, for example, saying in 1886 that he 'would give up Mr Childers and would select the gentleman named by your Majesty, Mr Campbell-Bannerman, for the War Office'.[118]†

Sometimes it was the Queen's interventions which determined whether some politician should get a minor or a major office. Thus in 1880, when it had become clear to Gladstone that either Joseph Chamberlain or Sir Charles Dilke must be given Cabinet office, it was the Queen who determined that the former should enter the Cabinet as President of the Board of Trade, and the latter remain outside as Under-Secretary of State for Foreign Affairs. She objected to both as Radicals, but Dilke was in her eyes guilty of a grave offence, that of making

* In 1880 she refused her *agrément* to the Marquis de Noailles, because of his scandalous life, becoming French Ambassador to the Court of St James [113]

† He was Gladstone's third choice for the job, Ponsonby dryly recording on a letter from the Queen dated 1.ii.86: 'Mr Gladstone asked me not to send him unpleasant letters at night as it prevented him sleeping. He was much put out at the Queen's objection to Childers for War Office.... Wouldn't hear of Harcourt for that position. Queen wouldn't hear of Childers. I showed him in' [119]

Republican speeches, albeit nine years earlier. Chamberlain was, at the time of those speeches, also a Republican but does not seem to have expressed Republican views in public until a few years later.[120]

The Queen's hostility to Dilke had such important practical consequences that the episode deserves detailed treatment. He did not get even his Under-Secretaryship in 1880 (he was particularly well versed in foreign affairs) without having to write two letters, the first disavowing Republicanism in general terms[121] and the second eating, so to speak, a second helping of humble pie in specific relation to the criticisms he had made of the Civil List in 1871.[122] Even so a watchful royal eye was ever on him. 'Is it true', the Queen asked Gladstone in March 1882, 'that Sir C. Dilke and Mr Fawcett did not vote for the Pce Leopd's annuity? If so . . . it must put an effectual bar to their ever being Cabinet Ministers.'[123] When a proposal that Dilke should be given Cabinet office was renewed at the end of the year, the Queen, still not satisfied even by two letters of recantation, argued that his Republican views had not been publicly withdrawn:

> Does he still maintain these views? If so, he cannot be a Minister in the Govt. of a Monarchy. Has he changed his principles? If so, there can be no difficulty in avowing it publicly.[124]

This pressure was not fair. Dilke had publicly abandoned his earlier attitude in the course of the Election campaign of 1874,[125] and this fact was part of the explanations offered before he joined the Government of 1880. Moreover, what had been asked for on that occasion was either 'a written explanation' or a speech in Parliament 'on the subject of his very offensive Speeches on the Civil List and the Royal Family . . .'.[126] The former having been supplied, it was unfair to ask for a speech as well two years later. Moreover the Queen refused to have

Dilke, as the Prime Minister suggested, as Chancellor of the Duchy of Lancaster and only accepted him as President of the Local Government Board. Several days after the appointment she wired Gladstone:

> Pray remember that I accepted Sir C. Dilke on condition he took an early opportunity making recantation or explanation of his former crude opinions.[127]

Another assurance was forthcoming. But a week later the Queen wrote to Gladstone that 'she had no confidence in Sir C. Dilke as yet and his conduct and language will be very carefully watched by her . . .'.[128]

In May 1882, Dilke wrote despondently to Gladstone: 'I think the Queen's object is to keep me out of the Cabinet for her life, and in this I think she can succeed.'[129] In fact she delayed Dilke's entry into the Cabinet for nearly three years. Her first meeting with him had been in the Crystal Palace in 1851 when he was only eight. She stroked his head and, 20 years later, remembered doing this, adding that 'she supposed she must have rubbed the brains the wrong way'.[130]*

The question of office for Labouchere, another leading Radical, in the Queen's view 'that horrible lying Labouchere',[132] arose over the formation of Gladstone's fourth Ministry in 1892. The Queen began by positively refusing[133] to take him; became 'very anxious not to see him in office on account of his personal character';[134] but ended by agreeing to his having 'some subordinate post, which would never bring him into my presence'.[135] Gladstone, however, took it upon himself not to offer Labouchere any post.[136] The latter's own view of this decision was given to a constituent in a letter which was published in *The Times*:

* Forty years later the 72-year-old Queen met another small boy with a great political future before him, Hugh Dalton, Socialist Chancellor of the Exchequer from 1945 to 1947, then aged four. The dialogue which ensued has a piquant fascination [131]

Dear Mr Tonsley   August 19, 1892
    The Queen expressed so strong a feeling against me as
one of her Ministers that, as I understand it, Mr Gladstone did not think it desirable to submit my name to her.
                    Yours truly,
                    Henry Labouchere[137]

What does all this amount to? To some extent the facts, particularly those about the prolonged exclusion of Dilke from
Cabinet office and the successful exclusion of Labouchere from
any office whatsoever, speak for themselves. Still, valid general-
isations are elusive. The truth of the matter lies in the nature
of the processes involved. The making of a Ministry, or making
changes in one, is not a simple process of a Prime Minister
choosing the best man, in his view, for each job. Some men are
so powerful, by virtue of their position in the Government
Party, that they cannot be denied office. *Ipso facto*, therefore,
they can pick and choose among the offices available. They
can, and do, make compacts with each other to bring pressure
to bear on the Prime Minister to allocate offices in accordance
with their wishes. A Prime Minister, in short, whatever the
theory, does not in practice have a clean slate on which to
chalk his appointments. Rather do all sorts of considerations
have to be weighed in all sorts of balances. In other words,
the distribution of offices involves an intricate negotiation in
which many different persons have to be consulted and con-
ciliated. Among them in the Victorian period was the Queen,
and she took full advantage of the system to press her views,
sometimes successfully, sometimes not. It would have been
next to impossible at the end of the day, when the structure
was complete, to say in terms of each person in it that his
presence was solely because of the wish of this or that other
person. But to say that the Queen's contribution to the final
result cannot be precisely measured, is not to say that it was

not substantial. On the contrary, her influence over appointments was very great indeed.[138]

The same difficulty, of measurement, of identification of her personal contribution (as in the case of the retention of Frere in South Africa)[139] arises when one attempts to sum up and evaluate the other side of her political activities, her unremitting stream of opinion on all the political questions of the hour, great and small, domestic and overseas, legislative and administrative. Ponsonby, drafting comments on Gladstone's view of regal influence having been substituted for regal power,[140] made much of what he called 'dormant power':

> Take for instance her eagerness that some public denunciation of Railway carelessness should be published. It certainly was her persistence that induced Fortescue to write his circular; and then the country was full of it for days afterwards, Parliament founded debates on it, now a Royal Commission is sitting on the matter and possibly legislation may follow—and yet the Queen's name never appeared at all.
>
> In some ways the dormant power is so great that it might almost be dreaded if we had a bad and clever King and a weak Minister. This is most unlikely but I only allude to it to support my argument that the latent power exists.[141]

The Queen's influence could make itself directly felt in the sphere of legislation. Thus in June 1876, she was instrumental in securing the passage of a Bill to regulate vivisection.[142] Without her pressure on Disraeli this measure would not have survived the so-called 'massacre of the innocents' at the end of the Session.[143] On at least two occasions she virtually initiated legislation, the Public Worship Regulation Act of 1874 and the Royal Titles Act of 1876, under which she became Empress of India. But these were exceptional events and both, it will be noted, occurred when Disraeli was for the second time Prime

Minister with a substantial Conservative majority in the House of Commons, not that he was really keen on either measure.[144]* In general, however, it was not by this emulation of one of the roles of the President of the United States that the Queen made her influence felt. Nor could she, like an American President, veto legislation approved by both Houses. That was another power that had gone. But a 'veto precedent' remained,[146] that is to say that the Queen could and did object to legislation, or seek to modify its provisions, long before it was brought before Parliament. And over the administrative acts of the Government she could and did exercise a perpetual and wide-ranging vigilance.

Gladstone told Dilke, when he joined the Cabinet, that the 'many difficulties in that quarter... are in the main confined to three or four Departments'.[147] One may well think that the Queen's influence would have been more effective if it had been more restricted even than that, less frequent and more discriminating. As it was, she turned herself, as Lord Salisbury confirmed,[148] into a Department. In 1886 (when the Queen, it must be borne in mind, was 67) he complained:

> I could do very well with two departments; in fact I have four—the Prime Ministership, the Foreign Office, the Queen, and Randolph Churchill—and the burden of them increases in that order.[149]

Three years earlier Herbert Gladstone had told his brother Henry that the people who bothered their father 'more than all England' were 'the Queen and Lord Rosebery'.[150] If the Queen's activity was burdensome to Salisbury, how much more burdensome to Gladstone and his colleagues, and later to Rose-

* It was after the passing of the first of these two Acts, sent for the instant he arrived at Osborne, that he wrote to another lady that he could only describe his reception 'by telling you that I really thought she was going to embrace me. She was wreathed with smiles, and, as she talked, glided about the room like a bird'[145]

bery and his. If her opposition was burdensome, her coopera-
tion was helpful. Benjamin Disraeli, a great adventurer in
politics, went where he thought the power was, just as in our day,
on his own confession, and it was no discredit to him, did
Aneurin Bevan. Disraeli, a realist as well as a romantic, saw
that, as Guedalla put it, 'public business was undeniably facili-
tated by the maintenance of easy relations with the Crown. ...
A shrewd Prime Minister judged that the Queen was a valuable addition to the pieces on the board.'[151] Blake confirms this
point; 'however diminished and ill-defined' her powers, they
were 'sufficient for her good will to make a difference'[152] and
her ill will had 'a considerable nuisance value'.[153] Melbourne
and his Cabinet had found that true of William IV in the last
three years of his reign;[154] it was still true for Gladstone and
Rosebery and their Cabinets in the late Victorian period. Sir
Ivor Jennings' summation is: 'The impress of Queen Victoria's personality is evident on every page of the political history of England during her long reign. She was a clog on the
activity of every Liberal Government after 1841, and a stimulus
to every Conservative Government after 1868.'[155]

The struggle between the Queen and Liberalism was most
intense from 1880 to 1885. In 1883 Gladstone said, speaking of
his burdens, 'fiercely', to Rosebery: 'The Queen alone is
enough to kill any man.'[156] Rosebery laughed at this, but Gladstone added 'This is no laughing matter, though it may sound
so. ...' In 1884 Ponsonby wrote: 'The Queen reads carefully
the Ministerial speeches and immediately writes to Gladstone
if she observes the least threat against the House of Lords. ...
Hamilton complains to me that if these criticisms go on there
must be an Assistant Prime Minister to do nothing but read
[them] and expostulate with wild members of the Government.'[157]

It was once said that anyone could get a speech out of Gladstone, i.e., that he dissipated his energies by unnecessary re-

plies to unimportant criticisms. By the same token it could be said that too many people could get letters out of him too easily and the Queen was one of them. Once and once only do we find him deciding to 'take no notice of this rather foolish letter'.[158] In the Gladstone papers are 4,460 letters to the Queen; as Prime Minister between 1880 and 1885 there are 1,017, exclusive of letters about the formation of the Government and about honours and appointments. All were written in his own hand. Many must have required careful drafting.[159]

It is true that, as Lytton Strachey says, 'speech was the fibre of his being'.[160] It helped him to put his problems into words. At that time the Queen's share in many of the relatively minor processes of administration was great and, in contra-distinction from her argumentative utterances about high policy, not unhelpful. None the less, the war of attrition which the Queen waged against Liberal Governments had its effects. It put the Constitution under strain in a manner reminiscent of the strain on the American Constitution when the President is of one Party and the Congress of another. The Queen had not, like the House of Lords from 1911 onwards, a legally defined 'delaying power', but she could cause delays (as with Dilke's appointment to the Cabinet).[161] She slowed things up; she wore men down. Rosebery was, no doubt, a weak vessel and his position as Prime Minister most unhappy in many ways. None the less, his difficulties with the Queen were among the causes of a breakdown in health.[162] He was a chronic insomniac, but even Gladstone lost sleep, literally, on many occasions because harassed by the Queen.[163] Francis Birrell wrote: 'The failure of the 1880 Administration can be largely attributed to the time wasted quarrelling with the Court.'[164]

The weakness and inconsistency of Disraeli's 1874 Administration in handling the Eastern crisis can be largely attributed to the Queen's influence. He and his Cabinet allowed themselves to be driven this way and that by various influences, and this was one of them. From 1876 to 1878, in Viscount Gladstone's opinion, she 'was the driving force behind the Government'.[165] Ponsonby observed that: 'Taken from her point of view she is more determined and energetic than her Ministers.'[166] Colonel Wellesley, Military Attaché at St Petersburg, after an audience with the Queen, said 'he thought [she] knew as much as Lord Beaconsfield and had far more defined and clear ideas of her views than Lord Beaconsfield and Derby . . .'.[167]

When the Administration was still in its infancy, the Foreign Secretary, Lord Derby (the 15th Earl), wrote to the Prime Minister:

> Nobody can have managed the lady better than you have; but is there not just a risk of encouraging her in too large ideas of her personal power, and too great indifference to what the public expects. I only ask: it is for you to judge.[168]

Disraeli had rubbed the lamp too hard. In 1878 Derby neither asked nor judged, but resigned. Another Cabinet casualty in the same year, Lord Carnarvon, reviewing the course of events which led to his resignation, wrote of the situation in the spring of 1877:

> A new and great power now made itself felt. For some time the Queen, in personal communications with various members of the Cabinet, had brought her influence to bear —I have little doubt that the original impulse proceeded from Disraeli; but that as the [Russo-Turkish] war proceeded . . . he was no longer able to control the force which he had called into being. . . . He on more than one occasion in Cabinet described himself as unable to check or moderate the pressure exercised by the Queen upon him and the Government, and . . . I am disposed to believe that this was partly true. Be this, however, as it may the personal impulse was exercised much more strongly on individual members of the Government, and in some cases

with remarkable effect. . . . The object and purpose of these communications were all in the same direction—active and armed support of Turkey. . . .[169]

Carnarvon resigned on 24 January 1878. On 27 May he confidentially confided in Gladstone something of what had been going on, of how Cabinet Ministers had repeatedly 'been sent for to receive "wiggings" from the Queen' and how communications had from time to time been sent 'to the Cabinet warning it off from certain subjects and saying that she could not agree to this and would not agree to that . . .'.[170] Gladstone held strongly to the view, which the Queen did not accept as correct,[171] that the Cabinet should be a unity in its relations with the Sovereign* and, in a memorandum marked 'Secret', described Carnarvon's second point as an 'outrage', which he blamed on Beaconsfield's influence.[173] Carnarvon has put on record at least one specific instance of a Cabinet meeting opening with a communication from the Queen 'urging us very strongly to stand by the principle . . . that any advance on Constantinople would free us from neutrality . . .'.[174]†

One final point about Queen Victoria's political role. It must be re-emphasised[176] that the only Victorians to whom it was known were those 'in the know'. The great mass of her contemporaries could only judge the quantum of her activity by the number of her public appearances. They therefore must have thought, at any rate from 1861 onwards, if they thought about

* Morley, Gladstone's disciple and biographer, was expressing his views when he gave in his *Walpole*, in 1889, what was, in its day, a classic description of the 'principal features of Cabinet government . . . the first is the doctrine of collective responsibility. . . . The Cabinet is a unit—a unit as regards the sovereign, and a unit as regards the legislature. Its views are laid before the Sovereign and Parliament, as if they are the views of one man . . .'[173]

† Another royal missive to the Cabinet (19.iv.77) is given in full in Monypenny and Buckle, *Life of Disraeli*, II, 1004–5. We shall see that Edward VII once or twice threatened to write a letter to the Cabinet, but did not in fact act on that intention[175]

the subject at all, that the Queen lived rather a lazy life. *Leaves from Our Journals in the Highlands* must have contributed to this impression.[177] The Queen herself saw the book as to some extent a substitute for public appearances[178] and attributed her seclusion to 'her *overwhelming work*' rather than her sorrow or ill-health: 'From the hour she gets out of bed till she gets into it again there is work, work, work—letters, boxes, questions, etc. ...'[179] But this paper work was not known to the public and, partly because of that ignorance, a wave of Republicanism swept across the country in the 'seventies. In 1871 Disraeli defended the particular way in which she discharged her duties, in a Harvest Festival speech at Hughenden. He attributed to ill-health her failure 'to resume the performance of those public and active duties which ... brought her into constant and active touch with her people', but went on to dwell on the exemplary discharge of 'much higher duties':

> I will venture to say that no head of any department in the State performs more laborious duties than fall to the Sovereign. ... There is not a despatch received from abroad nor one sent from this country which is not submitted to the Queen. ... Those Cabinet Councils of which you hear ... often call for her critical remarks necessarily requiring considerable attention.[180]

Gladstone thought ill of this utterance. In his opinion, Disraeli had done the Queen and the country 'a left-handed service' by it: 'The right aim is to keep her up to work; he has done all in his power to let her down.'[181]

In the next year, however, the year of the second edition (with a long new Introduction) of the *English Constitution* Bagehot, despite Disraeli's speech, saw no reason to change his description of the Queen as 'a retired widow'. He had indeed written that 'the courtiers of Queen Victoria are agreed as to the magnitude of the royal influence. It is with [them] an accepted secret doctrine that the Crown does more than it

seems.'[182] But this clue was, seemingly, not followed up. Nor
did many people follow up such clues to the Queen's politics as
that she paid a well-publicised visit to Hughenden, but never
visited Hawarden; the announcement in the Court Circular in
August 1892, that she had accepted Lord Salisbury's resignation 'with regret', or Labouchere's letter to Tonsley.[183] Sir
Philip Magnus comments that '... the new British democracy
accepted, casually and characteristically, as authoritative, an
amateur's definition of the altered relationship between the
sovereign and the executive'.[184]

Bagehot, however, was better informed than other 'out-
siders'. Typical of their opinions were those of Frederick Harrison, Editor of *The Fortnightly Review*, writing in that paper
at the moment of maximum popularity for Republicanism:

> ... the sovereign is as much bound to keep his feelings to
> himself as any well-bred young lady. In consequence the
> influence of the throne, whatever it may be socially is
> nothing politically....

'If the Crown were', he wound up, 'to insist on personally
nominating a minister ... the very lawn of the bishops would
ruffle in wrath.... We may, however, be perfectly tranquil,
no sovereign is likely to attempt any gambles with the constitution any more than the Queen's coloured horses are likely
to kick to pieces the gingerbread coach. Are we poor people
not to laugh?'[185]

The last laugh was not with Harrison. The academics seem
to have had more of the root of the matter in them than the
journalists. Dicey in 1885 wrote:

> ... no one of the King's predecessors, nor, it may be pre-
> sumed, the King himself, has ever acted upon or affected
> to act upon the maxim originated by Thiers, that 'the
> King reigns but does not govern'.... No one really sup-
> poses that there is not a sphere, though a vaguely defined

sphere, in which the personal will of the King has under the constitution very considerable influence.[186]

Maitland, lecturing in 1887–8 on 'Public law at the present day', said:

> Few indeed are the people who really know how much or how little the Queen's own wishes affect the course of government. I strongly suspect that her influence is rather underrated than overrated by the popular mind.[187]

He said also that if, at that time, when Salisbury was Prime Minister, '...Gladstone insisted on constantly having the Queen's ear...our Constitution would soon be topsy-turvy'.[188] Little did he know that in 1886, when the roles were reversed, Salisbury, as we have seen,[189] did have the Queen's ear constantly. And Disraeli had it too, from his resignation in 1880 until his death the next year.

But if the extent of the Queen's political activity was not widely known among contemporaries, still less was the strength and ferocity of her Party views. Dilke, in the letter already quoted from,[190] after emphasising the extent of the Queen's interference when Liberal Ministers were in power, went on:

> But it is very doubtful how far her interference is unconstitutional, and it would be quite impossible to prove it, unless Mr Gladstone, for example, were to publish her letters—a not very likely supposition.[191]

That supposition was even more unlikely than Sir Charles, or anyone else, could possibly have thought. Gladstone's fourth son, Herbert (Viscount Gladstone), revealed that his father's diary for 2 January 1898 (he died on 19 May) contained a definite injunction for silence 'about his personal relations with the Queen in the later years of his life'.[192] From this injunction Viscount Gladstone and his elder brother Henry (Lord Gladstone of Hawarden) felt themselves absolved by G. E. Buckle's

unfolding of the Queen's side of the story, first in the last four
volumes of the official *Life of Disraeli* and then in the second
series, which he edited, of *The Letters of Queen Victoria*. But
the fact remains that it was Gladstone's intention to be loyal
to the Queen even in death. In spite of the heavy burden she
put on him, he retained a high regard for her personally and
an abiding reverence for the institution she embodied. A strong
element of the Conservative always remained in him. He loved
Lords overmuch, putting far too many Whig aristocrats into
his Cabinets ('Scottish toadyism' was his enemies' description
of this trait), and it was with reluctance that he became the
enemy of the House of Lords. Of the Crown, fortunately for
it, he was always the best possible friend. Indeed his concern
for it was, as we have seen, a major factor marring his relations
with the Queen, for it led him into pressing her, to an extent
which she greatly resented, to make more public appearances
and to provide proper employment for the Prince of Wales.
(He attached more importance to this than did Disraeli.)[193] He
had as great a horror as the Queen herself of Republicanism.
He told her à propos of the Republican wave of 1870–1, that
his object was not merely meeting it 'by a more powerful display of opposite opinion, but... getting rid of it altogether,
for it could never be satisfactory that there should exist even a
fraction of the nation republican in its views'.[194]

Ten years later, rather agitated and mournful, he said to
Sir Henry Ponsonby, to whom he always spoke freely:

> Formerly I saw no reason why Monarchy should not go
> on here for hundreds of years, but I confess that the way
> [it] has been brought forward by the late government in
> political and foreign affairs has shaken my confidence and
> I dread any shock that may weaken the power of the
> Crown with the rising mass of politicians. ... I dread ap-
> pearing in antagonism to the Crown, which I am not, for

this could encourage both now and hereafter those who are dangerous to the Monarchy.[195]

Lady Ponsonby, Sir Henry's wife, the most intelligent person in Court circles, said to her husband: 'If they don't take care Gladstone will show his teeth about Royalty altogether, and I wouldn't answer for its lasting long after that.'[196] If that was true in September 1871, how much more true was it from 1880 onwards. Republicanism could easily have been revived. If Gladstone had told what he knew, almost certainly the reign, and the Monarchy itself, would have been ended. As it was, he allowed the Monarchy to show to the people a mask which did not resemble its real face. In the fullness of time the face came to resemble the mask. Sir Philip Magnus goes so far as to say that 'the main share of the credit for cutting the modern pattern of British democratic kingship is due to Gladstone . . .'.[197] It was mainly because of his restraint that a new reign began on 22 January 1901. 'We all feel a bit motherless today', wrote Henry James, 'mysterious little Victoria is dead and fat vulgar Edward is King.'

4

Edward VII

POLITICAL ROLE IN GENERAL

Sir Charles Dilke's summary of Queen Victoria's politics, quoted from more than once in the previous chapter,[1] was followed by comments on the heir apparent with whom, at the time he penned them (1882), he was frequently and closely in touch:[2]

> The Prince is, of course, in fact a strong Conservative and a still stronger JINGO, really agreeing in the Queen's politics and wanting to take everything everywhere in the world and keep everything, if possible, but a good deal under the influence of the last person who talks to him, so that he would sometimes reflect the Queen and sometimes reflect me or Chamberlain.... He has more sense and more usage of the modern world than his mother, whose long retirement has cut her off from that world, but less real brain power.[3]

Only on one major political matter during his mother's reign did the Prince of Wales differ from the Queen, and that was the Schleswig-Holstein question. Newly married to a Danish Princess, he was passionately pro-Danish and anti-Prussian. It was natural that he should have sided with his wife's country and against his elder sister's. (The Princess Royal had married Frederick, Crown Prince of Prussia, in 1858.) The Prince of Wales got on notably well with his brother-in-law, but the Prussian aggression against Denmark in 1864 coloured Edward's views about foreign politics for the rest of his life.

This point will be returned to in its proper place.[4] One may meanwhile note, however, that as King he overruled his Foreign Secretary's objection to the publication[5] of Royal correspondence about the Danish Duchies. He wanted to show that a claim to influence the conduct of foreign policy was in accordance with precedent.[6] As a young man he told a friend that he meant, when he came to the throne, to be his own Foreign Minister.[7] But it is fair only to take this as an indication of his interest in foreign affairs.

On Edward VII's accession, Lord Salisbury continued as Prime Minister until July 1902, when he was succeeded by A. J. Balfour, who continued in office until December 1905. Balfour was one of the few members of the younger generation of politicians who had not been in awe of Queen Victoria.[8] Indeed, perhaps because he was a philosopher as well as a politician, she was, almost unbelievably, a little in awe of him.[9] Neither did the new King feel at ease with the new Prime Minister, somewhat aloof in manner and so vastly his intellectual superior.

When a great new issue in British politics was raised, that of Imperial Preference, Edward VII's initial reaction to the idea, in October 1902, was favourable: '... the suggestion, if carried out, will be popular with the great bulk of the population over here, as well as, of course, with the Colonies.'[10] He went on, however, to counsel against 'any premature decision' and for 'the fullest consideration'. This advice did not come amiss to Balfour, but when it came to the politics as opposed to the policy he moved fast, carrying out an over-clever manoeuvre by which he secured the simultaneous resignation of Joseph Chamberlain, the protagonist of Imperial Preference, and of the Free Trade Cabinet Ministers whilst retaining the allegiance of a key figure, the Duke of Devonshire (the former Lord Hartington). At the start of this upheaval the Prime Minister sent, on 15 September 1903, a cipher telegram to the

King at Balmoral saying that his own policy of 'tariff retaliation' against foreign countries would cause less disruption in
the Government than any other.[11] The King was therefore
startled to receive another cipher telegram the next day announcing at least four resignations from the Cabinet.[12] A
prompt answer from Balmoral read: 'The King considers it
most important that he should see Mr Balfour without delay,
so as to discuss the future appointments in the Cabinet caused
by resignations.'[13] The answer to that was not a departure for
Scotland (when in 1931 another Cabinet was breaking up
George V left Balmoral for London) but a telegram from
Downing Street requesting permission to announce the resignations.[14] It was an essential part of Balfour's manoeuvre that it
should be rapidly known that the Duke of Devonshire, although a Free Trader, had not resigned along with the Free
Trade Ministers who had done so. The King, however, replied:
'I cannot approve of resignations being announced until I have
thoroughly discussed the matter with you. . . . This great haste is
to be deprecated and appears to be unnecessary. Moreover, it
would not look well in eyes of Public that a matter of such
importance should be settled without my having seen Prime
Minister.'[15] To this the Prime Minister replied that the King's
message had arrived too late to prevent the resignations being
announced. A few days later, after a visit to Balmoral, he submitted, from London, his list of new appointments. Brodrick
was to be moved from the War to the India Office and it was
about the nomination of a new War Secretary that the King
was most concerned.[16] To the name of Arnold-Forster he 'objected in the strongest possible terms'.[17] But Arnold-Forster got
the job.

This Cabinet crisis at the end of September 1903, was the
first major political crisis of King Edward VII's reign. We see
him in the wings, anxious to move to the centre of the stage,
but kept in the wings, not even very politely, by the producer

of the play. Balfour could not afford a moment's delay in his
fast-moving plot, but one may also surmise that, a political
Humpty Dumpty, seated somewhat insecurely on the top of
the political wall, he wanted to settle as soon as possible the
question, as between Prime Minister and Monarch, of who
was to be master.

Edward VII had already had two warnings of Balfour's
toughness, once over a brush with Brodrick about a Court Mar-
tial sentence which the King unsuccessfully tried to have miti-
gated,[18] and again when he wanted to give the Garter to the
Shah of Persia and this proposal was opposed by the Foreign
Secretary, Lord Lansdowne.[19] On both occasions the King had
a good case and influential support; on both, however, Balfour
intervened decisively and effectively in support of his Ministers.

Attention may be conveniently drawn here to Fulford's point
—and he has made many special studies of these subjects—that
'Liberals or progressive politicians are generally more considerate to royal persons than are Conservatives'.[20] A. J. P. Taylor
adds chapter and verse:

> The Right always regards itself as 'the loyal party'; there-
> fore it does not need to take any notice of the King's ob-
> jections. Even when Carson set up a seditious and rebel-
> lious organisation in 1912, its members pledged themselves
> as 'loyal subjects of His Gracious Majesty King George V'.[21]

Sir Sidney Lee saw it as a 'curious irony' that 'it was the Conservative Party, the traditional "Church and King" party,
which, during King Edward's short reign, made the most re-
sounding attacks on what was left of the royal prerogatives'.[22]
He notes on the other hand that the Liberal Ministers were
readier than their predecessors to consult the King's wishes in
'matters which touched his amour propre'.[23] Just as, in the post-
War period, there has often been a tendency for the Right to
be at greater pains to conciliate the Trade Union movement

than the Left, so perhaps there was a tendency throughout the period covered by this book for the Left to be at greater pains than the Right to conciliate the Crown. Certainly, as we have already seen, Gladstone was more considerate to the Crown than Balfour. We shall see that Asquith was more considerate than Bonar Law.[24]

In discussing the new King's relations with Liberals Sir Charles Dilke can again have the first word:

> The only two subjects on which the Prince of Wales agrees with any Liberals are (1) Randolph Churchill, (2) the Government of London.[25]

With Lord Randolph Churchill the Prince had in fact some violent 'ups and downs'. His Liberal attitude on the government of London derived, one may infer, from his friendship with Lord Rosebery who, in 1889, became the first chairman of the London County Council. With Rosebery too, Edward, as Prince and King, had some (rather petty) 'ups and downs'.[26] But he was not the only Liberal to be a personal friend. Lord Carrington (later Marquess of Lincolnshire) was a close one, although on his side there may have been an element of sycophancy in the friendship.* It was, however, the right wing of the Liberal Party that was represented in the Prince's intimate social circle.[28]

In 1868, at the age of 27, the Prince of Wales deplored Gladstone's advent to power and thought his plan for the disestablishment of the Irish Church endangered 'the safety of the Crown itself'.[29] But he recognised Gladstone's genius and came to prefer him to Disraeli, whose sense of irony 'always set the Prince of Wales on edge'.[30] This was despite Disraeli's wooing, not only of the Prince, but also of the Princess,[31] whom he

---

* It was Marie Mallet's opinion that 'Lord Carrington is most good-natured but to my mind something of a snob, he literally grovels before the meanest Royalty and makes an extraordinary fuss with all of us merely because we can date our letters "Balmoral" '[27]

courted with the same deftness which had proved successful in
the case of the Queen.

None the less, Edward's friendship with politicians, like his
mother's, to a great extent waxed and waned in accordance
with his views on their politics. He was unhappy about meeting
Sir Henry Campbell-Bannerman socially because he was 'pro-
Boer'.[32] In July 1901, he asked both Lord Salisbury[33] and Lord
Rosebery[34] whether he should ask Sir Henry to cease encourag-
ing the Boers. Both advised him not to. Lord Carrington's intervention eased the personal relationship between the King
and the Leader of the Opposition and quite a friendship grew
up at Marienbad in July 1905.[35] The King probably liked Ban-
nerman personally more than Balfour,[36] but the political relationship was always uneasy. Lord Knollys, the King's Private
Secretary, wrote to Lord Esher in March 1906, about the new
Prime Minister:

> Between ourselves, I don't think the King will ever like
> C-B politically. I do not believe that the latter understands
> him any more than Mr G. understood the Queen.[37]

It is to Edward VII's credit that he let Sir Henry have a free
hand with his appointments in December 1905, only intervening in the choice of political members of the Royal House-
hold and of Lords Lieutenant.[38]

In March 1906, Winston Churchill, Under-Secretary for the
Colonies, incurred royal wrath for a speech in the House,
widely held, but with very little justification, to have been an
offensive criticism of a Tory hero, Lord Milner. The King
described Churchill's conduct as 'simply scandalous' and, in
another letter, wrote of his 'violent and objectionable language'.[39] On 20 August 1906, however, the King wrote to
Churchill, in his own hand, that he was glad that the Minister
was becoming *a reliable minister which can only be attained
by putting country before party'.*[40]

Campbell-Bannerman was succeeded as Prime Minister in
1908 by Asquith. The King never really took to Asquith. He
disliked his manners[41] and also thought him 'very weak'.[42] By
that year Churchill was again in trouble with the King, for
making speeches about foreign policy, and Lloyd George
(Chancellor of the Exchequer) was out of favour for the same
reason.[43] By 1909 the King was as much on edge with Asquith,
and even Grey, as with Lloyd George and Churchill.[44] The
King was 'seriously annoyed' by the Chancellor's Limehouse
speech (30 July 1909). He saw it as grossly vulgar, 'full of
false statements, of socialism in its worst and most insidious
form and of virulent abuse against one particular class'
and almost 'an insult to the Sovereign . . .'. But what could the
Sovereign do about it other than tell his Private Secretary to tell
the Prime Minister that he would 'have to consider whether it
will not be his duty to write a letter to be read at the Cabinet'?[45]
In fact, he was disarmed by a 'dignified and temperate letter'
from the Chancellor.[46] He admired Lloyd George's skill as a
conciliator in industrial disputes,[47] but severely condemned his
support of Women's Suffrage, saying to Asquith, 'I shall have
no more to do with him than what is absolutely necessary',[48]
and Lloyd George was never chosen as 'Minister in attendance'
on Edward VII.[49] His much more broad-minded son invited
Lloyd George to Balmoral within three months of his accession.[50]

In September 1909, the *Glasgow Herald* published a letter
to a correspondent from Lord Knollys, addressed from Balmoral, which was a snub to Winston Churchill. It was re-
published in *The Times*. Churchill had spoken at Leicester on
4 September of Balfour from time to time emitting 'four or
five columns of insipid equivocation which the newspapers,
whose proprietors he has taken the precaution to make into
barons, hasten to claim as another epoch-making pronounce-
ment'. Knollys' point was that the creation of peers remained a
royal prerogative. He knew perfectly well, however, that this

prerogative was exercised on the Prime Minister's advice. It is understandable therefore that Churchill wrote to his wife that Knollys and the King 'must really have gone mad.... This looks to me like a rather remarkable Royal intervention and shows the bitterness which is felt in those circles.'[51] The King was in fact in Norway at the time[52] and so it seems virtually certain that he had no pre-knowledge of Knollys' letter. This 'Royal intervention' was in fact, therefore, that of the Private Secretary.

The King's objections, as in his mother's case, were not to Liberal men but to Liberal measures, policies and attitudes.[53] (None of his differences with her had their roots in politics.) Thus he liked Lord Crewe, but had no sympathy for his politics which 'mystified and vexed' him.[54] Edward's latest, brilliant biographer, Sir Philip Magnus, says (the context is social rather than political) that 'his outlook was always conservative'.[55] His earlier, official biographer, Sir Sidney Lee, thought Dilke's description of him as 'a strong Conservative' and so on, a crude characterisation.[56] But Sir Sidney also states that:

> The main political opinions to which the Prince was faithful through life, reflected Lord Palmerston's creed....[57]

And that, surely, is a variation without a difference. His mother's political opinions have already been described as Palmerstonian.[58]

We have already seen that, when Prince of Wales, Edward deplored the formation of a Liberal Government in 1868 and strongly criticised its principal measures. He was strongly anti-Russian and anti-Gladstonian at the time of the Eastern crisis.[59] In 1882 he 'did his utmost to persuade the Government to use force against Egypt'[60] and in 1889 'expressed a fervent wish to Baring and others that the British would stay in Egypt for ever ...'.[61] Under Rosebery's influence he supported both the

third Reform Bill (he even wanted to vote for it in the House
of Lords)[62] and the idea of a moderate reform of the House of
Lords.[63] To Irish Home Rule 'he was most strongly opposed',[64]
describing its advocates as 'abominable agitators'.[65] Shortly after
the defeat of the first Home Rule Bill, he asked Gladstone for
various honours for various friends. The latter commented that
the Prince had acted with tact and forbearance, but had no
claims 'as being friendly'.[66]

As King, Edward was 'of course, not a Home Ruler'.[67] He
was opposed to the legalisation of peaceful picketing by the
Trades Disputes Act of 1906.[68] (Six years later George v was
wanting it made illegal again.[69]) He thought the Education
Bill of the same year 'deplorable'.[70] He thought that the House
of Lords should be based upon the hereditary principle,[71] and
that Ministers should not advocate its abolition.[72] John Burns
was criticised for making this a plank in his electoral platform
in 1906.[73] The King at the close of his life was pondering a plan
to solve the constitutional crisis by giving peerages to the
eldest sons of Liberal peers.[74] He had 'a strong dislike' of the
1909 Budget.[75] He was against Women's Suffrage.[76] He was, as
already indicated, against the grant of self-government to the
Transvaal,[77] and thought the legislation for the Union of South
Africa premature.[78] He found the Morley-Minto reforms in
India distasteful,[79] and opposed, vigorously but vainly, the appointment of Mr S. P., later Lord Sinha, as the first Indian
member of the Viceroy's Council.[80]

In 1899 Edward wrote to Lady Warwick:

> As regards the Czar's idea of disarmament throughout all
> nations, it is the greatest rubbish and nonsense I ever
> heard of. The thing is simply impossible![81]

Eight years later he was 'disgusted' by the Prime Minister's
contribution to the first number of *The Nation*, advocating dis-
armament discussions at the second Hague Conference.[82] For

once at one with the German Emperor, he described the discussions, when they materialised, as 'humbug'.[83] It is in accordance with opinions of this kind and the responsible military opinion of the time, and also, for once, the policy of the Liberal Government, that he should 'rejoice' at the quashing of a Channel Tunnel Bill.[84] Gladstone, that great 'European', had been a strong believer in the desirability of a Tunnel.[85]

When the Unionist Party split on the issue of 'Tariff Reform', the King sided with the Free Traders,[86] i.e., with the conservative Conservatives. At the opera in August 1903, he spoke strongly, and indiscreetly, against 'the taxation of the food of the poor', so much so that the Duke of Devonshire turned to Lord Balfour of Burleigh and said: 'We must really get this man on the stump.' The discussion had started about the Motor Bill, and in that context the King had said that he was 'all in favour of taxing the rich'.[87] He pressed in vain for a Royal Commission on the whole tariff question.[88] He deemed the Chinese Labour Bill 'a necessary measure';[89] he was indeed 'enthusiastically in favour of what the Opposition called "Chinese Slavery" '.[90] In March 1905, echoing almost verbatim his mother's sentiments six years previously,[91] he spoke with asperity of Opposition speeches about South Africa as unpatriotic.[92]

We have seen that not only did the Prince share the Queen's political attitudes during her reign, but also that, in so far as the same issues continued, as for the most part they did, into his own, the King maintained her attitudes. His affection for her, despite what he called her 'jobations', had been great, his respect and admiration enormous. Sharing his mother's political attitudes, envious of her great political influence, Edward VII quite consciously tried to model his political role on Victoria's.[93] He probably realised more quickly than his advisers that this aspiration could not be fulfilled.

Lord Knollys and Lord Esher wanted Edward VII to be as

much consulted by Ministers as his mother had been; in particular they wanted this consultation to take place before the questions concerned came to the Cabinet. But this was a system which had had its hey-day in the Prince Consort's time; it had been on the wane as early as the 'eighties.[94] Influenced by Knollys and Esher, the King pressed a claim to see Cabinet papers at the formative stage of policy-making and thereby predictably precipitated a decision against it; 'it is impossible for us to yield in a matter of this kind', Balfour wrote in February 1904.[95] None the less, Esher, in September 1905, was complaining to Knollys of 'the want of painstaking care on the part of the Ministers to take full advantage of the admirable monarchical system as it was worked by Peel and Aberdeen'.[96] The historical reference no doubt derives from the fact that Esher was then engaged on editing for publication the Queen's letters, from her accession in 1837 up to the Prince Consort's death in 1861, for the express purpose of demonstrating what he, and no doubt the King also,[97] thought the rightful place of the Crown in the Constitution.[98] Between 1853 and 1856, in Lord Esher's view, the Queen and the Prince 'were the real Ministers of the Crown, and even Palmerston, now and then, had to take a back seat'.[99]

As late as December 1907, Esher was still saying that 'according to the ancient usage which has prevailed for 60 years' the King had a right to be consulted on all important questions before Cabinet decisions were reached. He added that 'the practice which prevailed under the Queen should be adhered to, because the position of the Sovereign should be altogether independent of the personality of the Monarch, if the Monarchy is to stand. The King's personality is the great factor nowadays, and this is a stumbling block in the way of his successors.'[100] Plainly this was only true if the man was to be fitted to the job, whereas in the nature of the case top jobs have to be fitted to the man. The Monarchy was not going to survive through

being permanently fitted into an unalterable mould. Hindsight
lets us see that the King's personality was indeed 'the great
factor' in enabling the Monarchy to stand, but not in the sense
of his playing as influential a political part as the Queen.
Rather did his personality bring about, as will appear,[101] a
significant and beneficent change in 'the position of the Sovereign'.

Our hindsight, however, includes not only a view of Edward
VII's reign as a whole, and a view of him and his predecessors
in perspective (neither of which views could have been seen by
Esher and Knollys), but also a view of his successors' reigns
which shows the palpable untruth of Edward VII's personality
proving a stumbling block to them. Our hindsight, in other
words, is to that extent a foresight quite unattainable for Esher
and Knollys. None the less, we may justifiably criticise the de-
ficiencies of their own backward looks and indeed criticise
them for looking back as much as they did. Their reading of
the past was often wrong; there were signs and portents in
their own times which they failed to perceive.

Knollys, to turn more particularly to him, believed that the
old system had broken down, temporarily only, because the
Queen had lost grip on it in her old age and because Sir Arthur
Bigge, her Private Secretary since 1895, was not as competent
as his predecessor, Sir Henry Ponsonby, or, it may be inferred,
his successor, Knollys himself. But we have already seen that
the Queen's grip did not begin to slacken until late in 1900,[102]
and there is plenty of evidence that Bigge was much more up
to the Private Secretary's job than Knollys.[103] Writing to Esher
in 1906, Knollys referred to an instance of the Queen's being
passed over in 1899 and went on:

> Matters having gradually fallen into this unsatisfactory
> state, it has not been easy for the King to put them again
> on a proper footing . . . the difficulty the King has to con-
> tend with is that some Ministers settle questions . . . with-

out the King...knowing of it—I am sure without the
least wish to pass him by, but through ignorance or care-
lessness.[104]

But from the point of view of Ministers, there were more solid
reasons for passing the King by than that. One was the enormous increase in the volume and complexity of Government
business[105] and the consequent increase of pressure on them.
Another was a change, or perhaps a recognition of a change, in
the office of Prime Minister. That office was 'unknown to the
law' until Edward vii in 1905 put the Prime Minister in the
fourth place in the Table of Precedence (below, surprisingly,
both Archbishops and the Lord Chancellor). More and more,
then, the relations between the Sovereign and the Government
were not between him and Ministers, and at the formative
stage of policy-making, but between him and the Prime Minister, acting as spokesman of a Cabinet which had already
made up its mind.[106]

So Edward vii's attempt to be another Queen Victoria was,
to a substantial extent, bound to fail, if only on that account.
The failure was made complete by his age, his personality, and
his lack of experience.

Edward vii was 59 when he came to the throne, and he had
in fact long been too old to learn new habits, though there was
the advantage that, obviously, he knew more political person-
alities than his mother had done in 1837. (Only one of his
predecessors, William iv, had been older on his accession: it
was not an auspicious precedent.) He was often ill; he spent at
least three months of each year abroad, normally without a
Minister in attendance.[107] His power to influence domestic
events was *pro tanto* diminished.[108] He grumbled repeatedly, in
the manner of his fictional contemporary, James Forsyte, that
his Ministers told him nothing,[109] but in the last resort, for this
state of affairs, he had primarily himself to blame. He was not
(Dilke was right) as intelligent as his mother, though a better

listener.[110] He was, for the matter of that, less clever than the Kaiser, and knew it.[111] He had not his mother's passionate interest in public affairs; his range of political interests was narrower; he was more active, but less industrious. He had little application; he was easily bored. Edward VII, wrote Margot Asquith in her diary, 'devotes what time he does not spend upon sport and pleasure ungrudgingly to duty'.[112]

The new King had not been trained for his position. Gladstone's first major breach with the Queen came through a struggle to secure a real job for the Prince of Wales in Ireland (no one seems to have thought of employment for him in Wales), but the Prince did not range himself on the Prime Minister's side in the battle.[113]

Queen Victoria, because she rightly thought her heir indiscreet, persistently refused him access to State secrets. As late as 1882 she vetoed a plan for his seeing copies of the secret Foreign Office telegrams, although they were seen by the Private Secretaries of all Cabinet Ministers.[114] It was not until 1892 that the whole range of State papers were made available to him.[115] Lord Rosebery's gift of the 'gold key' to the 51-year-old heir to the throne was as important to him as a father's gift of a latchkey to a son of 21 or under.

The factors of his personality and lack of experience were linked. His education had been badly bungled. His mother weighed him in the scales against his father and found him wanting. The scales which gave that result were accurate, but it was unfair to make such a measurement and attach significance to it. Few men could have measured up to the Prince Consort in brains and character. But the Prince of Wales was open to criticism by less exacting standards. He was notoriously indiscreet. In December 1871, Lord Granville (Foreign Secretary), who liked him[116]—most people did—discussing with Sir Henry Ponsonby the possibility of allowing the Prince to see diplomatic despatches, wrote:

And as to really confidential matters, will they remain
secret? He asked me to keep him informed during the
war. One evening I got four messages from different
friends telling me to be careful. One of my first notes to
him had been handed round a dinner party.[117]

Fourteen years later, Lord Granville, again Foreign Secretary,
wrote to the Prime Minister:

The Prince of Wales is thoroughly though unintentionally
indiscreet—and he is especially abusive of our Foreign
Policy—and I doubt his being a little better informed
would make much difference—The Queen would I should
think strongly object to regular reports from the Cabinet.[118]

As King he became a reformed character in respect of this kind
of indiscretion; no one could be better trusted to keep a
secret.[119]

The Prince, however, had been indiscreet not only in the
sense of being someone who would betray confidences but also
in the sense of being 'unwise in his talk'.[120] He was extremely
unwise in his talk in Berlin on the occasion of the Emperor
Frederick's funeral,[121] and continued to make diplomatic gaffes
as King. In the summer after his accession, when he was to
visit the German Emperor at Homburg, the Foreign Secretary
(Lord Lansdowne) equipped him with a series of confidential
notes on the political topics which the Emperor might raise.
These the King took out of his pocket and handed to his
nephew. Fortunately there was nothing in the paper likely to
cause real harm to Anglo-German relations.[122] Staying at
Copenhagen in 1904, the King told the Russian Minister to
the Danish Court, Isvolsky, that one object of the Anglo-
Japanese alliance had been a desire to stop Japan going to war
with Russia and that we had tried to do so. This was not true
and the Government was correspondingly embarrassed.[123] In
1909 he made a speech in Naples at a dinner to the King and

Queen of Italy, fortunately not reported, in which he referred to a non-existent Anglo-Italian alliance.[124] In general, however, his speeches as King, even when impromptu, which they usually were,[125] and in a foreign language, were perfect for the particular occasion. Manifestly, however, as a diplomatist he required very careful briefing.

The new King was, then, ill-prepared for his position. But if any one factor is to be singled out to explain his failure to emulate his mother's use of her position it must be that of his laziness. He was prepared to garner information in conversation, especially if it was well spiced, but he was not prepared to sit down and read or write, certainly not for any appreciable length of time. Victoria made her influence felt by an immense two-way flow of paper. Her views were forcibly and vividly, however ungrammatically, expressed. Edward was no desk worker. Such letters as he did write are unbelievably dull. Not only did he never turn a phrase, but he made most of his points by the quotation of stale clichés. By his own methods he became a more influential monarch than could have been foreseen, but his political influence was noticeably less than his mother's. Balfour, in February 1901, wrote:

> The King will take up a good deal more of his ministers' time than did the Queen. . . .[126]

That prediction proved wrong. Balfour himself, as we have seen, did his best to make it so.

For all these various reasons, therefore, Edward VII exercised little or no influence on the 'high politics' of his reign. Home politics in any case did not interest him.[127] Specifically the controversy over the 1902 Education Act bored him.[128] (Perhaps this was because the sectarian overtones of the controversy prevented him, and others, perceiving how great a reforming measure it in fact was.) Nor did Colonial questions interest him.[129] His interest in Ireland seems to have been limited to his opposition to Home Rule. He was badly received there in 1885 and did not go again until the State visit of 1903. India (although he had made an extensive visit there as Prince of Wales) did not have for him the magic it had for the Queen-Empress. Like her, however, he was continuously interested in defence and in foreign policy. But unlike her[130] he was deeply interested in the Royal Navy. (The Queen's name had never appeared in the Navy List, but on the day of her funeral the King ordered that his should appear at its head and be followed by those of his personal naval staff.[131]) Moreover, again in marked contradistinction to his mother, the King, in both Army and Navy matters alike, was well-nigh consistently 'upon the side of the reformers'. 'By throwing his vast social influence' on their side, says Sir Philip Magnus,[132] 'he played a salutary role.' Again: 'He swayed a public opinion in which the qualitative element must be distinguished from the quantitative ... the known attitude of King Edward was important politically because it influenced that of the upper class.' Sir Sidney Lee says that in 1902 the King 'headed the advance guard of Army reformers'.[133] It was only in this field that he worked hard on his papers in the manner of his mother.[134] It was only as an Army reformer that he in the least resembled his father. So great was the King's enthusiasm for this cause that when a new Secretary of State for War, H. O. Arnold-Forster, was appointed in 1903, he was summoned to the Palace virtually from a sick-bed, and arrived 'looking more dead than alive', so that he might have the benefit of his Sovereign's opinions before being 'got at' by the military side of the War Office.[135]

Even in his chosen fields of interest, however, the King met with constitutional rebuffs. A brush with Brodrick has already been mentioned.[136] Arnold-Forster exasperated him more than any other Minister.[137] He let the King have his way about uniforms, but, in his despite, abolished inter-regimental polo tournaments at home and instituted an Army Journal.

A really important matter was an Army Order of 1904 *inter alia* confirming the absolute control of the Chancellor of the Exchequer over the Army Estimates. The King 'raised a large number of objections'[138] but 'could obtain no satisfaction on points of substance'.[139] And this was because the Minister, as Knollys clearly saw,[140] had a trump card in his hand—resignation.

Another clash with Arnold-Forster came the next year. The King had declined to sign an Army Order pending a full discussion of it. The Minister wanted to be able to tell a Committee of the House of Commons that it was already in force. Accordingly, he sent his secretary ('a person of whom His Majesty has no cognizance whatever', commented Lord Esher) to the King's Private Secretary, on the morning of the afternoon on which the Committee was meeting, with a request that the Order should be signed before lunch. This written request was followed by a telephone message pointing out the embarrassment to the Minister of having to explain to the Committee that the Army Order in question was being held up by the King.

The King signed because he considered that he was being advised by the Minister to do so and could not constitutionally reject that advice. But the Minister apologised for the manner in which he had tendered it and the Prime Minister offered to ask him to resign if Lord Esher would take his place. Esher refused this position, for the second time. Arnold-Forster was therefore reprieved, and Lord Knollys was left to regret that 'a greater man than he is was sent about his business: Lord Palmerston'.[141] Balfour's secretary thought that Arnold-Forster's conduct implied 'an equality between the Minister and the Sovereign which one would have imagined to be repugnant to any one thought qualified to hold high office in the country'.[142] The Sovereign's conduct, however, had implied a different factual position.

It was as Prince of Wales, and under the influence of Lord
Hartington, who was Secretary of State for War from 1883 to
1885, that the King had first become interested in the cause of
Army Reform. It was natural that he should take it up with
the greatest possible vigour on his accession. Nothing then
seemed more important than speedy victory in the Boer War
and the Secretary of State for War was received almost daily in
audience. Within four years the King had almost ceased to give
formal audience to Ministers (with the exception of the Prime
Minister and Foreign Secretary and, occasionally, the War
Secretary), relying instead on conversation on purely social occasions.[143] In 1901, however, the Leader of the Opposition,
Campbell-Bannerman (a former War Secretary), perhaps ap-
prehensive of a new monarch increasing the royal power,
warned Balfour, as Leader of the House, that he might have to
ask a question about the constitutional control of the Army, if
frequent interviews with Brodrick continued.[144]

That gentleman, who had many reasons for sore feelings
about the King's dealings with his Department (including, in
the end, his being moved to the India Office against his
wish[145]) none the less in his memoirs wrote about the King's
'uncompromising determination'[146] to reform the Army and the
War Office and the excellent results obtained. In particular he
emphasised that the 'great monument of King Edward's military interest was the reform of the medical system ...'.[147] By
the end of the reign 'the efficiency and reputation of the Army
Medical Service'[148] had been transformed.

Victory in the Boer War was followed by a Royal Commission enquiring into its conduct. The King told the Prime Minister (Lord Salisbury) that 'this system of "washing our dirty
linen in public" the late Queen had a horror of, and the King
entirely shares the views of his beloved Mother'.[149] A year later,
however, in 1903, the King instigated the idea of a committee
of three, under Lord Esher's chairmanship, to make proposals

for the reconstruction of the War Office. The King stipulated that the committee should be appointed by the Prime Minister and not by the War Secretary and that the announcement of its appointment should specifically mention the royal approval of the project. To this Balfour agreed, but with misgivings, arguing that, if the royal approval of some Ministerial actions was to be expressed, no mention of it in other cases might be construed as disapproval and the Crown thereby involved, to its discredit, in controversy.[150]

Brodrick was, as we have seen, succeeded by Arnold-Forster and he, in his turn, in 1905, by the most famous and greatest of all War Secretaries (with the possible exception of Cardwell),[151] R. B. Haldane. He and the King had already had much to do with each other over the foundation of the Imperial College,[152] and the King now wrote to the Prince of Wales:

> Mr Haldane, with sound common sense and great power of organisation, ought to make an excellent War Minister, which is much needed as his predecessor was hopeless.[153]

In fact, Edward VII's attitude to Haldane proved ambivalent. The King enjoyed his company but did not give him the full support which, as we shall see, he gave to Fisher at the Admiralty.[154] This was partly because Fisher and Haldane were often at odds.[155] The King's opinion of the latter was at its lowest in the winter of 1907–8.[156] He described his War Minister as 'a damned radical lawyer and a German professor' and said that 'all confidence in him was gone'.[157] In March 1908, Asquith, who was deputising for the Prime Minister, was actually asked to move Haldane from the War Office.[158] In April the King was grumbling to Esher about the 'mental gymnastics of a clever lawyer'.[159] In June 1908, however, the King gave him covert support against the demands of Lloyd George and Churchill, backed by Fisher, for a reduction in the Army Estimates,[160] and thereafter the relations between the King and Haldane were good.

Edward VII's contribution to naval reform was greater than that which he made to Army reform, and can indeed be judged to be the greatest single achievement of his reign.[161] The nature of his contribution was to give his open* and steady support to Sir John Fisher (First Sea Lord from 1904 to 1910) and his principal policies. (His plea for free education at Osborne and Dartmouth in order to widen the field of officer-entry was dubbed socialist.[163]) It is highly probable that, without this support, Fisher's policies would not have prevailed. And it is not too much to say that, if they had not, the Great War might have been lost, at sea.

The Boer War had made manifest the need for Army reform. In the case, on the other hand, of the Navy, undefeated for centuries, the need for reform, though great, was less plain. It was made all the greater, and desperately urgent, by the building, from 1898 onwards, of a powerful German Navy. Fisher was the apostle of reform; the self-appointed 'leader of the opposition' was Lord Charles Beresford, during the time in question Commander-in-Chief, first of the Mediterranean and then of the Channel Fleet. The controversy between the two was bitter; high and low in the Navy took sides. Three successive First Lords, Lords Selborne, Cawdor and Tweed-mouth, were, during this crucial period of naval history, undecided and ineffective. The King's backing of the First Sea Lord took the place of that which they should have given.[164] (In 1908 he agreed to McKenna's appointment as First Lord on condition that Fisher remained First Sea Lord.[165]) Fisher was always ready to recognise that, without his Sovereign's support, he might not have gained the day. At the height of

* The King made Fisher his principal naval A.D.C., and, a little later, conferred the O.M. on him without consulting anyone [162]

the great controversies which raged between him and Beresford he wrote to the King:

> When your Majesty backed up the First Sea Lord against unanimous Naval feeling, against the *Dreadnought*—when she was first designed—and when your Majesty launched her, went to sea in her, witnessed her battle practice (which surpassed all records) it just simply shut up the mouths of the revilers as effectively as those lions were kept from eating Daniel! *And they would have eaten me but for your Majesty!*

'That', comments Sir Philip Magnus, 'was not mere hyperbole.'[166] 'The King has stuck to him wonderfully', wrote Lord Esher at the time: 'It is *so* difficult to stick to any one through storm as well as sun-shine.'[167]

The issues involved in the naval controversies of the Edwardian age seem arid now. Suffice it to quote Winston Churchill (twice First Lord of the Admiralty): 'There is no doubt whatever that Fisher was right in nine-tenths of what he fought for....'[168] It may be doubted if the King really grasped the issues. At an early stage of their relationship (in August 1904) Fisher complained that he had wasted '5 solid hours' in explaining them to him, adding: 'The worst of it is that the impression is not *lasting* with him. He can't grasp details.'[169] But—and Esher made the point to Fisher at the time[170]—this was not necessary. The King formed his view of measures largely through his view of men. With Beresford, once a close personal friend, he had had a violent quarrel. He did not side against him, however, for so unworthy and negative a reason. He gave Fisher his positive support because he had taken the measure of a man of genius.[171]

ROLE IN FOREIGN AFFAIRS

The contention[172] that the King's contribution to naval reform was the biggest single achievement of his reign may surprise those brought up on the legend of 'Edward, the peacemaker' or, in Germany, 'Edward the encircler': Edward, in any case, the creator of the Entente Cordiale. His latest, and best, biographer however, maintains that his personal influence was much less effective, albeit more conspicuous, in the diplomatic field[173] than in that of naval and military reforms. The conspicuousness came from his annual State or semi-State visits abroad. This was in complete contrast with his mother's pattern of foreign travel. She visited Germany frequently on family occasions and, for holidays, France and Italy. Her only State visit abroad had been to Paris in 1855. King Edward on the other hand travelled far more often, always with considerable display and much more widely. During his reign he visited (more than once in some instances) Austria-Hungary, Denmark, France, Germany, Greece, Italy, Norway, Portugal, Russia and Sweden. In short, the contrast between the mother's and the son's methods applied just as much to foreign as to home affairs.

It is noteworthy, however, that on only two of his foreign visits was Edward VII accompanied by a Cabinet Minister and on none of them by the Foreign Secretary. (Lord Selborne, First Lord of the Admiralty, went with him to Kiel in 1904, and Lord Crewe, Colonial Secretary, went with him on his last State visit, to Berlin in 1909.) On all the other journeys the King was invariably accompanied, as Minister in attendance, by Sir Charles Hardinge, although he was not a Minister but a Foreign Office official, Permanent Under-Secretary from 1906 until 1910. This arrangement was disapproved of by Lord

Lansdowne, Foreign Secretary in the Conservative Government, and later by Lord Esher,[174] but was acceptable to the Liberal Foreign Secretary, Sir Edward Grey.* Knollys held that a Cabinet Minister should have accompanied the King on his visit to the Tsar (accompanied by his Prime Minister and Foreign Minister) at Reval (now Tallin) in 1908 and rubbed in that point to Asquith once back in London,[176] but the King himself thought otherwise. He said that he did not want to feel like a prisoner, handcuffed to a warder, whilst conversing with his relatives through a grille.[177] The fact that the Government was prepared to agree with him about this, except on two occasions, is surely a measure of the lack of importance they attached to the King's conversations with the Heads of other States, even when politics were touched on.

It was the pageantry the King enjoyed, not the politics. When the Kaiser paid a State visit to London in 1907 the King declined to talk politics with him or any of his entourage.[178] When he visited the Kaiser the following month, Grey (mindful perhaps of the incident of 1901 when the King handed the Kaiser Lord Lansdowne's confidential notes[179]) prepared two memoranda on the Anglo-German naval questions, either of which the Kaiser could see. 'This', Hardinge later recorded, 'was really a very interesting innovation, since for the first time in history the British Government briefed the King to act as their spokesman in an interview with the Head of a Foreign State....'[180] The King himself saw the matter in another light at the time, minuting, 'This is, I believe, the first occasion on which the Sovereign has received instructions from his Government!'[181] Sir Philip Magnus writes that this royal activity of engaging 'personally while abroad in diplomatic discussions for which the Foreign Secretary assumed responsibility ... was

* He thought that Hardinge, in the course of royal cruises in 1906 and 1907, had done particularly useful work in settling disputes with Greece and Spain[175]

as useful to the Foreign Office as is a rich unusual sauce to a dull dinner dish...'.[182] But the technique makes it plain that it was the Government which was the master and the King the servant. That position was made completely clear at 1.30 a.m. on Saturday, 1 August 1914, when Asquith took a taxi to Buckingham Palace, got George v out of bed ('a brown dressing gown over his night-shirt') to sign a formal message to the Tsar asking him to defer Russian mobilisation: 'All he did was to suggest that it should be more personal and direct—by the insertion of the words "My dear Nicky" and the addition at the end of the signature "Georgie"!'[183]

Sir Harold Nicolson, who praises King Edward as a 'supreme diplomatist' (by which, in the particular context, he means someone who is obviously friendly and who asks no awkward questions) says also that he was 'too superficial to be a statesman'.[184] The King would probably have been content with this. He was pleased with himself for so relatively minor but definitely happy an initiative as inviting Clemenceau to meet him at Marienbad (in August 1907) just after he had visited the German and Austrian Emperors, telling Hardinge that 'the idea emanated from my fertile brain!!!'[185] Anything less than a large question of policy he did not even try to understand and, about questions of that sort, in Balfour's opinion 'he never made an important suggestion...'.[186] His triumphal visit to Paris, in May 1903, helped to prepare the way for the Anglo-French agreement of April 1904, but in the negotiation of it he took little or no interest.[187] But he knew where he stood. When, the next year, Germany put pressure on France to secure the resignation of the French Foreign Minister, M. Delcassé, a deliberate attempt at a public humiliation, the King telegraphed Delcassé pressing him not to resign.[188]

Edward VII in truth was neither statesman nor diplomatist. He lacked the former's ability to conceive a policy, the latter's patience in implementing one. He was a salesman of foreign policy, in modern parlance a supremely good Public Relations Officer; he did not create the Entente but he did create, to use another modern term, the 'climate' for its creation. As Paul Cambon, the French Ambassador in London said at the time: 'Any clerk at the Foreign Office could draw up a treaty, but there was no one else who could have succeeded in producing the right atmosphere for a *rapprochement* with France.'[189] The Kaiser could have produced, between 1898 and 1901, the right atmosphere for an Anglo-German alliance, but notably failed to do so.[190] To note that, and reflect on all that followed from the Kaiser's lack of achievement, helps to give the measure of Edward VII's positive success.

And this derived, it must be emphasised, from his own initiative. The idea of a visit to Paris in 1903 was his own idea, tepidly received by the British Government,[191] warmly by the French one.[192] When he left London on this, his first foreign tour as King, none of his own staff, possibly not even Hardinge, knew that his final destination was Paris. He went to France by way of Portugal and Italy so as to conceal his real object and by an appearance of 'dropping in' on the French on his way home, as almost a matter of mere geographical convenience, to avoid irritating the Germans. It was an adroit manoeuvre. The visit was, Sir Philip Magnus rightly says, 'his finest hour'.[193]

His finest hour had its finest moment, his speech at the Hôtel de Ville, on 2 May. It was short, it was apt, its last phrase ('. . . *Paris, où je me trouve toujours comme si j'étais chez moi*') 'brought the house down'.[194] The whole atmosphere changed completely during the visit. A Parisian Anglophobe complained of the behaviour of the crowds: 'The first day they behaved well; the second day they merely displayed interest; but the third day, *"c'était attristant—ils ont acclamé le Roi"*.'[195]

Roger Fulford emphasises that Edward VII had no 'specific aims in foreign policy'.[196] He had, however, his likes and dislikes. Possibly since his visit to Paris in 1856 as a boy of 15,[197] certainly from his early twenties onwards, he had always, except for the estrangement brought about by the Boer War,[198] liked France and the French and—his wife even more so—disliked Prussia and the Prussians. The formative political event in the building of these preferences was, as we have seen,[199] the Prusso-Danish war of 1864: 'The experience impaired for life his faith in the honesty of Prussia and stimulated his leanings towards Prussia's rival France.'[200] As early as June 1886, he expressed the opinion that 'the general interests of Europe could best be served by an *entente* between England and France'.[201] (This was a term which had first been used to describe Anglo-French relations between 1831 and 1846.) In 1878 he used it in public in Paris to describe, with a touch of optimism, the relationship then.[202] At that time he was congratulated by Lord Salisbury for his skill in influencing in our favour Gambetta,[203] to whom he had been introduced by Dilke.[204]

Things might have been very different if Edward's brother-in-law and friend, the German Emperor Frederick, had had a longer reign. As it was, his death in 1888 put paid to the Prince's idea of 'many years of useful and thoroughly congenial para-diplomatic activity'.[205] Frederick's successor, William II, was jealous of his uncle and the uncle, with good reason, disliked the nephew. (He was not best pleased, for example, to be called an 'old peacock' by the younger man.) Perhaps too he was jealous, of the younger man being a crowned head when he was only an heir-apparent, an Emperor when he was only a King. 'There was always a feeling of thunder in the air whenever the King and the Emperor were together.'[206] They were rivals for the leadership of European society, and the King was easily the winner of that competition. But, more than that, the personal antipathy between them exactly tallied with the political estrangement of the States of which they were Heads.[207] Was that altogether a coincidence? The stout, easy-going uncle was the embodiment in his own person of a State sated with Empire; the high-strung, assertive, restless nephew was as symbolical of a State still without, in its own view, its proper place in the sun.

When Lord Salisbury met the Tsar, at Balmoral in 1898, he was overheard saying: 'He is very different from the other Emperor!'[208] The last Tsar of all the Russias was a simple, indeed a feeble creature. It is not surprising that the King preferred the Russian to the German nephew and the Tsar the English uncle to the German cousin. (Nicholas II's mother was a sister of Queen Alexandra and he had married a niece of Edward VII.) Edward had desired friendship with Russia, with rare intermissions, ever since his first visit there (he made five in all) in the autumn of 1866,[209] telling Lord Derby then that he would be 'only too happy to be the means in any way of promoting the *entente cordiale* between Russia and our own country...'. (The occasion for this visit was the marriage of the Prince of Wales' sister-in-law Dagmar to the future Tsar Alexander III.) The Prince, when returning from Alexander II's funeral, was praised by Sir William Harcourt for establishing a sentiment for friendly relations with Russia 'in public opinion'.[210] The Government's decision in 1906 to try and remove differences between the United Kingdom and Russia, in the same way as they had done with France in 1904, delighted the King.[211] But with a good sense of timing he declined Grey's suggestion that he should facilitate the negotiations by an immediate visit to the Tsar. He based his objection on the revolutionary situation in Russia at the time (shortly before the dissolution of the Duma) and the view that such a visit would not 'for a while' be popular at home.[212] The Anglo-Russian Convention was signed in August 1907, and the King set the seal on the new relationship by a State visit to the Tsar in June 1908, 'the only visit ever paid by a British Sovereign to Russia'.[213]*

* This visit was extremely unpopular with sections of British Radical

Lord Hardinge later described the 1907 agreement with Russia as 'the triumph of King Edward's policy of which the Anglo-French *entente* was the first step'.[215] One must, however, again emphasise that the King had no policy. Holland Rose's, in fact very cautious,[216] attribution of the creation of the *entente* to Edward VII was, according to Balfour, to embody 'in serious historical work a foolish piece of gossip...'.[217] His Government's foreign policy, continued by the succeeding Liberal Government, happened to be in accordance with the King's inclinations. For this policy he was therefore an excellent showman, but he did a first-class public relations job wherever he went, Germany included. His speech at the Berlin Rathaus, in February 1909, captivated an audience disposed to be hostile in much the same way as his speech at the Hôtel de Ville in Paris in May 1903.[218] But his heart was not in his work. In France and Russia it was known that the King of England was positively and wholeheartedly in favour of the *ententes*.[219] Unfortunately and inevitably this was known in Germany too. To the extent, therefore, that the King soothed French and Russian nerves, he disturbed German ones. Furthermore, his justi-

---

opinion. Arthur Ponsonby, then a Liberal M.P., Keir Hardie, the Leader of the Parliamentary Labour Party, and Victor Grayson, an Independent M.P., were not invited to a royal garden party because they spoke and voted against it in the House of Commons. Grayson and Hardie were quickly forgiven, but Ponsonby had given greater offence, because as Sir Henry's son and himself a former page of Queen Victoria, it was thought that he should have known better. Eventually his brother Frederick, the King's Assistant Private Secretary, extracted an apology from him, much as Granville had extracted one from Dilke.

Social ostracism because of political dislike had been practised by Queen Victoria—and imitated by others. In 1879 she did not, despite a remonstrance from Disraeli, invite Mr and Mrs Gladstone to the wedding of one of her sons, the Duke of Connaught. After 1886, says Sir Robert Ensor, 'London Society, following the known view of the Queen, practically ostracised Home Rulers'.[214] Gladstone was unpopular with the London mob, as well as with London Society, to the extent of being hooted at in the streets, when at the height of his popularity in the North of England and in Scotland.

fiable indignation at the Austrian annexation of Bosnia–Herze-
govina in 1908 was interpreted in Vienna as an attempt to
break up the Dual Alliance and he was strongly attacked in the
Austrian Press.[220] Sir Robert Ensor indeed holds that the German legend of an attempted British encirclement of Germany
arose directly out of King Edward's foreign tours, allied to
over-estimates of his political power.[221] In particular, the meeting with the Tsar at Reval alarmed the Germans. In fact, we
have it from Sir Harold Nicolson, who began his career as a
diplomat and whose father, then our Ambassador to Russia,
was present throughout, that 'the two sovereigns did not discuss politics at all . . .'.[222]

There can be no doubt that the King's intentions were pacific. He was not a mischief-maker in international affairs, still
less a war-monger.[223] In so far as he failed to prevent war, that
is a criticism, not of his work, but of the whole system of
alliances. Moreover, in so far as the 'para-diplomatic activities'
of a constitutional King had bad results the blame must fall
on his Government. There was not the same certainty in
Europe of their policy as of his feeling. It was only when Bel-
gium was invaded that British Ministers made up their minds.
Because they were undecided, they could not educate public
opinion in the new shape of things. *Ententes*, with a Russian
tyranny and a corrupt French Republic, were not popular. But
Grey did not even tell all his Cabinet colleagues of the Anglo-
French military conversations, started in 1906, until 1912. A
Government with a clear policy could have assigned to the
King a far more useful and important role in public relations
in the field of foreign policy than that which, lacking their
guidance, he had to devise for himself.

An important general point seems to be involved. The theory
of constitutional Monarchy is that the Sovereign acts on the
advice of his Ministers. But what is he to do if advice is not
forthcoming? At least twice Edward VII was led to complain

that he had asked for advice, admittedly in minor matters, and not got it. The first time was in 1903, when the question was whether or not he should visit the Pope; the second in 1907, when the question was whether or not to accept the Transvaal Government's offer of the Cullinan Diamond.[224] He could justifiably have complained of lack of advice about far more important matters and, in general, of little more use being made of him as King than as Prince of Wales. German Ministers overestimated his power, British Ministers under-estimated his skill. He himself probably over-estimated the quantum of the conciliation which he personally could achieve, whether in foreign or in home[225] affairs.

THE CONSTITUTIONAL CRISIS, 1909–10

The home politics of Queen Victoria's reign closed for her, as we have seen,[226] with a 'golden evening'. King Edward, in the evening of his reign, was often depressed by the anxieties of home politics.[227] He did not like the domestic measures of the Liberal Government; he did not like the strife which attended them;[228] above all he disliked strife centred on his own personal position. That, however, was just what he had to contend with as, in 1909, a great constitutional crisis came to dominate the political situation.

On 30 November in that year the House of Lords rejected the Finance Bill (the 'People's Budget'), the first time they had rejected the Finance Bill of the year for more than 200 years. This rejection, in the Government's view, 'filled the cup'. It became their policy to implement a House of Commons Resolution of 1907 stating that, within the limit of a single Parliament, the legislative will of the House of Commons should prevail. The question, however, was whether the very legislation necessary to implement the 1907 resolution could be passed without the use, to secure the necessary majority in the House of Lords itself, of the royal prerogative to create peers.

In 1906 the King had sought to mediate between the Prime Minister and the Archbishop of Canterbury in the controversy over the Education Bill,[229] precisely because it involved a conflict between the two Houses of Parliament and so threatened to involve the Crown.[230] His mother had successfully mediated between Prime Minister and Archbishop over the Irish Church Bill of 1869,[231] but Edward's intervention, so partisan was the mood on both sides, was unsuccessful. Roy Jenkins' comment must, however, be noted, that the King urged compromise by both sides rather than a recognition by the Lords of the relevance of the recent Liberal electoral victory.[232] He renewed his attempt at an agreed educational settlement in 1908, but again unsuccessfully.[233] In the same year he intervened in the controversy between the two Houses over the Licensing Bill. This intervention was on quite a different basis from that two years earlier, as he urged Lord Lansdowne, Conservative Leader in the House of Lords, to secure the Government's Bill at any rate a Second Reading in his House.[234] The interview was held, with the Prime Minister's approval, on 12 October 1908.[235] The Lords rejected the Bill on Second Reading by 272 votes to 96 on 25 November. The King deplored this vote.[236]

In March 1909, he was not, according to Lord Esher,[237] 'much frightened' by what Lloyd George told him of his Budget, and in September Lord Esher wrote: 'I don't think the King objects to the Budget, but he dislikes intensely the style of certain speeches.'[238] In Sir Sidney Lee's opinion, on the other hand, his dislike of the Budget was strong.[239] In October, after securing the agreement of the Prime Minister, he summoned Balfour and Lansdowne (Leaders of the Opposition in the Commons and Lords respectively) and sought to persuade them to restrain the Tory Peers from throwing out the Budget.[240] To that course of action he was 'strongly opposed'.[241] Again he was

unsuccessful, Balfour and Lansdowne offering specious ex-
cuses for being unable to commit the Opposition in the Lords,
much as Lansdowne alone had done the previous year in respect of the Licensing Bill.[242] When the deed was none the less
done, a General Election inevitably followed.

Opening the Government's campaign, in the Albert Hall on
10 December 1909, Asquith made an important statement
which seemed clear but was in fact equivocal, perhaps foolish:

> We shall not assume office and we shall not hold office
> unless we can secure the safeguards which experience
> shows us to be necessary for the legislative utility and
> honour of the party of progress....[243]

These words could have meant merely that his Government
would not continue without the passing of a Parliament Bill.
It was, however, widely assumed that they meant that he had
already obtained from the King the so-called 'advance guarantees', i.e., his promise that, if the Government won the Election
and thereafter could not pass its Parliament Bill without the
creation of Peers, the necessary number would be created. In
point of fact the Prime Minister had not at that time even
raised the point with the King. He had, however, received
from His Majesty's Private Secretary, Lord Knollys, a letter,
dated 28 November, saying that '... to create 500 new Peers,
which I am told is the number required [to coerce the House
of Lords] would practically be almost an impossibility, and if
asked for would place the King in an awkward position'.[244]

Knollys was wrong on the first point, i.e., the impractica-
bility of creating Peers on a large enough scale (Asquith had
his list of potential Peers ready),[245] but right on the second, i.e.,
that a request for such a creation would place the King 'in an
awkward position'. To accept it would make him unpopular
with the Unionist Party, to reject it would make him unpopular with the Liberal, Labour and Irish Nationalist Parties. In

such a dilemma the safest course for a constitutional King would have been to act strictly on the advice of the Government of the day. Knollys, however, at first at any rate, did not see the matter as simply as that. He considered that to agree to a creation on the scale required was tantamount to the destruction of the House of Lords and would also gravely, perhaps fatally, impair the prestige of the Monarchy by such an enlistment of it on the Liberal side in politics. In these circumstances he thought the King should abdicate rather than agree.[246] What he thought would happen after that is not clear.

Knollys' views are important because it was primarily to him that the King turned for advice on this thorny subject for the little of his life that was left to him. If he had lived longer and Knollys had not changed his mind (as in fact he did in the next reign) it is possible that the King, acting on his advice, would have embroiled the Crown on the Unionist side in politics with consequences fatal not merely to its prestige but to its existence. A 'King's Party' might win one Election, but it could not always win, and when it was beaten the King would be beaten with it.[247] As the crunch approached many Unionists became increasingly angry, first with Edward VII and then with George V, for submitting to the will of the Liberal Government. But it was not in the nature of Conservatism to go on from that to Republicanism. For the King, however, to have declined to act on the advice of his Government, even in such unprecedented and controversial circumstances, could easily have touched off a Republican movement on the Left, far stronger than that which had raised its head in the 1870s.

Presumably the King knew of Knollys' letter of 28 November 1909. A little later, however, and after Asquith's Albert Hall speech, a far more decisive, indeed a supremely decisive, royal intervention was made, albeit in a curiously off-hand manner. On 15 December 1909, Knollys sent for Vaughan Nash, Asquith's secretary, whose report of the meeting reads:

He began by saying that the King had come to the conclusion that he would not be justified in creating new
Peers (say 300) until after a second General Election and
that he, Lord K., thought you should know of this now,
though, for the present he would suggest that what he was
telling me should be for your ear only. The King regards
the policy of the Government as tantamount to the destruction of the House of Lords and he thinks that before a
large creation of Peers is embarked upon or threatened the
country should be acquainted with the particular project
for accomplishing such destruction as well as with the general line of action as to which the country will be consulted
at the forthcoming Elections.[248]

In other words, the Election already in progress was to settle
primarily the fate of the Budget (which it would have done
anyway) and, whatever it showed about the electors' attitude
to the Lords' veto, a second Election was to be fought on that
issue—after the production of an actual Parliament Bill. Only
then could the King contemplate creating a large number of
Peers. In effect he was in 1909 rejecting, so far as he was concerned, the putting into practice of the Commons' resolution of
1907. The House of Lords had just insisted on a new constitutional doctrine, its right to reject the Budget unless sanctioned
by an Election; the King was now putting forward a new
constitutional doctrine, his right not to create Peers to pass a
Bill unless it had been sanctioned by an Election. What led
him to this decision is something of a mystery. Lord Esher had
written to Lord Knollys, on 1 December 1909, saying that the
King should firmly refuse any pledge to make Peers before the
Election then impending.[249] But it is a far cry from that to refuse to make any without another Election.

At any rate, the King's communication of 15 December
must have been a considerable blow to the Prime Minister. It
had scarcely been foreshadowed by the earlier letter; it came too

late, with the Election campaign already under way, for any argument to have much point. Asquith was, however, as deeply loyal to the Monarchy in these trying circumstances as Gladstone had been in the trying circumstances of his day. The Election won, and the new Parliament met, he gave his followers, to the surprise of many of them (in a speech in the House of Commons, on 21 February 1910), the unpalatable information that he was without the 'guarantees':

> In my judgment it is the duty of responsible politicians in this country, as long as possible, and as far as possible, to keep the name of the Sovereign and the Prerogatives of the Crown outside the domain of party politics. If the occasion should arise, I should not hesitate to tender such advice to the Crown as in the circumstances the exigencies of the situation appear to warrant in the public interest. But to ask, in advance, for a blank authority, for an indefinite exercise of the Royal Prerogative, in regard to a measure which has never been submitted to, or approved by, the House of Commons, is a request which, in my judgment, no constitutional statesman can properly make, and is a concession which the Sovereign cannot be expected to grant.

Did these words express a policy which Asquith had all along intended to follow, or did they express a complete and graceful acceptance of the King's point of view? The Liberal Chief Whip (the Master of Elibank) said that, in consequence of them, Asquith's standing with his followers fell very low.[250] His latest biographer, Roy Jenkins, moreover criticises him for hesitancy between January and April 1910, thus (as it happened) preventing 'the issue being pushed near to a conclusion during the lifetime of King Edward'.[251] It does seem possible that the King's intervention, in December 1909, pushed the Prime Minister off his usual steady stride. He fought the Election of December 1910 with much greater vigour than the

January one. Winston Churchill complimented him on this at the time.[252] Perhaps indeed Asquith had made a mistake in not introducing a Parliament Bill before the first Election of the two. That would have been in accordance with the precedent of 1831 when the production of a Reform Bill preceded the Election of that year.

The final development in King Edward's lifetime came in April 1910. The Cabinet's decisions were communicated in a letter from the Prime Minister of 13 April and announced by him in the House of Commons next day in almost identical language:

> If the Lords fail to accept our policy ... we shall feel it our duty immediately to tender advice to the Crown as to the steps which will have to be taken if that policy is to receive statutory effect in this Parliament. What the precise terms of that advice will be, it will of course not be right for me to say now, but if we do not find ourselves in a position to ensure that statutory effect will be given to this policy in this Parliament, we shall then either resign our offices or recommend a dissolution of Parliament, and let me add this: that in no case would we recommend dissolution except under such conditions as will ensure that in the new Parliament the judgment of the people as expressed in the Election will be carried into law.

The sting was in the tail. If the King was to have his second Election, with Asquith still Prime Minister, he must give the 'advance guarantees'. His only alternative was to accept Asquith's resignation, appoint, if possible, Balfour to succeed him, and give the latter the Dissolution which he had refused the former. The mention, however, of the Government's policy receiving 'statutory effect in this Parliament' leads one to suppose that Asquith may have been hoping to avoid the second Election. Whether he would have succeeded in persuading the King to agree to a creation of Peers on the scale necessary with-

out another Election, we shall never know. The Prime Minister
'had a good talk with the King' on 28 April 'and found him
most reasonable'.[253] Edward VII felt a little unwell on the 30th.
Six days later he was dead. The real drama of his reign was
not any intervention in foreign affairs, but the 'unresolved
drama of its tragic close'.[254]

Asquith at the time was on holiday on the Admiralty yacht.
He received the news in the early hours of 7 May: 'I went up
on deck', he wrote later, 'and I remember well that the first
sight that met my eyes in the twilight before dawn was Halley's
comet blazing in the sky. . . . I felt bewildered and indeed
stunned.'[255] Even more so did the new King. Perhaps only
Elizabeth I or Charles I had succeeded to a more troubled in-
heritance.

5

George V

THE CONSTITUTIONAL CRISIS, 1910–11

George v had in many ways been better prepared for the Throne than Edward vii, but the father had not discussed with the son the difficult problem which he had immediately to face. 'I had no idea', George v told Lord Derby two years later, 'how my father would have dealt with the request [for the creation of peers], he never mentioned the subject to me at all....'[1] Edward vii was not expecting so sudden a demise; he could not, therefore, have been expected to have prepared a political will and testament. But it is strange that a father and son who in most ways were close to each other should not have discussed the biggest topic germane to their profession.

Worried as Edward vii had been by the menace of a constitutional crisis, George v, younger, relatively inexperienced, and a worrier by nature,[2] was even more worried by it. Whether or not the all-important decision which the new King took, six months after his accession, to give the 'advance guarantees' would have been taken by the old one is a wholly speculative question. At the time of his death, Edward vii had, almost certainly, not made up his mind about it; after all, in May 1910 there was still no need to do so. As we have seen, he was motivated by dislike of strife rather than by loyalty to his Government. He disliked, too, not so much the provisions of the Parliament Bill, as the idea of 'destroying' the House of Lords by a creation of Peers on a large scale. But who is to say that in November 1910 he would have refused to give 'advance guarantees', accepted Asquith's resignation, put Balfour in and granted him a Dissolution? Lord Knollys told George v that he had given him the same advice as he would have given Edward vii and that he would have taken it.[3] But Knollys, as we shall see, had changed his mind since the old King's death. Sir Arthur Bigge,* who had been Queen Victoria's Private Secretary and was at this time Private Secretary to the King jointly with Knollys, was surely right to say:

> This quoting what a dead person would do is to me most unfair, if not improper, especially to the King, who has such a high opinion of his father's judgment. But might I not equally have urged that I was perfectly certain Queen Victoria would have done what I advised?[5]

Bigge's advice was to refuse the request for 'advance guarantees'. One cannot help, however, picturing the Queen, intensely disliking a Liberal measure, but (as with the abolition of Army Purchase by Royal Warrant in 1871) relishing the chance of a display of Prerogative powers on a grand scale. Lord Esher thought she would have acted as her grandson did.[6] Roy Jenkins thinks it 'a probability'.[7]

George v shrank from the decision which seemed likely to be forced upon him. He hated the prospect of alienating one half of his subjects whichever way he made it; he greatly disliked (as his father had done) the prospect of a creation of Peers on the scale which would be required. To be responsible for so dramatic and yet in a way so ridiculous an action at the behest of his Ministers would, he felt, be for him a humiliation. Many Unionists saw the matter in the same light. 'Was it right', Sir Harold Nicolson pictures them arguing, that the King 'should be forced, under the menace of resignation, to stultify his posi-

---

* He was created Lord Stamfordham on 23 June 1911. The King thereafter continued from time to time to call him Bigge, e.g., in his important diary entry of 10 August 1911 (see below p. 130). At the Court of Queen Victoria Bigge was nicknamed 'Betternot' because that was so often his counsel[4]

tion and to render himself a puppet...by conferring peerages upon some five hundred unknown and unnamed gentlemen selected by the Master of Elibank?' This was to expose the Crown to an 'unwarranted humiliation'.[8]

For the first six months of his reign, however, George V was deliberately spared the need for a decision. On Asquith's initiative, despite some opposition on his side of the House,[9] a conference was held between leaders of the Liberal and Unionist Parties to try and reach an agreed settlement of the constitutional issues which had been at stake for the previous two years. The conference failed. By the beginning of November 1910, therefore, the position was the same as it had been in May, i.e., the Government had to decide whether to advise another Dissolution and the King had to decide whether to accept that advice, conjoined as it was bound to be, in the light of the Prime Minister's declaration of 14 April,[10] with a request for 'advance guarantees'.

Asquith showed the new King, as he had his father, every possible consideration. The constitutional conference, as we have just seen, is a case in point. The King, in his turn, quickly came to like and respect the Prime Minister. But now a misunderstanding arose between the two men, perhaps because the Prime Minister's approach to the King was over-delicate. Asquith went to Sandringham on 11 November in order to prepare the King's mind in a general way for what was to come. It may be guessed that he shrank from abruptly facing a man under his own roof with unpleasant issues.* The King noted in his diary:

> He reported that the Conference had failed and he proposed to dissolve and have a general election and get it

---

* In the same house, 38 years earlier and for the same reason, Gladstone had avoided altogether an enormously important topic, the employment of the Prince of Wales in Ireland, which he thought might be distasteful to his host[11]

over before Exmas. He asked me for *no guarantees*. I suggested that the veto resolutions should first be sent up to
the H. of L. and, if they rejected them, then he could dis-
solve. This he agreed to do.[12]

The King had made a useful and constructive suggestion and
the Prime Minister had readily accepted it.[13] To the former,
however, the important point was that which he underlined
in his diary. The fact that at this time he was not asked for
guarantees meant, for him, that he was never to be asked for
them. His dismay was therefore great when Lord Knollys,
meeting Asquith in London, on 14 November, found 'to his
surprise', as he reported to the King, 'that what he *now* advocates is that you should give guarantees *at once* for the next
Parliament'.[14]

Bigge telegraphed to Vaughan Nash the next morning:

> His Majesty regrets that it would be impossible for him to
> give contingent guarantees and he reminds Mr Asquith of
> his promise not to seek for any during the present Parlia-
> ment.[15]

The latter part of this telegram perhaps indicates a confusion
between guarantees being sought during, and for, the present
Parliament and guarantees being sought during the present
Parliament for the next one. The King, like others, was apt to
find Asquith's phraseology ambiguous.[16] It was, in fact, lucid
but subtle. There was no ambiguity about the opening phrase
of his own telegram. The King had refused his Prime Minister's request. Asquith and his colleagues, however, wisely
ignored that initial reaction.

The Cabinet proceeded to formalise in a minute (15 November 1910) their advice to the King. The 'advance guarantees'
were formally asked for, but the giving of them was to be kept
secret 'unless and until the actual occasion should arise'.[17]
Asquith himself was convinced that it never would, saying to

his wife: 'If we are beaten at the General Election the question will never arise, and if we get in by a working majority, the Lords will give way, so the King won't be involved.'[18] He said the same thing, often, to his daughter: 'His constant pre-occupation was the position of the King.'[19] We shall see how very nearly in the following summer Asquith's prediction was fulfilled and how surprising and exceptional were the circumstances which prevented its fulfilment.

What is also surprising is that, the Prime Minister having in effect said in April that he would not fight another Election without 'advance guarantees', the opposition should have been surprised to be told the following August that they had been given before the intervening Dissolution. Balfour had felt sure that 'the so-called guarantee' would be secret and had undertaken that the Government would not be questioned about it by himself or Party leaders.[20] To that extent there was 'a conspiracy of silence'. By and large, however, people at this time seem to have been as obtuse about following up what clues there were to political activities behind the Royal scenes as had been the Victorians about following up the comparable clues offered them.[21]

The Cabinet minute of 15 November was sent to the King with a covering letter from Lord Knollys strongly recommending its acceptance. He described it as 'couched in studiously moderate terms' and went on:

> I feel certain that you can safely and constitutionally accept what the Cabinet propose and I venture to urge you strongly to do so. What is now recommended is altogether different in every way from any request to be allowed publicly to announce that you have consented to give guarantees. It is a great compromise on the part of the Cabinet, made entirely to fall in as far as possible with your wishes and to enable you to act conscientiously.[22]

It will be seen that what the argument hinged on in Lord

Knollys' mind, and seemingly induced an eleventh hour change of mind on his part, was the proposal that the 'advance guarantees' were to be kept secret 'unless and until the actual occasion should arise'. On the other hand, this was the aspect of the matter which most troubled the King himself. Eleven months later Lord Esher recorded him saying:

> What he especially resented was the promise extorted from him that he would tell no one. He said: 'I have never in my life done anything I was ashamed to confess. And I have never been accustomed to conceal things.'[23]

He also resented the fact that, when he was finally and definitely asked for the guarantees, the Prime Minister came to him accompanied by Lord Crewe, the Leader of the House of Lords. Asquith may have felt this to have been politically appropriate, and/or that the presence of a personal friend of the new King would ease a painful discussion. But to the King it seemed as if a witness to his word was thought necessary.[24] Twenty-one years later the King spoke of this episode to Lord Crewe when he came to give up his last Ministerial appointment. The tone was chaffing, but one can fairly deduce that his Ministers' attitude to him at that time still rankled. Lord Crewe said that they had not treated him well.[25]

That a man, and a singularly straightforward one, should have resented the secrecy imposed on him is understandable, but for a statesman it was justifiable to impose it. The secrecy which the King resented achieved just what it was intended to do. It kept his name out of the furious public controversy which was then proceeding. If the Prime Minister had only had the interests of the Government to think of, he might well have gained by announcing the pledge the moment it was given.[26] What the King was much more entitled to resent than the secrecy of the guarantees was their extraction in advance of the Election results. He could have maintained that he could and should have been trusted to accept the Government's advice to create Peers if and when such advice was actually tendered; that to 'tie him down' in advance of 'the actual occasion' was a reflection on his trustworthiness and indeed on his honour. Bigge argued this at the time[27] and stuck to it later. For example, in a letter of August 1911 to a friend, he wrote:

> Had the Prime Minister and the Cabinet known His Majesty as well as I do they could have trusted him to act rightly and constitutionally whenever the circumstances might make it necessary for him to do so. They would thus have saved him from being obliged to enter into a secret understanding as to his course of action in what was at that time a mere hypothetical contingency.[28]

But this was to take an unrealistic view of human nature and especially human political nature. The Prime Minister had publicly pledged himself in April not to enter another Election without the 'advance guarantees'. When, 'a few weeks later', the King asked Asquith why secrecy had been stipulated, the latter referred him to his April pledge and said definite private assurances were necessary, 'otherwise he would have broken his word'.[29] Even if no such pledge had been made, no Government, in the circumstances of Asquith's Government in November 1910, could have entered into the Election campaign which began at the end of that month without a definite understanding, not necessarily written, of the kind that George v in fact gave. 'Asquith', writes Jenkins, 'could hardly be expected to be certain that the King would behave in a way which almost the whole Unionist Party professed to believe was unconstitutional'.[30] Asquith and his Cabinet did not know the King as well as Bigge did. The latter had been his Private Secretary for nine years; Asquith had been his Prime Minister for only six months. By the mid-twenties every responsible

British politician knew that the King could always be trusted to do the straight thing.

On the evening of 16 November 1910, George v wrote in his diary:

> After a long talk I agreed most reluctantly to give the Cabinet a secret understanding that in the event of the Government being returned with a majority at the General Election, I should use my Prerogative to make Peers if asked for. I disliked having to do this very much, but agreed that this was the only alternative to the Cabinet resigning, which at this moment would be disastrous.
>
> Francis [Knollys] strongly urged me to take this course and I think his advice is generally very sound. I only trust and pray that he is right this time.[31]

Thus was taken a decision which Winston Churchill regarded as probably 'the most important' exercise 'of the personal discretion of the Sovereign in interpreting the Constitution'.[32]

One wonders what would have happened if the King had taken Bigge's advice rather than Knollys'. Would Asquith have at once resigned or might Bigge, by virtue of his long and close knowledge of the King, have been able to persuade the Prime Minister that, with such a man, there was no need of 'a secret understanding'?

It will have been seen how touch-and-go had been the outcome of the negotiations between Cabinet and King. At Sandringham, on the morning of 15 November, it was the advice of one Private Secretary, Bigge, not to give the guarantees that the King was taking (as witness Bigge's telegram to Nash quoted above); back in London by the evening of the 16th he had come to an opposite decision on the advice of the other Private Secretary, Knollys (as witness the second paragraph of the diary entry quoted in the preceding paragraph here). For Bigge, wise as he was, it was apparently a matter for great and enduring regret that the King took Knollys' advice.[33]

Underlying this sudden and dramatic change of mind on the King's part was the equally sudden and dramatic change of mind on Knollys' part. What, however, made the conclusion of the drama even more 'touch-and-go' was that Knollys, in giving his advice, suppressed an important part of the evidence.

On 27 April 1910,* eight days before the death of Edward VII, an important meeting was held at Lambeth Palace at the invitation of the Archishop of Canterbury (Randall Davidson) but on Knollys' suggestion. The principal invitee was Balfour and the principal object of the meeting was to ascertain his attitude to a possible refusal of the guarantees by the King. Lord Esher, whose delight it was to take part in every such back-stage negotiation, was also present. At this meeting Balfour made it clear that, if the King refused Asquith's proposal, he was ready to take over his office 'and immediately ask the King to grant him a dissolution'.[35] Knollys so informed Edward VII.[36]

This information conveyed to the old King in April should have been conveyed to the new King in November. It was very important. It meant that, if George v refused his Government's advice, an alternative Government was in all probability available, for what was true in this respect on 27 April was still, presumably, true on 16 November. Plainly there were powerful arguments against replacing Asquith by Balfour on that date, but it was surely the duty of the Private Secretary to inform the Sovereign that 'Balfour was willing'. We do not know what the King meant by saying that Asquith's resignation in November 1910 would have been 'disastrous'. It is, however, difficult to believe that he would have used that ad-

---

* This is the date given by Lord Esher. Sir Harold Nicolson gives the date as 29 April, but this was derived from a paper in the Royal Archives not written until 1923.[34] Lord Esher's date is therefore to be preferred

jective if he had known that another Administration could have been formed.

Knollys in 1910 was an old gentleman of 73, not notably competent or clear-headed[37] at the best of times, and in May no doubt had been much agitated by the death of his master. All the same, it is difficult to find a good reason for his failure to impart this vital information to the new King in November. Did he assume that the old King had passed it on to his son? Can it be that Knollys' Liberalism caused him to betray his duty to his Sovereign, that of presenting to him all the facts of the case? Or can it be that he thought it his duty not to present this one fact in order to make sure that what he was convinced was the right decision was taken? Similar questions arise in respect of Lord Esher's role on this occasion. He had been at the Lambeth Palace gathering; he was close to the new King and to Knollys. Did Esher assume that Knollys had reported to George v the Leader of the Opposition's attitude earlier in the year? Lord Esher thought 'accidental' the 'suppression' of vital information 'of what the Opposition thought in 1910 of the general situation, and of what the King ought to do'.[38] Sir Harold Nicolson, however, states that Knollys assured George v 'that Mr Balfour would in any event decline to form an administration'.[39] This was not *suppressio veri*, but *suggestio falsi*.

It is not surprising that on 1 August 1911 Balfour wrote to Bigge (by then Lord Stamfordham) indignantly denying that he had been unwilling to form a Government in November 1910.[40] (With Knollys he became so angry that he thereafter refused to meet him socially.) Balfour even maintained that, given certain premises, he could have won the ensuing Election. The King too was very angry when he discovered that Balfour's attitude had been concealed from him. Just when and how he became aware of Knollys' lamentable lapse is not clear. He told Lord

Derby on 20 August 1911 that in November 1910 he had been given to understand that Balfour would have refused to form a Government and that he now knew that that had not been true.[41] Lord Stamfordham had recorded as early as December 1910 assertions by Balfour of his willingness to take office the previous month.[42] It would not have been in Stamfordham's character to withhold information of this kind from the King, even if his advice to him had been the same as Knollys'. At any rate, it was to Stamfordham that the King from now on gave his whole confidence. Although Knollys did not formally re-tire until March 1913, the diarchy in the Private Secretaryship had in fact come to an end long before that. As late as Novem-ber 1913 the King was still concerned that he might have made a mistake three years previously, talking 'very excitedly', to Lord Esher, 'for 1½ hours, still over-weighed by the idea that if he had refused the guarantees in November 1910 all the present troubles would have been obviated'.[43] In January 1914 the King minuted the account in the Royal Archives of the Lambeth Palace meeting of April 1910:

> It was not until late in the year 1913 that the foregoing letters and memoranda came into my possession. The knowledge of their contents would, undoubtedly, have had an important bearing and influence with regard to Mr Asquith's request for guarantees on November 16, 1910.[44]

After the momentous decision then made, the constitutional crisis moved more swiftly, though slowly by the standards of our own times, to its conclusion. On the same day that the King gave his pledge, the Parliament Bill was introduced into the House of Lords. It was given a second reading on 21 November, but died a natural, albeit temporary, death, when Parliament was dissolved on the 28th. The presentation of the 'project' was in conformity with Edward VII's stipulation to Asquith.[45] The December election results were almost exactly the same as the January ones. The Parliament Bill was re-introduced in March, reached the House of Lords in May, but by July had been 'changed out of all recognition' in Committee.[46] On the 14th, therefore, the King was advised that he must exercise his Prerogative 'to get rid of the deadlock and to secure the passage of the Bill'.[47]

This advice was slightly premature for there was still the chance that, if the Commons rejected the Lords' amendments and insisted on the passage of the Bill in its original form, the Lords would give way. The King, very sensibly, suggested that they should be given this chance. Once again the Prime Minister readily accepted his suggestion. Indeed it seems surprising that Asquith should, even momentarily, have contemplated any other course of action. He had, as we have seen,[48] supposed that if the Election gave him a working majority, the Lords would give way. It had, but they had not. Nevertheless the chance remained that public knowledge of the November pledge would make it unnecessary to implement it.

By this time, however, all previous calculations had been upset by the resolve of a number of Unionist Peers to 'die in the last ditch' rather than let the Bill through. These Peers therefore became known as the 'Ditchers' (or sometimes 'Die-hards'*) in contradistinction to the 'Hedgers', who were prepared to be governed by the advice of their Party leaders and 'hedge'. The exact numbers of these two groups were not known, and the outcome of the debate and division in the Lords was therefore a highly speculative matter. That division, however, would determine whether or not the King would have to create Peers. If the Ditchers prevailed, it was certain that a creation of Peers would follow. The King, even if he had not already been pledged to this in such an event, would have been bound at that moment by political necessity apart

---

* ' "The Die-Hards"—as they call themselves rather arrogantly taking the title of one of the Peninsular Regiments...'[49]

from any question, to quote Stamfordham, of 'acting rightly', to accept Ministerial advice to make such a creation. There would have been no practical alternative to doing so. The Unionist Party was now split, but if the Ditchers triumphed it was not contemplated by any one that their effective leader, Lord Willoughby de Broke, a good platform speaker but a lightweight politician,[50] still less their nominal leader, the 87-year-old Lord Halsbury, could be called upon to form a Government. Balfour, the official leader of the Unionist Party, would almost certainly[51] have been prepared to form a Government in November 1910, but was certainly not prepared to form one from January 1911 onwards.[52] The operative factor in the situation subsequent to that date was that a third Dissolution was impossible.* The King was well aware of this.[54]

In these circumstances his hope of avoiding what he still regarded as the 'humiliation' of a large-scale creation of Peers for a particular political purpose was that the Ditchers should prove to be the minority in the Division lobbies. As that supreme moment of the crisis approached his wholly natural anxiety about it led him to be over-active, to see too many people (contrary to what he knew would be Knollys' advice),[55] to bombard his Ministers with letters, not all of them wise. But these were minor blemishes on the royal record. George v's main effort, in these final days of the crisis, was to do all he could to make plain the consequences of a Ditcher victory. First of all he urged that the existence of the guarantees should be made known to Balfour and Lansdowne. This was done orally by Lord Knollys on 19 July and in writing by Asquith the next day. The ban on the secrecy of the guarantees was thereby raised and the Opposition led to foresee the inevitability of its defeat by what, in their rage, they regarded as at

---

* In a different context, but one apposite to the situation in 1911, Balfour later coined the splendid phrase: 'No Constitution could stand a diet of dissolutions'[53]

best (in the words of their censure motion in the House of Commons) 'a gross violation of Constitutional Liberty',[56] at worst (in the words of Austen Chamberlain) 'revolution nurtured in lies, promoted by fraud, and only to be achieved by violence'.[57] On 25 July the Speaker had to adjourn the House of Commons when the Prime Minister was deliberately howled down as he tried to state the Government's policy on the Lords' amendments.

Lord Crewe, in the House of Lords, on 7 August, spoke of the King's 'natural and legitimate reluctance' in giving the guarantees. But at Court this caused alarm, for it was foreseen, probably rightly, that such wording might lead the Ditchers to suppose that the Government was bluffing. Lord Morley was therefore furnished with a letter from Stamfordham which, as deputy for Lord Crewe, he read out in the House of Lords on the day of the division (10 August). The key sentence ran:

> If the Bill should be defeated tonight His Majesty will assent to the creation of Peers sufficient in number to guard against any possible combination of the different parties in opposition, by which the Parliament Bill might be exposed a second time to defeat.

Lord Selborne asked for this to be read again. Morley did so and added: 'Every vote given against my motion will be a vote for a large and prompt creation of Peers.'*

Even so the Government won by a majority of only 17. Apart from Liberal votes, they also received votes from 13 Bishops and 37 Unionist Peers. 'We were beaten', said George

---

* Morley's motion was 'that this House do not insist upon the said amendment', i.e., the crucial one excluding certain categories of Bills from the normal operation of Clause 2 of the Parliament Bill restricting the delaying power of the Lords in respect of Public Bills other than Money Bills to a period of two years. This amendment has come to be known as 'Lord Lansdowne's amendment'

Wyndham, 'by the Bishops and the Rats.' That day the tem-
perature had reached 110° Fahrenheit. At Buckingham Palace
the King stayed up in the sweltering heat to await the result.
He wrote in his diary:

> At 11.0 Bigge returned from the House of Lords with the
> good news that the Parliament Bill had passed.
>   So the Halsburyites were thank God beaten! It is indeed
> a great relief to me and I am spared any further humilia-
> tion by a creation of peers. . . .[58]

He left London the next day to join a shooting party at Bolton
Abbey; before the end of the month he was anxious to get back
to London to be available for consultation about the national
railway strike, the first of its kind.[59] The equable Asquith returned to London from the country at about the time the King
was leaving London. If the Bill had been rejected, he had been
prepared to return one hour earlier than would otherwise have
been the case.[60] Even more detached, in mind and body, was
Balfour. On 10 August he was in Paris en route for Bad Gas-
tein. 'Politics have been to me quite unusually odious . . .', he
wrote to Lady Elcho.[61]

IRELAND, 1912–14

The end of one crisis, however, only led straight to the opening of another. The procedure prescribed by the Parliament
Act, that of passing a Bill after a delay of two years despite
Lords' opposition, was now to be used to secure Home Rule
for Ireland. That probability had indeed provided the motive
force for the Irish Nationalist Party's support of the Parliament
Bill and for the passionate Unionist opposition to it. Asquith
introduced his Home Rule Bill in April 1912. If the processes
prescribed by the Parliament Act were to be followed, it was
bound to become law by the summer of 1914.

But were these processes to be followed? The King was put under heavy pressure by the Unionist Party to depart from them in two respects. He was urged, in the first place, to bring about yet another Election before the Bill passed finally through Parliament; in the second place, and in the last resort, to refuse the Royal Assent to it. The second proposal, although related to a more distant point of future time, seems to have been made before the first.

Both these proposals now seem fantastical at first sight, but history cannot be written simply from the point of view of the *fait accompli*. At the time the situation presented itself to contemporaries as substantially one without valid precedents. Moreover, history is all too easily written from the point of view of the Party which won. The Unionists were half the British nation. The two main Parties each held 272 seats in the new House of Commons. From the Opposition's point of view the Liberal Government had forced the King to take action importantly aiding the Liberal cause;[62] they were fully entitled, as they saw it, to do all in their power to prevent further revolutionary legislation. They argued, in particular, that the Parliament Act had suspended an important part of the Constitution. The Act contained a preamble (inserted to prevent Grey's resignation) stating an intention, to this day honoured in the breach, to substitute for the House of Lords as 'it at present exists a Second Chamber constituted on a popular instead of hereditary basis'. The Opposition regarded this pledge as part of a bargain which the Government should honour, failing which the rest of the bargain did not have to be honoured. (Asquith did not reject this doctrine out of hand.)[63] In the Opposition's view it followed, *inter alia*, that the right of veto hitherto possessed by the House of Lords had now passed temporarily to the Crown.[64]

Among those who said this was Lord Halsbury, an ex-Lord Chancellor,[65] but the matter became more serious when the

same point was made by the new Leader of the Opposition,
Bonar Law. (He had succeeded Balfour in November 1911.)
He made it in a speech as early as January 1912,[66] which 'properly disturbed' the King[67] and to the King's face—which
'turned red'[68]—at a dinner party in Buckingham Palace in
May 1912. Not for Law were the scruples about conduct to a
host which had led Asquith to tread too delicately at Sandringham in November 1910.[69] When the King expressed the hope
that 'there would be no violent scenes this session' his guest
said to him:

> Our desire has been to keep the Crown out of our struggles,
> but the Government have brought it in. Your only chance
> is that they should resign within two years. If they don't,
> you must either accept the Home Rule Bill, or dismiss
> your Ministers and choose others who will support you in
> vetoing it: and in either case, half your subjects will think
> you have acted against them. . . . They may say that your
> Assent is a purely formal act and the prerogative of veto
> is dead. That was true, as long as there was a buffer be-
> tween you and the House of Commons, but they have de-
> stroyed this buffer and it is no longer true.[70]

At Balmoral in September 1912 Law modified his doctrine. He
envisaged that, if the Home Rule Bill passed through all its
stages under the Parliament Act and required only the Royal
Assent, the King would only give that 'on the advice of his
Ministers'.[71] At about the same time Balfour, now an apprentice 'Elder Statesman' and in any case clearer-headed than
either Bonar Law or Halsbury, was writing that, while a
refusal of the Royal Assent to the Home Rule Bill 'might be
represented as unconstitutional', for the King to change his
advisers was perfectly proper. Balfour's plan was that either
Rosebery or himself should preside as a caretaker Prime Minister over an Election on the Home Rule issue.[72]
   The King considered the question of whether to give or

withhold his Assent to a Home Rule Bill which reached him under the Parliament Act procedure to be a real one.[73] When the time for it to be decided seemed to come near, he consulted Lord Loreburn (Lord Chancellor from 1906 to 1912) and in conjunction with him drafted—this was as late as 31 July 1914 —a letter to the Prime Minister making it plain that, in spite of the novelty of the situation, the Royal Assent would be forthcoming. The draft letter,[74] however, did contain a request for written Ministerial advice to give it. In other words, the King finally made up his mind not to take Bonar Law's first advice (which had been to act on his own initiative when the Home Rule Bill came to him, however novel and controversial the circumstances), but to act in the manner established by custom stretching back to the reign of Queen Anne, further to be fortified, as Law had suggested, by positive and specific advice from his Ministers so to act. In fact the Royal Assent was given to the Home Rule Bill, after it had been voted through the Commons three times, on 17 September 1914. That Bill and the one for the Disestablishment of the Welsh Church were the first to become law under the procedure of the Parliament Act. Each was accompanied by another suspending the start of its operation until after the end of the war. Even so, in respect of the Irish legislation the domestic British bitterness was still so great that the Unionist Members walked out of the House of Commons in protest against, of all things, the postponing Bill.[75]

Great as was the pressure on the King to exercise a prerogative, which had been defunct as long as Queen Anne, and refuse the Royal Assent to the Irish Home Rule Bill, still greater was the pressure on him to secure another Election before it became law. The Unionist argument was that it had not been a leading issue at the second 1910 Election, their conviction that an Election on that issue in 1912 would win them a Parliamentary majority. Bonar Law, at Balmoral in Septem-

ber, had not only told the King that he should only give the
Royal Assent to the Home Rule Bill 'on the advice of his Minister', but also that, before acting on that advice, 'Unionists
would certainly believe' that he should ascertain whether he
could not 'appoint other Ministers who could advise him dif-
ferently and allow the question to be decided by the Country
at a General Election ...'.[76] By August 1913, the King had
come to accept the principle that a General Election should pre-
cede the enactment of the Home Rule Bill;[77] he had, in fact,
accepted the Unionist argument. His difficulty, however, was
in deciding how far he should go in pressing this on the Government. On 11 August he handed the Prime Minister a long
and able memorandum, written in his own hand, setting out
his anxiety about the trend of Irish affairs.[78] In this paper he
made no direct mention of the case for a pre-1914 Election. He
dwelt rather on the prospect of bloodshed, the difficulties of
his own position, and the possibilities of an agreed settlement.
Asquith took this paper away with him on 'holiday' and proceeded to answer it, in two parts, the following month.[79] Certainly the time and trouble he gave to his answer were genuine
compliments to the King's memorandum. Not thus had
Asquith answered a letter two years previously setting out the
new King's views on the industrial situation and calling in
particular for 'peaceful picketing' to be made illegal.[80] He cir-
culated that letter to the Cabinet, waited for the inevitably unfavourable replies, and then buried the proposal under the
weight of Cabinet disapproval.[81] This was a clever tactic: one
wonders what would have happened if Gladstone had treated
some of Queen Victoria's more foolish letters in the same way.

Asquith's first paper was concerned with the constitutional
position of the Sovereign. It is a classic statement of the traditional doctrines and practice, refutes the idea that the Parliament Act had in any way affected the King's constitutional
position, and concludes that, so long as he acted on the advice

of his Ministers, he was free from all personal responsibility 'for the acts of the executive and the legislature'. On this basis, in other words, force and meaning were given to the maxim that 'the King can do no wrong'. On this basis too

> however objectionable particular Acts may be to a large section of his subjects, they cannot hold him in any way accountable, and their loyalty is (or ought to be) wholly unaffected. If, on the other hand, the King were to intervene on one side, or in one case—which he could only do by dismissing Ministers in *de facto* possession of a Parliamentary majority—he would be expected to do the same on another occasion, and perhaps for the other side. Every Act of Parliament of the first order of importance, and only passed after acute controversy, would be regarded as bearing the personal *imprimatur* of the Sovereign. He would, whether he wished it or not, be dragged into the arena of party politics; and at a dissolution following such a dismissal of Ministers as has just been referred to, it is no exaggeration to say that the Crown would become the football of contending factions.
>
> This is a Constitutional catastrophe which it is the duty of every wise statesman to do the utmost in his power to avert.[82]

This memorandum did not remove the King's anxiety about his own position. His worry had been (Bonar Law's actual words seem to have stuck[83]): 'Whatever I do I shall offend half the population.'[84] It was indeed no real answer to say that, if he continued to act on Cabinet advice, the loyalty of large sections of his subjects who would find a Home Rule Act, to say the least, 'objectionable', '*ought*' to be wholly unaffected. The King replied, with wisdom perhaps greater than that of a politician, that, whilst fully accepting the proposition that he should act on Cabinet advice:

> I nevertheless cannot shut my eyes to the fact that in this

particular instance the people will, rightly or wrongly, associate me with whatever policy is adopted by my advisers, dispensing praise or blame according as that policy is in agreement or antagonistic to their own opinions.[85]

It is interesting to find that one politician, a Liberal Cabinet Minister to boot, John Morley, more than shared the King's point of view about this. Morley, like his Monarch, was 'distraught about the situation'. He sought 'quiet talk' about it with the Archbishop of Canterbury and confided in him (on 21 January 1914), 'guardedly', that he thought the King had a stronger position than Asquith and others had admitted 'inasmuch as there is only one House of Parliament at present, and the King's responsibility is therefore increased'. (This was a handsome, albeit private, admission of the rightness of the Unionist point of view.) Morley thought that if the King dismissed his Ministers by insisting on a Dissolution he might be acting unwisely, but thought he would not in that event be exceeding his legal rights—that was certainly true—or, arguably, be departing from his right course. Morley went on to say that, if there was a civil war, the public would blame the King for its outbreak:

He is the one man who (they will say) could have stopped it. He did not so act. Civil War came. The King must bear the responsibility for it.[86]

The Prime Minister's second paper, of September 1913, was about the prospective situation in Ireland. It raised, and rejected, the argument that there should be another Election before the Home Rule Bill became law. Not only would that make a mockery of the Parliament Act, but it would settle nothing. If the Government won, the problem of Ulster's resistance to the Bill would still remain. If it lost, there would be the problem of the rest of Ireland's resistance to the continuance of the Union.

The King replied to Asquith on 22 September 1913, with a memorandum which in length (1,500 words) and force is the most formidable remonstrance addressed by a modern British Monarch to his Prime Minister.[87] It is in manner more reminiscent of one of Gladstone's long, highly argumentative letters to the Queen than one of her sharp rebukes to him. There could be no better example of a King exercising, to the full, his right to advise and to warn.

With perfect 'intellectual good manners' the paper traverses many of Asquith's arguments and asks many searching questions, but concludes, as did the initial August memorandum, by emphasis on the need for an agreed Irish settlement.

About this the King ventured to be precise, suggesting the temporary exclusion of North-East Ulster from Home Rule. The Prime Minister answered this very long letter briefly (he was in any case due at Balmoral within a week), but he did comment favourably on this suggestion. Had he had it in mind from the start or had the King's pressure contributed to a change of attitude?

So far as the question of another Election was concerned, the King returned to the charge in February 1914, telling Asquith that an Election would 'clear the air', show whether the Government really possessed a mandate for Home Rule, and in any case relieve them both of responsibility for what followed. Grey and Haldane,[88] possibly also Morley,[89] had been in favour of Dissolution a few days earlier. Asquith, however, a statesman either on the 'down' of drift or on the 'up' of firmness, was now firm. He repeated the arguments he had set out in the correspondence of the previous summer, notably that responsibility for whatever might happen was not the King's but that of his Ministers. Lord Stamfordham recorded that:

> The King replied that, although constitutionally he might not be responsible, still he could not allow bloodshed among his loyal subjects in any part of his Dominions

without exerting every means in his power to avert it. Although at the present stage of the proceedings he could not rightly intervene he should feel it his duty to do what in his own judgment was best for his people generally.[90]

Asquith's answer to that observation pin-pointed the two significant ways in which the King could intervene. He could refuse the Royal Assent to the Home Rule Bill, which would be unconstitutional, or he could dismiss his Ministers. It is interesting that as late as 1914 a Prime Minister should have considered this to be a constitutional right of the Sovereign, however difficult to exercise in terms of political reality, and that the Sovereign should not have altogether disclaimed it. The King in fact replied 'that he had no intention of dismissing his Ministers, although his future action must be guided by circumstances'.[91] For the moment, in other words, the Prime Minister had repulsed the King's pressure for another Election, but the King had explicitly reserved his future position. He felt himself presented with odious alternatives. He either had to condone bloodshed or use the Prerogative in a highly controversial way, unprecedented since 1834, of dismissing his Ministers. On the personal level, he did not want to dismiss them. The liking and respect between King and Prime Minister were mutual.[92] Neither of them liked or respected Bonar Law.[93] Moreover, the King was better aware than the Leader of the Opposition of the dangers of the European situation.

George v was undoubtedly susceptible to the pressure put on him between 1912 and 1914 by Unionists, especially that of Irish Loyalists,[94] to abort the Home Rule Bill. It would be wrong, however, to represent this, or his anxiety about his own position, intense as that was, as the main motivating force for his great political activity over Ireland during those two years. Nor was he motivated by any special sympathy for the Union as such. (*Per contra* his father and grandmother had both, as we have seen, been passionately opposed to Irish Home Rule.)

Lord Crewe, writing from Balmoral in the autumn of 1913, shortly before Asquith's arrival at the Castle, reported to him that 'the King was sedulous, even in talking to me very intimately, to express no opinion against Home Rule'; he was more positive even than that, saying that 'It might be a very good thing' and that in any case some form of it was necessary because there was a Parliamentary majority in favour of it.[95]

No, George v was, above all, a man of peace: the driving force behind his great political activity in these two years was his desire to achieve a peaceful settlement and avoid bloodshed. Crewe, in the same letter, describes the King as 'haunted . . . by the feeling that, if he does not take off his coat and work for a settlement of some kind, and there is serious loss of life after the Bill passes, he will not only be held responsible by Opposition partisans, but will actually be so to some extent'.[96]

'Haunted' at Balmoral in September 1913, he was 'unhappy and pessimistic'[97] at Windsor in April 1914. His worry about Ireland kept him awake at night.[98] There seemed to him so little that he could do. In public, like King Magnus in Shaw's *Apple Cart*, he was limited to the tone of voice in which he uttered the words his Ministers put into his mouth. Opening Parliament on 10 February 1914, he 'laid great stress on the paragraph about Home Rule for Ireland, in which I appeal for a peaceful settlement'.[99] In private he could 'keep on bothering [the Prime Minister] as much as possible'.[100] It may well be the case—this is hard to assess—that the King's 'bothering' played an important part in making the Prime Minister eventually face up to the new issues of 1912-14, so different from those of 1910-12.[101]

The King's anxiety, however, perhaps made him overdo this bothering from time to time. In April 1914 Asquith received what he described as 'a rather hysterical letter from G.R.'[102] Jenkins describes it as 'an extreme example of royal pressure in favour of a particular policy'. The policy in question was

that of allowing the Six Counties indefinitely to contract out
of Home Rule. But that is, after all, what was in the end basically brought about, and it does not really seem in the least
hysterical to say:

> I repeat what I said to you last week, that I have every
> confidence in you. I have also absolute confidence in your
> ability to bring about a peaceful solution, whenever you
> put in force the great powers you possess.

The King was putting his finger on the principal cause of the
disastrous deterioration of the situation after 1912, the pas-
sivity of the Prime Minister. In the nature of the case he was
the most powerful piece on the board, but he made no decisive
move. Even so eminent a Liberal historian as Sir Robert Ensor
makes against Asquith the accusation that over Ireland 'down
to 1914 he still had no clear policy, but remained poised on
equivocations...'.[103] It is an eminent Conservative historian,
Robert Blake, impressively fair to Asquith, who suggests that
he regarded the movement led by Carson, in the light of his
personal knowledge of him as an old opponent in the Courts,
as largely bluff.[104]

No wonder that in late July 1914, the King jumped at his
Prime Minister's advice to hold a conference in Buckingham
Palace to attempt an Irish settlement. By then the question had
become one of the time limit (if any) for which Ulster was to
be excluded from the Home Rule Act and the definition of
Ulster for that purpose. The second part of this question was,
as Winston Churchill put it, one of toiling 'around the muddy
byways of Fermanagh and Tyrone'. The Prime Minister, for
one, thought that the question of area was all-important. 'Keep
your mind', he said to Archbishop Davidson on 30 June 1914,
'to the thought that the Area question is the only thing that
matters. All the rest is "leather and prunella".'[105]

The King opened the conference in person,[106] but the subsequent sessions were, at his suggestion—an important and valu-

able initiative[107]—chaired by the Speaker. Definition of area was the first item on the agenda and, no agreement having been reached on it, the conference broke down by 24 July without the question of time limit being even reached. The King, much upset by this,[108] could only seek to content himself with the thought that the meetings had at any rate created 'a more friendly understanding'.[109] He said goodbye to each member of the conference separately and privately, telling Redmond that he was 'convinced of the necessity of Home Rule'.[110] As the Speaker waited in the anteroom, in the company of Bonar Law and Lansdowne, for his turn to say goodbye to his Sovereign, he picked up *The Times* and learnt from it of the Austro-Hungarian ultimatum to Serbia: 'I called the attention of my companions to this very serious news which, as our Conference had sat early, they had not seen previously and we agreed that it foretold some very grave events.'[111]

The Home Rule Bill was, as we have already seen,[112] passed, for the third time, through both Houses of Parliament, but accompanied on this journey by another Bill deferring its coming into force until after the war. Civil war in Ireland was, in short, averted by the outbreak of European war and George v thereby rescued from a position which agonised him.

He was rescued by the outbreak of war from much else besides his worries about Ireland; 'he was relieved', says Sir Harold Nicolson, 'of central responsibility'.[113] This seems at first sight paradoxical, but we must remember that the main issues of domestic politics in the pre-war years of his reign were of a kind which largely turned on the way in which he should discharge his duties as a constitutional sovereign in unprecedented circumstances. Events, in other words, had put him, limelighted, in the centre of the stage, a solitary symbol of national unity. With the outbreak of war the nation became, pacifists apart, politically united and the importance of the King's political role correspondingly decreased. The limelight fell on the fighting men and their commanders. Only in communities in which in wartime the King takes command in the field is a King more important as a leader in war than in peace; a democracy with a titular Head of State has no special wartime role for him. (In the U.S.A., where the President is an effective as well as a titular Head of State, and always Commander-in-Chief by virtue of his office, the position is a different and special one.) Even in the Germany of 1914, where democracy only existed in embryo, the 'All-Highest' soon found himself with less power than in peacetime. The master of Bethmann-Hollweg became quite soon the servant of Hindenburg and Ludendorff. The Kaiser's first cousin, the King of England, one day at the centre of affairs, the next day found relative trivialities the subject matter of his communications to Ministers.[114] George VI, as we shall see,[115] in his time found himself, to his own intense chagrin, with not enough to do during the war.

Years afterwards Winston Churchill asked George V which had been his worst time, the constitutional crisis or the Great War.

'For me', he said, 'the most difficult was the constitutional crisis. In the war we were all united. We should sink or swim together. But then, in my first year, half the nation was one way and half the other.'[116]

The same was true of his three following years but, as civil war drew nearer, the stakes became higher, the passions more intense. Churchill could perhaps have asked another more acute question, perhaps indeed, for all we know, he did. It would certainly be interesting to know which time the King found worse, the constitutional crisis proper of 1910–11, or the Irish crisis of 1912–14. Sir Harold Nicolson's opinion is that the Irish problem 'faced him with an issue more disturbing even than the battle between the Commons and the Lords'.[117]

One may conjecture that the very difficulty of the central role which fell to George v in the four years before the war made him all the more willing, in accordance with his temperament and training—and his age—to adopt the role of complete neutrality which he played so well in post-war politics. The fact of his whole personality making him so naturally inclined to play that role, the contradistinction to his more responsible pre-war one which worried him is an important fact in the constitutional history of the British Monarchy. To it must be added the fact of the decisive rebuffs he received from Lloyd George as wartime Prime Minister.[118] The character of George v and the circumstances of the times combined to thrust on him, between 1910 and 1914, a role of ceaseless and important political activity. The Cabinet crisis of 1931 apart, his subsequent political role was a notably more passive one. 1914 proved a watershed in the political history of the British Monarchy just as it proved a watershed in the history of the British people and of the whole world.

POLITICAL ROLE IN GENERAL

The pace of these four years, particularly for a new and inexperienced Sovereign, had been breathtaking. On what sort of a man had this heavy pressure fallen?

Let us see him first as he was seen by Max Beerbohm in 1914, the time we have reached in our narrative. In a letter to his wife describing the State Opening of Parliament, Beerbohm wrote of:

> The little King with the great diamond crown that covered his eyebrows, and with the eyes that showed so tragically much of effort, of the will to please—the will to impress —the will to be all that he isn't and that his Papa *was* (or

seems to him to have been) . . . such a piteous, good, feeble, heroic little figure.[119]

When he died 22 years later Beerbohm wrote: 'I very genuinely mourn that transcendently decent and lovable King . . .'.[120] A. J. P. Taylor wrote of him:[121]

He was conscientious; he was decent; he was straight. These are high virtues. His strictly political activities showed the same virtues. . . .

Of these adjectives, the most apt is the recurring 'decent'. The King kept his head and his common humanity when men and women with stronger heads lost theirs and abandoned ordinary standards of decent behaviour. He thought the militant suffragettes 'insensate', but was disgusted by forcible feeding.[122] When he heard that conscientious objectors, against whom in the 1914–18 war almost every hand was raised, were being interned at Dartmoor he protested that 'their new condition of life will not be very different from that of imprisonment'.[123] When in 1918 a cry went up for the internment of all aliens, 'Intern me first', he said to Margot Asquith.[124] When the Government imposed 'differential treatment' on u-boat prisoners, a forceful warning was immediately sent to the Prime Minister:

Either they are criminals and should be tried and punished as such; or they are prisoners of war and ought to be treated accordingly. . . . The King yields to no-one in abominating the general conduct of the Germans throughout this war; but nonetheless he deprecates the idea of reprisals and retaliation; he has always hoped that at the end of the war we shall stand as a nation before the world as having conducted it as far as possible with humanity and like gentlemen.[125]

The language may be to a substantial extent Lord Stamfordham's, but the thought is that of George V. In the event the

Germans resorted to reprisals on British prisoners; the British Government had therefore to cancel their unwise instructions, and so the King's point was in practice gained.

He had to make it again, of course, in other circumstances. When the fighting in Ireland was at its height he asked the Chief Secretary 'if this policy of reprisals is to be continued and, if so, to where will it lead . . . ?'[126] The King thought the Black and Tans should be disbanded.'[127]*

He was always against a search for scapegoats. He believed in 'loyalty to public servants, who should not be thrown over by the government'.[129] For his own part he was consistently loyal to those who had served him well, however great any popular clamour against them. He was, for example, unswervingly faithful to Ramsay MacDonald.[130]

Victory in the 1914–18 war was for him an occasion for congratulations to Asquith as well as to Lloyd George. He insisted too that both should receive the same war medals.[131] In November 1918, the Prime Minister was pressed to include his predecessor in the British delegation to the Peace Conference.[132] (When Asquith lost his seat in Parliament the King saw to it that he was invited to all appropriate official ceremonies.[133] In 1924 the offer of an Earldom to him came from the King in the 'interregnum' between one Prime Minister and another, and so was patently a royal initiative.[134] At the same time Lord Stamfordham was writing to Haldane: 'The King directs me to tell you how deeply he appreciates all you have done to make our victory possible and how silly he thought the outcry against you'.[135] The King himself had given a conspicuous sign of his disapproval of that outcry, when it was at its height. On 26 May 1915 he received Lord Haldane (two days after he had

---

* 'Only once after 1922 is there any record of the King's views being mentioned in the Cabinet. This was [in 1924] when he took the strongest exception to the way in which Allenby, dressed in civilian clothes and backed by cavalry, had demanded reparations from the King of Egypt after the murder of Lee Stack'[128]

been driven from office) and personally conferred on him the Order of Merit.[136]

In his habits and in all personal matters the King was extremely conservative. In Naval matters, about which he was professionally knowledgeable (he had served in the Navy for 14 years), he had, as Prince of Wales, been a supporter of Beresford and an opponent of Fisher.[137] About at least two matters, however, he converted Fisher to his point of view.[138] In October 1914, the King had considerable misgivings about his re-appointment as First Sea Lord.[139] Edward VII's 're-actionary' views about India were shared by the Prince of Wales,[140] but by 1931 Lord Irwin, in whose appointment as Viceroy the King had played the leading part,[141] was being told that 'he deprecates as much as you do the attitude which the Conservatives, egged on by the retired diehards from India, are adopting'.[142]

None the less he was at the start of his reign, like his father and grandmother before him, a Conservative. In August 1911, he told Sir Frederick Ponsonby that one of his difficulties in giving the guarantees was that of being advised 'by the party whose views he did not support'.[143] He felt that the Conservatives were his natural allies.[144] He might not otherwise have been as much influenced as he in fact was by Bonar Law from 1911 to 1914. Jenkins suggests that what he really liked was 'a combination of "Whig men and Tory measures"'. ('Perhaps always', he adds, 'the ideal solution from a royal point of view'.)[145] From Asquith's standpoint he was, during that time, 'a little wobbly'.[146] Artlessly he wrote to his mother of his first Labour Ministers: 'They have different ideas to ours as they are all socialists. . . .'[147]

George V, however, was no doctrinaire. When Sir Herbert Samuel stuck to his Free Trade guns in October 1931, he was written off as 'quite impossible' and 'most obstinate'.[148] The King was not unsympathetic to the point of view of many

Socialist Ministers. He got on specially well with J. H. Thomas.[149] As early as 1919 he summed him up as 'a good and loyal man'.[150] The extremist member of the first Labour Government was J. P. Wheatley. He could be described as its Aneurin Bevan, and he held the same office, Minister of Health. The fact of 'a very interesting conversation with him' is recorded in the King's diary for 22 February 1924,[151] and after a long conversation with him on another occasion the King's comment was: 'I should have felt exactly as he does if I had had his sort of childhood.'[152] Tom Johnston, another Clydesider, who entered the second Labour Cabinet in March 1931, has testified[153] to his good relations with the King.

He had strong opinions of his own on many subjects. But he trained himself to subordinate them to his duties as a constitutional monarch.[154] In 1924 the septuagenarian Lord Esher, who had observed so much for so long, wrote of him: 'During fourteen years of a disturbed reign he has so far made no mistakes and has not alienated any body of politicians. That is a fine record.'[155] By the end of his reign he had altogether ceased to be a partisan. Sir Harold Nicolson writes:

Those who, whether as Cabinet Ministers or in some other capacity, had access to the King during the last decade of his reign, can still recall the smile and gesture with which, after indulging in some criticism, he would brush aside his own views as crumbs from the table, exclaiming: 'But all that, of course, is not for *me*.'[156]

George v became, in short, the model constitutional monarch, the keystone of the arch which had been being built for so many centuries.

Perhaps the severest test to which his impartiality was put was the formation and functioning of the first Labour Government. The Labour Party had become the official Opposition in 1922. The Election of 1923 left them with 191 seats in the

House of Commons compared with the Conservatives' 258 and the Liberals' 158. No such uncertain Parliamentary balance had been known since mid-Victorian times. Moreover, the Labour Party was then widely regarded as revolutionary. (In the first years of his reign the King had regarded 'socialism' as inimical to the Throne.)[157] All manner of people suggested all sorts of combinations by which they might be prevented from holding office.[158] But the three principal actors on the scene never hesitated as to their duties. Baldwin refused to ally himself with the Liberals to keep the Socialists out. Asquith was positive that, once Baldwin was defeated in the House, the King should send for MacDonald. The King himself was clear that Baldwin should not resign immediately but should face the new House of Commons. (Both of them changed their minds on this comparatively minor constitutional point in the comparable Parliamentary circumstances of 1929.)[159] Baldwin having done so, and having been defeated, the King considered it his undoubted constitutional duty to ask MacDonald, as the leader of the next largest Party, to form a Government. This commission was to be 'without strings'. Moreover, the King subsequently wrote that he 'never consulted Mr Baldwin in any way when he came to resign, nor asked his advice as to whom to send for'.[160] In 1913, as we have seen, George V was pressed to dismiss his Ministers and ask some 'elder statesman' to preside over a General Election. He resisted this pressure, but undoubtedly he was tempted to yield to it. Ten years later, put under comparable pressure, he did not for a moment hesitate to pursue the simple straightforward course, and the interesting thing is that there is evidence that the King made up his mind to this while Stamfordham, wise as he was, was still considering complicated alternatives.[161] In 1880 Queen Victoria had fought every inch of the way to prevent Gladstone, the undoubted choice of the people, becoming Prime Minister for the second time. In 1924 George V did not even contemplate stepping an inch away from the straight and narrow path of constitutional duty to prevent MacDonald, only the leader of a Minority Party in the House of Commons, becoming the first Socialist Prime Minister.

There was as much heart-searching among some pundits about the manner of the Labour Government's end as about its formation. Asquith held the view that 'the King was under no constitutional obligation to grant a dissolution to a Prime Minister not possessing a majority in Parliament'.[162] But this was in fact a self-interested view. The King was reluctant to give MacDonald a Dissolution in October 1924, not because of any abstruse constitutional consideration but for practical reasons which he took the trouble to record in his own hand.[163] He had been equally reluctant to agree to the dissolutions of 1918 and 1923, but it was not in his character not to give MacDonald what he had given to Lloyd George and Baldwin.

Ramsay MacDonald's undertaking to form a Labour Government, the first in British history, was given on 22 January 1924. It is something of a shock now to realise that that date was only 23 years from the date on which Queen Victoria died. 'I wonder what she would have thought of a Labour Government!', the King wrote in his diary after MacDonald had accepted his commission.[164] It is all too easy to think what she would have thought. By contrast her grandson's treatment of his new Ministers was scrupulously considerate and fair. He wrote to his mother on 17 February 1924:

> I have been making the acquaintance of all the Ministers in turn and I must say they all seem to be very intelligent and they take things very seriously ... they ought to be given a chance and ought to be treated fairly.[165]

One of the new Ministers, J. R. Clynes, has given a vivid account of their first reception by the King, a 'little, quiet man' who was 'kindness and sympathy itself'.[166] The year 1924 was the climacteric of George v's political career.

The suggestion has been made that the King's part in the events of August 1931 was unconstitutional; that he initiated the formation of the 'National Government' and that these actions of his were his most decisive intervention in the politics of his reign. No part of this triune statement is true.

To take the last point first, it is not true to say, as Sir Harold Nicolson does, that 'it was in connection with this crisis that King George assumed the greatest responsibility of his reign....'[167] It could be argued that sending for MacDonald in February 1924 was a greater one; it is certain that the giving of the 'advance guarantees' in November 1910 was far greater.

What is true is that the formation of the National Government under MacDonald aroused, understandably, extreme bitterness in the ranks of the Labour Party. Viscount Simon indeed wrote:

> The denunciations heaped upon MacDonald's head by many who had previously idolized him were the most violent I have ever known in British Politics.[168]

This, it must be remembered, is the judgment of a man who had had personal experience at a high level of the bitterness of British politics between 1911 and 1914. If the second Labour Government had been succeeded by a Conservative-Liberal coalition the post-crisis bitterness to the Left of it would have been nothing like so great. If MacDonald had joined, in a secondary position, a wider coalition than that, he would undoubtedly have been regarded as 'the lost leader', possibly even as a traitor to his Party. It was his stepping straight from the top place in a Labour Government to the top place in a Coalition Government, predominantly Conservative, which made him seem an arch-traitor. From that sprang the legend of his having been also an arch-plotter, with the child of his plotting, the 'National Government', conceived long before the events of August 1931.

The King came second to the Prime Minister as the whipping-boy the Left was in search of for the ignoble downfall of the Labour Government. Its formation, however, as will be seen, was not his brain-child. His part was that of midwife. His only personal initiative in those dramatic August days was, having on the 21st, with MacDonald's concurrence, left for Balmoral 'according to plan' he himself the next day decided to return to London.[169] In other words, he spent two consecutive nights in the train. He arrived at Euston at 8.0 a.m. on Sunday, 23 August: the right man, out of a sense of duty, in the right place. The events which interrupted his holiday had, however, been developing for many months.

The idea of a Coalition Government being needed to surmount the economic crisis was in the air from October 1930 onwards. At that time Sir Arthur Balfour, a member of the Economic Advisory Council, wrote to the Prime Minister advocating a decrease in the rates of unemployment benefit, as well as imposing import duties of between 10 per cent and 20 per cent, to avert national bankruptcy. Sir Arthur thought a Coalition Government would be needed to carry these measures.[170] On 11 July 1931, Sir Clive Wigram (who had succeeded Lord Stamfordham as Private Secretary on his death in March) warned the King in the gravest possible terms of the worsening of the international financial situation. He wrote:

> We are sitting on the top of a volcano.... A Minority Government will hardly be able to deal with the situation, and it is quite possible that Your Majesty might be asked to approve of a National Government....[171]

On 31 July Philip Snowden, the Chancellor of the Exchequer, told the House of Commons that he had received the report of the May Committee on economies in Government expenditure and that its recommendations could only be enforced by the House as a whole.[172]

The first specific suggestion for a National Government to carry out a programme on the lines of the May Report was not made by the King, but to him, shortly after noon on Sunday, 23 August, by Sir Herbert Samuel.[173] The King, it will be remembered, had returned to London early that morning. He saw MacDonald at 10.0 a.m. It was then agreed, and announced, that the King would see Baldwin and Sir Herbert Samuel to find out from them the position of their respective Parties. It is not clear whether this idea was the King's or his Minister's, but it certainly received the latter's sanction.

It was an accident that at this critical turning point Samuel came to the Palace before Baldwin. The latter could not be located.[174] Perhaps it was because Samuel came first that, according to Sir Clive Wigram, it was through this interview that 'His Majesty became convinced of the necessity for the National Government'.[175] Sir Herbert's argument was that 'the best solution' was that the requisite economies should be made by the existing or a reconstituted Labour Government; the 'best alternative' was a National Government under MacDonald.[176]

Late that evening MacDonald told the King that eight members of his Cabinet were against accepting the measures of economy specified by the New York bankers as a necessary pre-condition of their giving the credits asked for to check the growing flight from the pound. He therefore offered the resignation of his Government. The King asked him to reconsider the situation as 'he was the only man to lead the country through this crisis. . . .'[177] The Prime Minister then asked for a meeting of the King, Baldwin, Samuel and himself the following morning (Monday, 24 August). It was at this meeting, which the King opened and closed, and during the period of his absence, that the definitive decision to form a 'National Government' was taken.

The King's part in these proceedings was perfectly proper. The point is well put by Sir Herbert Samuel, perhaps, as we

have seen, more entitled to be thought the begetter of the new
Government than anyone else:

> Mr MacDonald's resignation was the necessary con-
> sequence of an irreconcilable division in his Cabinet. The
> King then acted in strict accordance with precedent in
> following the advice of the outgoing Premier: that was to
> bring into consultation the spokesmen of the two parties
> which together could furnish a majority in the House of
> Commons able to sustain a new Administration. The in-
> vitation to the Prime Minister to return to office, and to
> form a new Administration on an all-party basis, was the
> course advised by them.[178]

Herbert Morrison, one of the outgoing Labour Cabinet
Ministers, considers that there was no need for a 'National
Government'; all that it did could have been done by a Conservative-Liberal Coalition. Hence, in his opinion, the King's
action was unwise.[179] But that is not to say that it was unconstitutional.

No doubt the new Administration was much to the King's
taste. When in October it seemed likely to end, he did his best
to keep it going.[180] But the charge that he was its improper
promoter is baseless.[181]

The story of George V's relations with his two Labour
Governments illustrates his attitude to politics, his Conservative inclinations controlled by his determination to be fair. But,
as has already been said, he was, politics apart, conservative.
One aspect of this attitude was a respect for constituted authority
wherever it was to be found. He was, for example, strongly
opposed to the scrapping of the Simon Report.[182]

What was much more important as an aspect of this trait
was that he took the view (as did most of his contemporaries,
and notably Asquith)* that politicians should not interfere with

---

* The Cabinet's war role, under his chairmanship, is illuminated by his own
account of a meeting on 5 July 1916: 'Sir W. Robertson attended and with the

the conduct of war. Esher, who made a deep study of Defence questions, wrote to Fisher in 1907 of the Boer War:

> It was immensely to the credit of Lord Salisbury's Cabinet that they never interfered in 1899–1901, except on one occasion, when they appointed Lord Roberts to supersede Buller. That was a legitimate form of interference.[185]

George v gave Kitchener, as Secretary of State for War, the same unqualified and open support his father had given Fisher as First Sea Lord.[186] Kitchener and French, the Commander-in-Chief of the Expeditionary Force, were constantly at odds. The King backed the former[187] and indeed sized up the latter's defects for his command long before his Prime Minister did.[188] In November 1915, therefore, Asquith had the King's help in replacing French by Sir Douglas Haig.[189] He, it must be said, was an old friend of the Royal Family. He had proposed to Miss Vivian, a Maid of Honour to Queen Alexandra, when staying at Windsor Castle, and the wedding was in the private chapel at Buckingham Palace. Edward vii told the future Lady

---

aid of a large map described and explained to the Cabinet the operations in France so far as they had proceeded. His account was of a very reassuring character and gave general satisfaction. The Prime Minister then invited the attention of the Cabinet to the latest development in the Irish negotiations.'[183] As Prime Minister, says A. J. P. Taylor: 'though resolved on victory, he supposed that the only contribution statesmen could make was to keep out of the way, while free enterprise supplied the arms with which generals would win the battles'. Between the outbreak of war and the formation of the first Coalition he gave one war survey in the House of Commons, in which the campaign in France was not mentioned. After his fall from power in December 1916, he was still concerned to defend generals against interference by politicians rather than press for a more vigorous waging of the war. It was Churchill who twice attempted to survey the war in broad terms in the House of Commons (on 27 November 1914, and 15 February 1915), Churchill who on 22 August 1916 preached the doctrine of War Socialism. He won no support on any of these three occasions. Lloyd George was right to say on 23 June 1916: 'The Press has performed the function which should have been performed by Parliament and which the French Parliament has performed.' It is not true of the First World War, as General Groener said: 'The German General Staff fought against the English Parliament'[184]

Haig that her fiancé was his 'best and most capable General'.[190] But this is not to say that Haig was a toady, something which George v at any rate would not have welcomed.

The replacement of French by Haig was in accord with the Boer War precedent. An entirely new situation arose, however, when Asquith was replaced as Prime Minister by Lloyd George on 7 December 1916. The previous day Bonar Law told the King that Lloyd George and himself had long been convinced that the war was being mismanaged. 'To this', Lord Stamford-ham minuted:

> the King demurred and said that the politicians should leave the conduct of war to experts. Mr Bonar Law said that Robertson and the soldiers were all wrong, with the result that we have lost Serbia, Rumania and very likely Greece. The King expressed his entire disagreement with these views. . . .[191]

Here was a basis for endless conflict between George v and his new Prime Minister. Lloyd George's rise to supreme power was based on his energetic striving for a more vigorous waging of the war, in however unorthodox a fashion. He was an 'Easterner'. He was thus very far from seeing eye-to-eye with either the new Commander-in-Chief (Sir Douglas Haig) or the Chief of the Imperial General Staff (Sir William Robertson) and probably he had the balance of wisdom on his side. 'I never believed', he wrote later, 'in costly frontal attacks, either in war or in politics, if there were a way round.'[192] In blunter, more colloquial words, the Prime Minister's political methods involved the use of back doors rather than front ones. This had already been noted when he was Secretary of State for War, Robertson thwarting a manoeuvre in October 1916 to get Cabinet agreement to send divisions from France to Salonika by an appeal to the King and Asquith.[193] In March 1917 the new Prime Minister resorted, in Churchill's phrase, to a series of 'mystifying manoeuvres'[194] to secure one of his objects, a unified Allied command for the Western Front. He tried to impose this on Haig at an Anglo-French conference in Calais in February 1917, by what could be bluntly described as a trick.[195] But the King gave to Haig as c-in-c the same full backing that Edward VII had given Kitchener in South Africa,[196] and Haig reported the whole Calais manoeuvre in a long letter to the King.[197] The game of going through the back door was one, in fact, at which two could play. Haig's letter ended with, in effect, an offer of resignation. This was refused in the answer from Lord Stamfordham, who wrote, however:

> In conclusion I am to say from His Majesty you are not to worry; you may be certain that he will do his utmost to protect your interests. . . .[198]

The King had placed himself in a false position. A 'showdown' with the Prime Minister eventuated. The King 'remained obstinately convinced that high strategy was a matter for experts. . . '.[199] The Prime Minister for his part remained dissatisfied with the competence of his Generals. A manoeuvre for kicking Robertson upstairs was met by his tendering his resignation. Lloyd George was then told that the King strongly deprecated the removal of Robertson from the office of C.I.G.S.[200] The Prime Minister's answer was that 'he did not share His Majesty's extremely favourable opinion of Sir William Robertson' and that, if the King insisted on retaining his services, 'His Majesty must find other Ministers'.[201] The ace of trumps had been played and the game was taken. No Prime Minister ever had to play that card at the Palace again.

ROLE AS CONCILIATOR

In politics an Opposition can to a greater extent than a Government choose the issues on which it wishes to concentrate. The

Government must respond to the challenge of day-to-day events. A King is very much part of the Government, but he has rather more freedom than his Ministers to develop his own interests. This Chapter has so far recounted George v's reaction to the main political and politico-military events of his reign. He found them very worrying but also absorbingly interesting. But the subject which most interested him politically was the Empire. As Prince of Wales he had visited Australia, Canada, India, Newfoundland (then a separate country) and New Zealand. No other royal person had had anything like the same personal experience of the Empire.[202] The role he cast for himself as King was to make an intense interest in the affairs of the Empire which his father had on the whole neglected. Edward vii had had to be talked to very strongly by Balfour in 1901 to allow the Prince and Princess of Wales to travel out to open the first Parliament of the newly federated Australia.[203]

As early as August 1910, George v expressed his intention to have himself crowned at a Durbar in India and to visit every Dominion.[204] His idea of an Indian Durbar materialised in December 1911. Successive Prime Ministers, however, advised against visits to the Dominions.[205] It can be seen now that the King-Emperor was lucky to achieve a visit to India in the interval between the end of the crisis over the Parliament Act and the beginning of that over the Home Rule Bill. At no other time in the years from 1910 to 1914 would a prolonged absence of the Head of State from Great Britain have been possible. From 1914 to 1918 it was plainly out of the question. Moreover, an accident with a horse in 1915 permanently impaired his vitality.[206] It was perhaps in compensation for his own inability to carry out such a programme that George v arranged for the Prince of Wales to visit every Dominion between 1920 and 1924. He was at particular pains to keep up with Imperial affairs by correspondence and by receiving Dominion and

Indian statesmen on their visits to Great Britain. 'No British monarch', says Sir Harold Nicolson, 'has ever acquired so extensive a knowledge of the principles and details of Empire. . . .'[207] The topic engaged his mind even on his death-bed.

Another subject of which the King acquired more knowledge than any of his predecessors was that of industry. Edward VII made a few industrial visits every July, staying in a nearby country house,[208] but on the whole felt trade and commerce not quite worthy of the interest of royalty.[209] George V toured munitions factories on the Clyde, the Tyne, and elsewhere. Lloyd George, Minister of Munitions at the time, later praised this as a contribution to the war effort in words which have more than a formal ring;[210] and he praises as highly a series of visits to industrial areas which the King made in 1917.[211] It was principally George V's visits to munitions factories which led Sir Harold Nicolson to say: 'No previous Monarch has entered into such close personal relations with so many of his subjects.'[212]

Edward VII had been in a more exact sense than George IV, 'the first gentleman of Europe'—not that either was very gentle-manly. George V, as has already been noted, did not share his father's interest in, or prejudices about, foreign affairs. The Duke of Windsor tells us that 'by and large foreigners bored him'.[213] He paid a number of visits both as Prince of Wales and King to foreign rulers, but they were 'duty visits'. By 1926 he had reached the view that State visits had ceased to have any political importance[214]—or was this perhaps only a rationalisa-tion of his unwillingness to change his routine? Urged that summer by the Foreign Secretary Sir Austen Chamberlain, for political reasons to pay a State Visit to Spain, the King refused to go. As Prince of Wales, despite opportunities much greater than his father's, his lack of interest in foreign affairs had left him largely ignorant of them.[215] As King he conscientiously strove to remedy this defect and even, in contrast to Queen Victoria,[216] granted frequent audiences to the Permanent Under-Secretary of the Foreign Office.[217] George V got on better with William II of Germany than Edward VII had done,[218] and the relations between crowned heads who were first cousins were in any case likely to be easier than the specially difficult uncle–nephew relationship which had existed between 1901 and 1910.[219] The easier personal relations between Kaiser and King between 1910 and 1914 had, however, little effect on the course of Anglo-German political relations. George V did not say the wrong thing to foreign representatives,[220] but except in that way (not altogether unimportant) had little or no influence on foreign policy. The subject was one on which he rarely tendered advice to his Ministers.[221] Fulford gives us a ground for regretting this indifference: 'If there is truth in the assertion that in 1914 Germany was in the dark about British policy it is much to be regretted that Queen Victoria's grandson did not sit down and write to his first cousin in Berlin with the trenchant clarity of his grandmother.'[222] We have seen that he did write, on Ministerial advice and in Ministerial language, to his first cousin in St Petersburg.[223] Queen Victoria had kept up a correspondence with 'the most intelligent member of the royal family of every Court'[224] and it is possible that such links could have been used in 1914 as the forerunners of today's 'hot lines'.

George V struck out for himself, or rather his whole character and temperament struck out for him, one line in his discharge of his political role which was specially characteristic of him rather than his predecessors, though Victoria and Edward VII had occasionally played the same part, which was positive and which was of great importance. This was the emollient role of the King in politics, his self-appointed function of being, above all, a conciliator and a mediator, a lowerer of temperatures.[225]

We have already seen how he made three important contributions to conciliation during the constitutional crisis. At the meeting with Asquith on 11 November 1910, asked for a dissolution, he suggested that the Government's policy should first be submitted to the House of Lords.[226] On 22 July 1911, he suggested that, the Lords' amendments to the Parliament Bill being about to be considered by the Commons, the Lords should be given another chance to accept the Bill before the creation of Peers.[227] He also suggested that in any case the Lords' amendments should not be rejected *en bloc*.[228] All these three suggestions were accepted.

When the crisis over the Parliament Bill was followed by the one over the Irish Home Rule Bill, the King's role was, as we have already seen, again one of mediation. His supreme effort, the Buckingham Palace conference of July 1914, failed, as had the constitutional conference between Liberal and Conservative leaders held in 1910.[229] But it established a new pattern for inter-Party conferences. (Perhaps the whole pattern stemmed from the series of meetings at Balmoral in the autumn of 1913, between the King and the principal figures of both Government and Opposition, culminating in a dialogue between Bonar Law and Churchill, simultaneously guests under the royal roof.[230]) Three more were held in George v's reign, all at Buckingham Palace. The first was on the subject of compulsory military service on 24 August 1915. Its members were Asquith, Balfour, Grey and Kitchener and the King was present throughout. 'What, of course, affects him most', wrote Asquith,[231] 'is not the abstract merits of the question, but the growing division of opinion and the prospect of a possible political row.' This conference too was a failure. On the other hand a Conference held on 6 December 1916, presided over by the King and attended by Asquith, Balfour, Bonar Law, Lloyd George and Arthur Henderson, led to the formation of the second wartime Coalition with Lloyd George as Prime Minister.[232] Similarly, as we have already seen, a conference held on 24 August 1931 between MacDonald, Baldwin and Samuel, opened and closed by the King, led to the formation of the 'National Government'.[233]

George v gave important encouragement to Baldwin in the 1924–9 Parliament in carrying out his policy of industrial conciliation.[234] When, however, the suggestion was made, during the General Strike of 1926, that the King should summon another Buckingham Palace Conference to establish a 'Committee of Reconciliation', his reply was that 'he absolutely declines to entertain the idea of intervention on his part, except of course at the request of the Prime Minister'.[235] On the other hand, no more carried away by patriotic frenzy than in 1914–1918,[236] he criticised a strident article in the *British Gazette* and warned the Government against legislation to prevent Trade Union funds being used in support of the Strike. His warning had its effect; the proposal was dropped.[237]

It is, however, in connection with Ireland that the King's conciliatory efforts were most notable and most successful. He had none of the anti-Irish prejudice of his father and grandmother. Her visit to Dublin in 1900 was, according to Sir Frederick Ponsonby, his idea.[238] Early in the Spring of that year he was talking about the impropriety of the Queen going to Italy at that time. 'I thought', Lord Esher recorded, 'that he talked a good deal of sense.'[239] As King he was every whit as much concerned for the welfare of his Irish as of his British subjects. His own official visit as Duke of York in 1897 had given him a strong conviction, whether right or wrong, that, despite the politicians, there was an understanding between the Irish people and the Crown.[240] An official visit to Dublin as King in July 1911 was 'a triumphant success.'[241]

From 1912 to 1914 George v was hag-ridden by the prospect of an Irish Civil War. His unending efforts during those two years to achieve a peaceful settlement were unsuccessful; he resumed them when renewed attempts to solve the problem were made from 1917 onwards. His biggest post-war contribu-

tion was his Belfast speech of 22 June 1921, at the opening, by
the King in person, of the new Parliament of Northern Ireland,
created by the Government of Ireland Act, 1920. The King's
Speech was not the usual statement of Ministerial intentions. At
the King's instigation the draft prepared by the Irish Office
was rejected by the Prime Minister and a new speech was written
by Sir Edward Grigg. It was wider in scope and faithfully
reflected the King's personal sentiments. For that reason, in
delivery it sounded completely personal and made a powerful
emotional impact on those who heard it. But the noble and
emollient phrases read with such obviously intense conviction
in Belfast were heard also in Dublin. The most remarkable of
them, an echo, unconscious perhaps, of Gladstone's appeal at
the end of his Second Reading speech on the first Home Rule
Bill for 'a blessed act of oblivion' was an appeal 'to all Irish-
men . . . to forgive and forget'.[242] It was the changed atmosphere
created by this speech, as much as the changed policy announced by it,* which made possible the negotiations which in
the end led to the Anglo-Irish Treaty.[244] Lloyd George said as
much.[245] A. J. P. Taylor has written that this initiative of
George V 'was perhaps the greatest service performed by a
British monarch in modern times'.[246] When the Treaty had
been signed the King told his Prime Minister that Lord Morley
had told him 'many years ago' that he would see the day when
the Conservatives would grant Home Rule.[247]

Behind the scenes of the negotiations which led up to it
George V played a notable and beneficent part. When in August
1921 de Valera rejected the British Government's proposals, the
King described him as an impractical 'dreamer and visionary',
but immediately added that he hoped the Cabinet would do
nothing in a hurry: 'The great thing is to prolong the negotia-

* In the House of Lords on the previous day (21 June 1921) Lord Birkenhead
had made a Government declaration of war *à outrance* against Sinn Fein[243]

tions and keep the truce as long as possible.'[248] He made an important personal contribution to their continuation when they were again on the verge of breakdown in September. The Assistant Private Secretary's record of what happened at Moy Hall on 7 September 1921 deserves full quotation:

> The Prime Minister told His Majesty that various members of the Government, including the Viceroy and the Secretary for Ireland, have advised the despatch of a sharp note amounting almost to an ultimatum, in reply to Mr de Valera's communication. It had been suggested that a time-limit should be fixed.
>
> The King very strongly deprecated any action on these lines, which would be interpreted as an attempt by a large country to bully a small one into submission, and would undo at once all the good that had been done.
>
> The Prime Minister laid before the King the draft of his proposed reply. His Majesty suggested numerous alterations in the text—the elimination of all threats and contentious phrases (e.g. 'dominion status')—and the invitation to Sinn Fein representatives to meet the Prime Minister at once for further negotiations.
>
> The Prime Minister then withdrew, and in company with Sir Edward Grigg, drew up a new draft to conform to His Majesty's wishes, the conciliatory wording of which was in marked contrast to the aggressive tone of the original one.[249]

The amended reply, accepted almost verbatim by the Cabinet, was handed over at Inverness the same afternoon and opened the way to the final negotiations. Was not this piece of re-drafting as important a contribution to peace between nations as the Prince Consort's re-modelling of the despatch of December 1861 to the United States Government,[250] of which so much has been so rightly made? George v had done as much to avert a continuation of war (for war it was) with Ireland as his grandfather had done to avert a war with the United States.

In surveying and praising George v's role as a political mediator it is only fair, however, to recall a contemporary note of misgiving. It is one to which weight must be given because it came not merely from a Prime Minister but one who had an exceptionally sound judgment on all constitutional problems. In January 1910 Asquith told the King that 'it is not the function of a Constitutional Sovereign to act as arbiter or mediator between rival parties and policies; still less, to take advice from the leaders of both sides, with a view to forming a conclusion of his own'.[251] This warning was uttered in the context of a proposed meeting of the King with Lord Lansdowne to ascertain the Unionist position after the second Election. Asquith's point was the difficulty of distinguishing between 'desiring knowledge' and 'seeking advice'. He did in fact reluctantly agree to the interview and this decision was surely wise. There is no constitutional objection to the Sovereign gathering information in any quarter,[252] either directly or through his Private Secretary. Indeed, it is one of the latter's most important duties to keep him well informed of all trends of opinion. No doubt Edward VII and George V were right, if only as a matter of courtesy and straight dealing, in consulting the Prime Minister before seeing Opposition leaders.[253] Edward VIII was constitutionally correct in obtaining his Prime Minister's permission to seek the opinions of individual Cabinet Ministers about his marriage as opposed to the advice of the Cabinet as a whole.[254] But once the advice of the Cabinet is asked for, or tendered, it must be followed. If it is not, the whole position of British Constitutional Monarchy as it has been built up over so long a period of time would be imperilled.

As to the rightness or wrongness of royal mediation in itself, commonsense seems to say 'no harm in trying'—subject to the same ultimate proviso that it is the prerogative of Ministers to decide. Fulford, however, thinks that George V, though never a partisan and consistently striving to be fair, attempted 'an adroitness of manoeuvre which was completely foreign to his nature and in truth beyond his capacity'.[255] It is this eminent specialist's opinion that 'on each occasion ... when the Sovereign attempted to act as a solvent on issues where the frenzy of parties offered no solution, his efforts ended in complete failure'.[256] Fulford sees Knollys and Stamfordham as holding distinctly different conceptions of the Crown's role, the former regarding it as having a right to warn but a duty to support the Government of the day, the latter seeing it as being above politics and so having a right to an, as it were, positive sort of neutrality.[257] Stamfordham's view, Fulford suggests, lay behind the royal role from 1913 to 1918, after which King and Secretary, in the light of the rebuffs to their attempts at conciliation, became 'reluctant to take a stand against the politician'.[258] (If this view be sound in respect of British domestic politics, it does not seem to square with the King's post-war role in respect of Ireland.) Whatever interpretation may eventually be adopted on this point, it seems certain that, as already indicated,[259] the British Monarchy in its political aspect underwent a 'sea change' in the 1914–18 period and indeed one, in historical and comparative terms, 'into something rich and strange'.

SUMMING-UP

The death in 1892 of Albert Victor, Duke of Clarence, the Prince of Wales' eldest son, was, for the British nation, a merciful act of providence.[260] The prospective Albert I was a gormless individual. His younger brother, the Duke of York, who took his place in the line of succession to the throne and in due course ascended it, was certainly not an intellectual but had plenty of intelligence. It could have been said of him, as later it was said of another, that he was 'a modest little man with much to be modest about'. But George v's intelligence has been as underrated as was, at first, Clement Attlee's. (There are other points of similarity between the two: a terse and yet utterly unambiguous prose style, for example.) It must be remembered, however, that George v's career, until 1892, had been that of a Naval Officer and that he had no doubt imbibed the tradition of his Service that any display of intellectual capacity was something 'not done'.

His Naval upbringing had another more important effect. As he told MacDonald when he first became Prime Minister, 'little expecting to occupy his present position, he served in the Navy for fourteen years—and thus had opportunities of seeing more of the world and mixing with his fellow creatures more than would otherwise have been the case. . .'.[261] In short, George v, on his accession, knew more of his fellow men than Edward vii had done on his. The father knew, intensively and extensively, the world of high society, both at home and on the Continent; the son knew something of the real world. (His two successors, in their time, because of their experiences in the 1914–18 war, were to know still more.) George v's official biographer writes: 'No British Monarch before his time had manifested so constant, or so obviously sincere, a liking for his poorer subjects',[262] and again: 'More than most of his associates he earnestly desired a world of social justice.'[263] Thus we find him in 1921 appealing to the Government to help the unemployed 'with the same liberality as they displayed in dealing with the enormous daily cost of the war'.[264]

An American historian, Professor H. R. Winkler, sums up George v as the 'King who made the monarchy democratic'.[265] The same writer adds that he 'also made it enormously stronger'. And this was despite the immense changes which occurred in the world during his reign.[266] During that time many other institutions were changed out of all recognition or altogether disappeared. Most of the other monarchies came to an end. He did more than just let the ship of British Monarchy

SUMMING-UP 167

ride out the storms; when he gave up the command he left the ship in better trim than he found it. Is it not proof of this that it survived so easily the storm of the abdication crisis which blew round it within a year of his death? And what storms there were in his life! Before the war, the crises over the Parliament Bill and the Irish Home Rule Bill; after it, the General Strike and the crisis of August 1931. Above all, there was the war itself which, more than any other single event, changed, besides so much else, the whole order of British society. In a sense, the Edwardian age ended, not in 1910, but in 1914; indeed it could be said that substantial features of the Victorian age lasted until 1914. There was no Georgian age; there was the war, and before and after the war. (Since the war, we have thought more in terms of decades than of reigns.) The deluge did not come after George v; it came in his reign and to him. Writing of the survival and strengthening of the British Monarchy during the period from 1910 to 1936 Winston Churchill makes the logical point that 'a fact so prodigious, a fact contrary to the whole tendency of the age, cannot be separated from the personality of the good, wise and truly noble King....'.[267]

George v made mistakes, of course. He became over-excited and therefore over-fussy in August 1911.[268] At his best over Ireland, he was at his worst in backing the Generals against the politicians during the war.[269] It was a mistake not to send a message of sympathy to MacDonald when his wife died in 1911.[270] A clinging, after the manner of Queen Victoria, to a vestigial piece of the Prerogative led to unnecessary difficulties and self-assertiveness over the appointment of Sir Isaac Isaacs as the first Australian Governor-General of Australia.[271] By and large, however, we can see George v, with A. J. P. Taylor, as 'a model of constitutional rectitude'.[272]

There are echoes of former reigns. Baldwin is told that the appointment of Austen Chamberlain as Foreign Secretary

would be very welcome to the King.[273] It was with George v
that there originated the invitation to Lord Irwin, later Lord
Halifax, to become Viceroy of India.[274] A complaint to Mac-
Donald about a speech of Lansbury's[275] is reminiscent of Queen
Victoria complaining to Gladstone about utterances by Joseph
Chamberlain or Dilke,[276] of Edward vii complaining to Asquith
of speeches by Lloyd George or Churchill.[277] But the tone of
George v's complaint was milder. Lansbury was convinced to
the end of his life that he had been excluded from the first
Labour Cabinet at the King's request.[278] This belief is not con-
firmed by Sir Harold Nicolson. In the second Labour Govern-
ment, Lansbury, in the Cabinet, had happy relations with the
King.[279]

Like his father, George v had occasion to grumble about
being kept in the dark by his Ministers.[280] He wrote in his own
hand to Asquith to complain, but in a sympathetic way, about
inadequate information on Parliamentary proceedings in
November 1912.[281] He wrote to Lord Stamfordham in June
1917:

> Very glad that the Government are going to grant an
> amnesty to the Irish prisoners.... I see it is to be an-
> nounced in the House today and I have never been asked
> for my approval. Usual way things are done in present day.
> I had better join the King of Greece in exile.[282]

A telegram to Lloyd George in 1921 deserves quotation, not
merely as an example of the King's determination to end the
war with Ireland, but also as an example of a tone utterly
different from that in which Queen Victoria had addressed
her Prime Ministers only a generation or two previously:

> Just received Mr De Valera's telegram of the 17th. I can-
> not help thinking that it is intended to be conciliatory....
> Has he not made rather a good point...? I only send this
> being anxious to avoid any chance of the extremists attri-

buting to you responsibility for the abandonment of the
Conference. My one wish is to help you in this most difficult situation.[283]

George v did his duty in the matter of public appearances and
proved a 'natural' for broadcasting; his first broadcast was on
Christmas Day 1932. But he did not court popularity; he did
not pander, as has already been pointed out, to popular passions.[284]

But the people of Britain came to sense the nature of his contribution and they admired it. They showed their appreciation
of the King and his work when he was dangerously ill in 1928
and again on the occasion of his Silver Jubilee in 1935. They
perceived, in advance of fuller evidence, that he had fashioned
the matrix of a 'new model' monarchy. In its history the break
between Edward vii and George v was far more decisive even
than that between Victoria and Edward vii. If the story of the
constitutional growth of the British Monarchy over the last
century has a hero, he must, great as must be our admiration
for George vi, be George v. It is a considerable achievement to
have set a pattern of political behaviour which has lasted so
long.

6

Edward VIII and George VI

THE ELDEST SON

The story of the reign of Edward VIII is mainly the story of the
personal drama with which it ended. It is in these terms that he
himself, and many other writers, have described it. That, at the
time, the King's mind should have been preoccupied by his
personal problems is natural and understandable. It does seem
worthy of remark, however, how little the missed possibilities
as King seem later to have preoccupied the Duke of Windsor,
his mind dwelling rather on his conduct of the abdication crisis
in a manner reminiscent of Napoleon's preoccupation at St
Helena with Waterloo. Even if, however, the reign had had
a different end, if the events leading up to the abdication had
not occupied so much of it, the history of a reign lasting only
from 20 January to 10 December 1936 could scarcely be
expected to provide much factual evidence of the regnant's
attitudes and intentions.

It has been suggested that the King's tour of South Wales
was an act of defiance of his Government, that a much pub-
licised remark, vague but well-intentioned, made in the course
of it ('Something must be done') was a deliberate criticism of
Ministers, that the new King was, in short, striking out a line
for himself as a man of the Left. All this the Duke of Windsor
has himself denied.[1] George V, as we have seen,[2] was much
more interested in industrial conditions than Edward VII, and
Edward VIII was proportionately even more interested than his
father. But he had also been trained, and trained himself, in his

father's habits of political impartiality. By the time of his accession it entailed 'no particular strain' on him to be above politics;
discretion had become instinctive.[3]

This is not to say that Edward VIII's own views were Radical.
A Radical Crown Prince may be a fairly common phenomenon,
but a Radical King is a rarity. Kingsley Martin has written:
'The weakness of Edward was that he was not sure what he
wanted to do.'[4] The Duke of Windsor's own summary of his
political attitudes at the moment of his accession reads:

> Had an assessment been made at the time of my private
> views on various issues of the day, it would have been
> revealed, I am sure, what would have been classified as a
> distinctly conservative outlook.
>
> I believed, among other things, in private enterprise, a
> strong Navy ... a balanced budget, the gold standard, and
> close relations with the United States. . . . I was not a sup-
> porter of the League of Nations. . . . I was all for Mr
> Winston Churchill in his campaign to rearm Britain, al-
> though I was against anything, including the controversial
> imposition of sanctions, that might tend to throw the Italy
> of Mussolini into the arms of Hitler.[5]

The tale of the abdication has been told so often as to become
tedious and, in constitutional terms, it signifies very little. The
British Government, Opposition, and people[6] (and the
Dominion Governments) all thought the question of who should
become Queen of England was not a merely personal one for
the King to decide. There was no 'politicians' ramp' to elimi-
nate a too democratic King. When an intimate friend told
Baldwin that this idea had appeared in the American papers:
'All lies of the Hearst Press', he snorted. He had seen a photo-
graph in the Hearst papers in which they had combined
separate photographs of Queen Mary and Mrs Simpson, who
had never met, and made them appear as walking together.[7]
During the abdication crisis Walter Monckton played perfectly

the part of go-between whilst retaining the respect and confidence of King and Prime Minister; Monckton's biographer has written that 'nowhere in his papers is there any hint that he believed that the discussions ... were influenced by a conspiratorial tendency on the part of Baldwin'.[8] Edward VIII as a constitutional King could not insist on his view of Mrs Simpson's suitability to succeed Queen Mary. He could either accept Ministerial advice or abdicate. He chose the latter course and no amount of printer's ink on any amount of paper can make the essence of the matter any more complicated than that. Basically his attitude was consistent throughout the abdication crisis. He was unwaveringly determined to marry Mrs Simpson. He hoped that he could remain King and his wife be Queen, but if Mrs Simpson could not be Queen he would not be King.

Nor is it surprising that Edward VIII made the choice he did. Because he was unconventional in some respects it did not follow that he would be unconventional to the point of defying the Constitution's major convention in respect of his own role, that a King can only act on the advice of his Ministers. In this crisis he respected too its minor conventions, seeking, for example, and obtaining the Prime Minister's agreement to consult two personal friends in the Cabinet, Samuel Hoare and Duff Cooper.[9] 'There has never', said the ex-King,* in his farewell broadcast from Windsor Castle on 11 December 1936, 'been any constitutional difference between me and them and between me and Parliament. Bred in the constitutional tradition by my Father, I should never have allowed any such issue to arise.'[10] A King can show no greater love for a Constitution than to lay down his Crown for it.

The temptation to do otherwise must have been strong. Great

---

* His official style at that moment was 'His Royal Highness, Prince Edward' and he was introduced as such to his radio audience by the Director-General of the B.B.C., Sir John Reith. His Royal Highness was created Duke of Windsor by his successor on 27 May 1937

popular newspapers were on his side,[11] and so conceivably was time. A 'King's Party'* was in the making. To play for time so that such a Party might grow, and to use the Beaverbrook and other newspapers as levers on public opinion, were obvious courses of action for a King determined at all costs to retain his Throne. Moreover, such courses of action had powerful advocates, notably Churchill and Lord Beaverbrook. It must, on the other hand, be stated that the argument about time was possibly invalid and that the one about publicity cut both ways. Hugh Dalton shortly after the event, and with his opinion based on much evidence, wrote:

> The pro-King demonstrations were only froth. . . . Moreover with each day of delay public opinion moved against the King. And I realized that the full forces of propaganda and incitement against Mrs Simpson were not un-loosed.[13]

However these things might be, the King, in point of fact, throughout the abdication crisis secluded himself at Fort Belvedere rather than run the risk of arousing a public demonstration on his behalf by showing himself in London.[14] He fought for a chance to continue to do the job for which he had been trained, and which he had wanted to do, but he fought with his hands, by his own decision to stick to the Constitution, tied behind his back and his tongue gagged. It was only after the battle had been lost that he broadcast to the people and then in studiously muted tones.

And he fought in this way because from the start his 'instinctive desires' were 'to dampen the uproar' and 'avoid the responsibility of splitting the nation . . .'.[15] As the crisis deepened he continued to hold this thought in the front of his mind. He reflected that 'By making a stand for myself, I should have left the scars of a civil war'.[16] It was not for him to jeopardise the

---

* Sir Ivor Jennings describes the Conservatives of 1886 as the 'Queen's party'[12]—but they did not know that they were

institution of the Monarchy on the issue of his personal happiness;[17] if he were to fight with less scruple, and win, 'the cherished conception of the Monarchy above politics would have been shattered...'.[18] Lord Beaverbrook, passionately pro-King, because passionately anti-Baldwin,[19] has recorded the King's anxiety 'to avoid any suggestion of conflict with Baldwin'.[20] Baldwin himself had earlier said to a friend: 'Whoever writes about the Abdication, must give the King his due. He could not have behaved better than he did.'[21]* An observer close to the course of events, Sir Edward Peacock, saw 'a certain wavering in the King's mind a short time after Winston's call', a temptation to fight for his rights, quickly followed, however, by a restoration of the resolve in no circumstances to 'be a party to a constitutional crisis, or any other move that would weaken the Constitution or cause trouble between the Crown and its Ministers'.[23]

The man who, to his credit, behaved as he then did, the man whose political outlook was such as he himself has described it,[24] would never have made 'the first radical King'.[25] He did not aspire to that role. In his second book, he writes that if his reign had run its full course, its mood and texture would possibly have followed more that of Edward VII than that of George V.[26] Possibly indeed (his character certainly resembled his grandfather's more than his father's) but that is not to say very much. Edward VII, as we have seen, was a good showman but not a great political figure. George V, for all his personal conservatism, successfully presided over a constitutional revolution which changed completely the character of the British Monarchy.

Edward VIII, rightly styling himself as the King next in line

---

* At the time the King gave the Prime Minister his due. He did not have to say in his farewell broadcast: 'The Ministers of the Crown, and in particular, Mr Baldwin, have always treated me with full consideration'; in private, at dinner on 6 December, he 'spoke with gratitude of Stanley Baldwin's kindness and help'[22]

to his grandfather, saw himself, as, at most, Edward the Innovator, not Edward the Reformer.[27] He was very pleased to have
been described as 'Britain's Best Salesman'.[28] He had hoped to
concentrate on what he knew best, to remind the people, 'in
the limited ways' open to him, of their 'Imperial stake in world
trade' and to throw 'the prestige and glamour of the Crown's
solicitude around the workaday matters of commerce'.[29] High
drama prevented the fulfilment of these humdrum aspirations.
The constitutional caravan moved on.

THE SECOND SON

When the Duke of York, later King George vi, got married,
he received from his father a letter which remarked: 'You have
always been so sensible and easy to work with and you have
always been ready to listen to any advice and to agree with my
opinions about people and things, that I feel that we have
always got on very well together (very different to dear
David).'[30]

The always getting on very well together was perhaps, in the
way of all flesh, more apparent to the father than to the son,
but the similarity of opinions was real and so too was the difference between the younger and the elder brother. The former
was later to say of the latter, though he said nice things too,
that he 'had never had any discipline in his life'.[31] It was not for
nothing that the new King took the title of George vi. His
intention was that his behaviour as King should be as nearly as
possible the same as his father's.[32] The widowed Victoria aimed
to model her political role on that of the Prince Consort, but
played in fact an entirely different part. Edward vii's model
was his mother, George v's his father, but each in fact
developed a quite different pattern. Of the five monarchs who
figure in this narrative only Edward viii consciously aspired to

be an innovator.[33] Of the five, George vi alone successfully copied his model, in his case his father. Moreover, as things worked out, there were important parallels between the major events of the two reigns. The son did not have a great constitutional crisis thrust upon him as he took over, but in the third year of his reign had, like his father in the fourth year of his, to face a World War. The Second World War precipitated, like the first, immense social changes of which, politically, in Britain Labour Governments, this time majority Governments, were the most prominent visible manifestations.

It was sensible of the son to imitate the father. It was not only what the majority of his people wanted but also what came naturally to him. The fifth and sixth Georges had fundamentally similar characters, minds and temperaments. Both loved family life. To a great extent they shared the same interests and the same relaxations. They both liked a regular pattern in life and much the same pattern. They expressed their thoughts in similar language. From the style, or even the handwriting, it would not be easy to distinguish a letter from one or the other. Both had a simple religious faith, both had a high sense of duty, both were worriers. The differences between the two were mainly of degree. The son was more religious than the father, was even more of a worrier and, unfortunately, less strong. It might not be untrue to say that his anxieties were the cause of his premature death.[34] He had a long history of illnesses; his was, alas, 'a bad life'.

Both, moreover, had had similar upbringings, as naval officers. (George vi saw active service at the Battle of Jutland.) Both were second sons and did not expect to succeed. Whereas, however, George v was heir-apparent for the 10 years of Edward vii's reign, George vi can only have come to realise that the throne was his definite destiny a few weeks before his brother's abdication. He had not, in short, been trained for the job. On the first night of his reign his heartfelt cry to his cousin and, probably, 'closest personal friend',[35] Lord Louis Mountbatten, was: 'Dickie, this is absolutely terrible. I never wanted this to happen; I'm quite unprepared for it. David has been trained for this all his life. I've never even seen a State Paper. I'm only a Naval Officer; it's the only thing I know about.'[36]*

The new King's first political initiatives were brushed aside by his Ministers. The first of all was a suggestion, in September 1938, of a personal appeal for peace to Hitler, on the basis of 'one ex-Serviceman to another'.[38] Lord Halifax, the Foreign Secretary, referred this suggestion to Chamberlain, the Prime Minister, and it does not seem to have been heard of again. In October, however, the Prime Minister agreed that a large-scale appeal for voluntary national service should be inaugurated by a broadcast by the King. This time the Governor of the Bank of England, Montagu Norman, stepped in to advise against the idea on the ground that such a broadcast might lead to a slump on the Stock Exchange.[39] In November a suggestion by the King of a personal letter to the King of Italy, to express satisfaction at the coming into force of the Anglo-Italian Agreement concluded in April, was rejected by the Government as premature.[40] When the Nazi-Soviet Pact was signed in August 1939, the King saw the possibility of gaining advantage from it in terms of better relations with Japan and therefore mooted the idea of 'a friendly message direct to the Emperor'. The Foreign Office, however, ruled this out on the ground that it might merely lead to a rebuff.[41] A little later Mackenzie King, the Prime Minister of Canada, revived the idea of a direct appeal from the King to Hitler, but Chamberlain was again procrastinatory.[42] The King's last attempt to make a personal contribution to the preservation of peace was in April 1940. He

---

* Forty-two years previously the new Tsar, Nicholas II, first cousin of George V, had used astonishingly similar language on succeeding at 26 a father who had died at 46. 'Sandro, what am I going to do...? I am not prepared to be a Tsar. I never wanted to become one. I know nothing of the business of ruling. I have no idea of how to talk to Ministers'[37]

then reverted to the idea of a personal letter to the King of Italy. He wrote and signed one, and it got as far as Paris before the Cabinet decided that it would be unwise to give in Rome an impression of doubt about Italian policy.[43]

The great climacteric in the King's career was his visit to the United States in June 1939. It was his first really important mission, and he made a success of it. Perhaps, however, it was even more important that it 'made' him.[44] Next to his wife, no one gave him more self-confidence than President Roosevelt. After an after-dinner conversation with him at Hyde Park about the international situation, the King paid a call on another house guest, Mackenzie King, and in the course of conversation with him asked: 'Why don't my Ministers talk to me as the President did tonight? I feel exactly as though a father were giving me his most careful and wise advice.'[45] The King took very full notes of his conversations with the President, which were specially notable as containing the germ of the later bases-for-destroyers agreement, and passed these notes on to the proper quarters.[46] But the really important result of these conversations, in addition to the boost to the King's self-confidence, was the foundation of a firm friendship between him and the President. A cordial correspondence, only ended by Roosevelt's death, was started many months before the more famous one between the President and a 'Former Naval Person' began and played a useful part in lubricating the machinery of Anglo-American relations. At the White House, on Christmas Day 1941, Roosevelt spoke to Churchill and his other guests of the royal visit two-and-a-half years previously, saying that 'this had been a beginning of the coming together of the two English-speaking races, which would go on after the war'.[47] Roosevelt and Churchill had first met only in August of that year.

None the less, George VI's first important political letter was a contribution of a very different sort to Anglo-American relations. It was written to Joseph Kennedy, the United States

Ambassador, on 12 September 1939,[48] and consisted of a polite but plain rebuke to the Ambassador for views he had expressed the previous day about the war not being worthwhile. The King, after thinking the matter over, felt it important firmly to re-state the British position. He showed the letter, before its despatch, to the Prime Minister.[49] But the idea of sending it and the form of the argument were clearly his own.

A fresh and effective authority was also shown a little later to another foreign representative, General Mehmet Orbay of Turkey. A Franco-British-Turkish treaty of alliance had been initialled on 28 September 1939, and thereafter General Orbay came to London as head of a military mission with an extensive 'shopping list' of armaments, without the supply of which his country was not prepared to put the new treaty into force. In the circumstances of the time the General could only be offered words instead of guns. The words, however, spoken by the King in private audience on 11 October, which Orbay had expected to be little more than a formality, were so powerful that he cancelled his plans to leave London, and the treaty was signed on 19 October. General Ismay, Military Secretary to the Cabinet, wrote to Sir Alexander Hardinge, the King's Private Secretary:

> It has been quite impossible to let him [Orbay] have cer-
> tain important items of which we ourselves are woefully
> deficient. Consequently, one cannot but think that he
> would have gone away a disappointed man, if it had not
> been for the tremendous impression created upon him by
> his private audience with the King.[50]

From about this time onwards a great deal of use was made by the Government of the King as a mouthpiece in negotiations with other Governments, much as, but more than, use had been made of Edward VII in the diplomacy of his time.[51] Personal letters were written to King Boris of Bulgaria on

22 September 1939,[52] and on 12 October 1940,[53] and played a part in keeping Bulgaria neutral until March 1941. A telegram to the King of the Belgians on 26 May 1940 appealed to him, in vain, not to become a prisoner of the Germans.[54] A telegram sent on 22 June 1940 to President Lebrun, appealing to him not to let the French fleet run any risk of falling into enemy hands, failed, owing to the disorganised state of Anglo-French communications at the time, to reach him until after the action at Mers-el-Kebir.[55] A personal appeal to Marshal Pétain on 25 October 1940, not to become a collaborator of Hitler, met with a dusty answer.[56] A melancholy letter from Prince Paul, the Regent of Yugoslavia, was answered on 15 November 1940 by a long letter in the King's own hand trying to put fresh heart into him.[57] An answer to an appeal for help from the King of Greece had to be delayed until after the start of General Wavell's offensive in Libya.[58] A final appeal to Prince Paul not to sign the Axis Pact was made in March 1941. 'I disliked the draft shown me and sent him a personal one of friendship', the King noted in his diary.[59]

From the early days of the war, however, the King's mind was occupied not only with the problem of maintaining Allied strength, but also with the problem of post-war reconstruction. His diary for 5 May 1940 shows him concerned with what he called 'an International Mission of help after the war'.[60] He prepared a paper on the subject, and it was agreed on 12 March with Chamberlain and Halifax that the King should write to President Roosevelt about it.[61] The President's reply was friendly and constructive. The King then went a step further and in August had a paper sent to the Foreign Office envisaging a joint Anglo-American welcome for a post-war European federation. This particular idea was thought to be too advanced for American opinion, but the King's initiative gave a considerable impetus to the British Government's study of the problems of post-war reconstruction, domestic as well as European.

It has been said above[62] that the start of the 1914 war lessened George V's problems and perplexities. On the other hand, Sir Harold Nicolson has made the general point that the position of a constitutional King is in some ways more difficult in war than in peace: 'Being the sole representative of the Nation as a whole, he may be expected, and even tempted, to voice not merely the will and virtue of his subjects but also their momentary moods and passions.'[63] In this respect, however, George VI had a smoother passage in the Second World War than his father had had in the first. The task of representing the nation was easier for him than for his father, inasmuch as it was a more level-headed nation that entered the war in 1939 than had done so in 1914. On the other hand, the period of endurance was longer, the peril greater, the sufferings of civilians greater. 'Total war', however, brought King and people together; the bombing of Buckingham Palace, with the King and Queen in it, made a popular couple still more popular. Their visits to Coventry and other bombed cities did much for civilian morale. George VI, who strove to share the sufferings of his people, was a far better 'leader' than Hitler, remote at headquarters. None the less the King constantly confided to his diary his disappointment at not being able to do more.[64] On 9 April 1940, the day of the German attack on Norway, there is in it the heartfelt cry: 'I have spent a bad day. Everybody working at fever heat except me.'[65]

The 'top management' of the 1939 War was better organised than that of the 1914 one. There were not the same conflicts between politicians and soldiers in which George V so unfortunately became involved. With strategy, therefore, there was no need for George VI to concern himself. He did, however, on one occasion exercise his constitutional right to 'warn' with a powerful letter to the Prime Minister criticising the idea of starting a new front in France as opposed to the extension of the one we already had in Italy.[66] The arguments were pungently put, but it was too late to go back on the decisions, whether right or wrong, of the Quebec Conference. On an earlier occasion, prompted by Sir Alan Lascelles (Private Secretary), he had warned his Prime Minister to much greater effect, stopping him from observing the operations of D-Day, 1944, from a warship.[67]

George VI, on 7 May 1940, loyal to Chamberlain, asked him if it would help him 'if I spoke to Attlee about the national standpoint of the Labour Party, and say that I hoped that they would realise that they must pull their weight and join the National Government. . . . I told the P.M. that I did not like the way in which, with all the worries and responsibilities he had to bear in the conduct of the war, he was always subject to a stab in the back from both the H. of C. and the Press.'[68] The King's own candidate for the succession had been Lord Halifax* (who had been favoured also by Chamberlain, Attlee[70] and Dalton[71]) but he was soon firm friends with Churchill. Formal audiences were replaced by weekly luncheons; on two different days in February 1941 the King wrote in his diary: 'I could not have a better Prime Minister.'[72] The loyalty which he had shown to Chamberlain was now transferred to Churchill.[73] He resented criticism of him[74] and was distressed by the serious criticism which followed the loss of Singapore in February 1942.[75] Churchill, on his side, was deeply appreciative of the King's support, more so perhaps—because of his sense of history, his romantic feeling for Kingship that went with it, and his Conservatism—than any other Prime Minister since Disraeli. In answer to a congratulatory message on the final victory in Africa he wrote of his Sovereign's 'kindness and confidence' being 'a precious aid and comfort' to him.[76] The man who had been the staunch supporter of Edward VIII became the devoted admirer of George VI and even to think that

---

* The thought of being Prime Minister gave Lord Halifax 'stomach ache'[69]

perhaps the Churchill-Beaverbrook line at the time of the abdication had been wrong.[77]

The end of the war in Europe was quickly followed by the advent of a Labour Government in Britain and one with an overwhelming Parliamentary majority. But this did not produce the same alarm as the mere prospect of a first Labour Government, without a majority, had done in 1924. The event was one which the King took in his stride. His suggestion that Ernest Bevin rather than Hugh Dalton should be made Foreign Secretary was a factor—though not, according to Lord Attlee,* the decisive one—in the making of that appointment. A long letter to the King from the Prime Minister[79] in August 1947, explaining the Supplies and Services Act of that year, is reminiscent of Gladstone defending his legislation to Queen Victoria. Her great-grandson and his Socialist Prime Minister had, however, much in common, in terms both of personality and outlook on public affairs, and the relations between them were excellent. So also were the King's relations with the Foreign Secretary, though he 'did not often go to the Palace';[80] George VI found himself in accord with Aneurin Bevan[81] in much the same way as his father had done with John Wheatley.[82]

From the policies of his new Ministers the King, his biographer tells us, 'did not dissent in principle'.[83] In his talks with them 'he was not infrequently successful in presenting arguments which caused them to reconsider decisions at which they had already arrived...'.[84] If he had any warning to offer the Government it was one against undue haste.[85] Thus when, in Attlee's absence abroad, Herbert Morrison was acting as Prime Minister in November 1945, the King discussed with him 'the whole of the Labour Programme' and told him 'he

* 'He expressed an opinion about the Foreign Secretaryship in 1945, but did not press it and this was not the decisive factor in the making of the appointment'[78]

was going too fast in the new nationalising legislation. Bill drafting takes time, especially with a reduced staff.'[86] There was, it may be noted, no objection to nationalising as such.

For the first time in this study the question of the reigning Sovereign's political attitudes, which necessarily loomed so large at the start of it, needs only the briefest of mentions. George VI had, like his father and grandfather, his conservative inclinations, but Sir John Wheeler-Bennett claims him as a social reformer and 'a progressive in political thought'.[87] He would have liked the Coalition Government which had won the war to have tackled the immediate problems of the peace. He regretted the departure of Churchill from power as, it may be remembered, did many whose votes in the General Election of 1945 had helped to bring that about, but he was in no sense a partisan: 'His Majesty was not pro-Conservative or anti-Socialist.'[88] Under George VI the political impartiality of the Crown was established absolutely, firmly and finally.

The minor events of the reign of George VI bring, as in the case of George V,[89] echoes of former reigns. The new King was displeased at not being properly informed until the afternoon of Sunday 21 February 1938, of the momentous proceedings at the Cabinet the previous day, which led to Eden's resignation as Foreign Secretary. But the King himself, with his practical mind, suggested a way in which he could thereafter be more rapidly kept in touch with the course of Cabinet events, i.e., that the draft Cabinet minutes should be sent to him at the same time as they were sent to the Prime Minister.[90]

George VI, like George V, had a special interest in the Empire, fortified by a correct belief that the new constitutional developments in its structure involved the Crown in a special responsibility for Imperial affairs.[91] In his time he visited Australia, Canada, New Zealand and South Africa. He constantly regretted the fact of the moment never seeming ripe for a visit to India. In 1942 and 1943 he was distrustful of the advance towards Indian independence,[92] but by 1946 was reconciled to the principle of it whilst critical of its pace.[93] Just as in 1945 he played a secondary part in the appointment of Bevin as Foreign Secretary,[94] so in 1943 he played a part, and quite a large one, in the decision not to appoint Eden as Viceroy.[95] On 15 August 1947, the King of England ceased to be Emperor of India. The lack of fuss with which George VI gave up that title is in marked contrast to the fanfaronade with which Queen Victoria had assumed it.

The shortness of the life and reign of George VI tends to be overlooked. Queen Victoria died at the age of 82, Edward VII at 68, George V at 71. But George VI died at the age of 56. (There is almost a parallel with the death of the Prince Consort at 42.) He had reigned for 15 years and could reasonably have been expected to reign much longer. His brother, if he had not abdicated, would now (1969) be in the thirty-third year of his reign. Short, therefore, as was Edward VIII's reign of 10 months, so too in a sense was that of his successor. Similar difficulties in consequence arise in assessing it. George VI on his accession, as has been emphasised and as he himself fully realised,[96] had everything to learn about a job which he had never expected. But by July 1945, after the results of the Election had been declared, Lord Mountbatten wrote to him:

> You will find that your position will be greatly strengthened since you are now the old experienced campaigner on whom a new and partly inexperienced Government will lean for advice and guidance.[97]

If that was true in 1945, when he had just appointed his fourth Prime Minister, how much more true it would have become as the years went on. Even his father had only had experience of five Prime Ministers. Of the Cabinet Ministers at the moment of George VI's accession, only Malcolm Macdonald is still in public life. Of the members of Attlee's Cabinet at the moment of its formation in 1945, none became members of Wilson's Cabinet at the moment of its formation in 1964. (Wilson himself, James Griffiths and Gordon-Walker, were the only members of the new Cabinet who had been members of Attlee's when his Government fell in 1951.) In those circumstances not only the counsel of Earl Attlee but also that of George VI, if still on the throne, aged 68, might well have been valuable to the new Prime Minister.

In these respects George VI inevitably abides our question.

7

Postscript

Of the statesmen who have appeared on the stage of this story it is naturally the Prime Ministers who have played the principal parts. And of the Prime Ministers it is Gladstone who towers over the others. No man becomes Prime Minister of the United Kingdom—or President of the United States—four times for nothing, though any man who does so will have been, and will long remain, a centre of controversy. But to an important extent Gladstone plays the dominant part in this story on, so to speak, the statesmen's side because of the particular circumstances of his times. Churchill had many problems on his hands during the war, and on resuming the highest office in 1951, but he was far from finding George VI as burdensome as a gifted but temperamental and troublesome colleague. Gladstone, and Salisbury, had found Queen Victoria the equivalent of just such a burden. It is easy now to see, and his wife saw it at the time, how badly Gladstone handled his personal relations with the Queen; easy now to criticise him for taking her far too seriously (perhaps he was really afraid that too much pressure would produce an abdication?); easy now to forget how utterly different was the constitutional 'climate' of his age from ours. On the other hand much credit must be given to him for foreseeing a political role for the Monarchy which it fully and finally assumed only during the reign of George VI, and for his part in preparing the way for so great a change.

On the Sovereigns' side, the dominant part is played by

Queen Victoria, dominant not because of any positive contribution to the development of the Monarchy's political role but because of her formidable, endlessly fascinating and fundamentally likeable personality. But George v now appears as a more considerable public figure than his grandmother. Wisely or unwisely, he sought to play a significant part as a conciliator, but, what was more important, he tightly controlled his own political views not only in public but in private. The two Edwards, if only because of the shortness of their reigns and their particular personal circumstances, played less important parts than Victoria or George v. Inevitably the evidence about George vi's contribution is thinner than that for his predecessors, but the evidence already available seems to establish him firmly as, politically, the very pattern of a modern Monarch.

What was the trend in the exercise of the Monarchy's political influence between 1868 and 1952? Most notable is the decline and, finally, disappearance of partisan interventions. The initial shock of the revelation of Queen Victoria's partiality was very great. It no longer surprises us. The extent and intensity of it remain, however, astonishing. Since 1901 the trend towards a real political neutrality, not merely a matter of appearances, has been steady, reign by reign.

Other points are clear. Influence in respect of political appointments has notably diminished. So, too, has any special role in foreign policy. This is partly the result of special circumstances. Until 1914 foreign policy was, almost exclusively, a matter of European policy and only four European States were Republics (Switzerland since the start of its independent existence, France since 1870, Portugal since 1910, and San Marino). The rest of Europe was presided over by what was virtually a European Royal Family, and family relationships consequently played a large part in the relationships between European States.

In the case of administration and policy in respect of Home, Empire and Commonwealth, and Defence affairs, however, the matter is not so simple. The story is again one of decline, but not of fall. There is no evidence that by 1952 the Crown's role in relation to these matters had become wholly passive, the Sovereign a mere puppet with strings moved by Ministers. True, the Sovereign had come not only to do, but to do with a good grace, what his Ministers advised him. He had not, however, become a complete cipher.

For the smoothness of the transition from the earlier to the later state of affairs, particular credit must be given to two Liberal and two Socialist Prime Ministers: Gladstone, Asquith, MacDonald and Attlee. All four were proponents of major political and social changes but all four were also, in a larger sense, traditionalists. (Churchill, Conservative but ex-Liberal, was almost more of a traditionalist than anything else.) Lloyd George was the first plebeian Prime Minister and one with a Radical record, but he held office only by Conservative support. Even so he treated his Sovereign with a lack of consideration and, on occasion, a downright 'toughness'. (Balfour and Chamberlain preferred politely to ignore.) A clash between a Radical Prime Minister with no feeling for the Monarchical tradition and a Sovereign hostile and obstructive to Radicalism would have produced a very different course of events from that recounted.

In my end is my beginning. Historians should have special insights into the present, and indeed the future, as well as the past. But they are tethered by facts as goats are by sticks: the grazing in both cases is sharply limited. It is not for the historian to speculate about the parts that may now be played behind the scenes; nor is it necessarily for him either to applaud the political system which has over generations been built up or to propound major changes in it. On this occasion at any rate it is enough for an apprentice historian to follow in the footsteps of a master (G. M. Trevelyan) and 'point like a showman to the things of the past, with their manifold and mysterious message'.

Appendix

THE SOVEREIGN'S PRIVATE SECRETARIES, 1861–1953

1861–1870	General Sir Charles Grey
1870–1895	Colonel Henry Ponsonby
	(General, 1872; Knighted, 1879)
1895–1901	Colonel Sir Arthur Bigge
1901–1910	Sir Francis Knollys
	(Lord Knollys, 1901)
1910–1913	Lord Knollys and
	Sir Arthur Bigge (Lord Stamfordham, 1911)
	jointly
1913–1931	Lord Stamfordham
1931–1936	Sir Clive Wigram
	(Lord Wigram, 1935)
1936–1943	Sir Alexander Hardinge
1943–1953	Sir Alan Lascelles

Bibliography

PRINCIPAL PUBLICATIONS CONSULTED

Similar details of other publications are given at the point where they are first mentioned in the References

Asquith, Margot, *Autobiography*, 2 vols., Penguin ed., 1936

Bagehot, Walter, *The English Constitution*, O.U.P., World's Classics Series, 1928*

Balfour, A. J., *Chapters of Autobiography*, Cassell, 1930

Balfour, Michael, *The Kaiser and his Times*, Cresset Press, 1964

Bassett, R., *1931: Political Crisis*, Macmillan, 1958

Beaverbrook, Lord, *Men and Power, 1917–1918*, Hutchinson, 1956

Beaverbrook, Lord, *The Abdication of King Edward VIII*, Hamish Hamilton, 1956

Bell, G. K. A., *Randall Davidson, Archbishop of Canterbury*, 3rd ed., O.U.P., 1952

Birkenhead, Lord, *Walter Monckton*, Weidenfeld and Nicolson, 1969

Blake, Robert, *The Unknown Prime Minister*, Eyre & Spottiswoode, 1955

Blake, Robert, *Disraeli*, Eyre & Spottiswoode, 1966

Brett, Maurice V. (Editor), *Reginald, Viscount Esher, Letters and Journals*, 4 vols., Ivor Nicholson & Watson, 1934

---

* The Fontana Library edition, 1963, has a brilliant and important Introduction by Mr R. H. S. Crossman.

Cecil, Lady Gwendolin, *Life of Lord Salisbury*, 3 vols., Hodder
    & Stoughton, 1921
Chamberlain, Sir Austen, *Politics from Inside*, Cassell, 1936
Churchill, R. S., *Lord Derby*, Heinemann, 1959
Churchill, R. S., *Winston S. Churchill*, Vol. 2, *Young States-
    man, 1901–14*, Heinemann, 1967
Churchill, W. S., *Great Contemporaries*, Fontana Books ed.,
    1959
Crewe, Marquess of, *Lord Rosebery*, 2 vols., John Murray, 1931
Dugdale, Blanche E. C., *Arthur James Balfour*, 2 vols.,
    Hutchinson, 1936
Ensor, Sir Robert, *England 1870–1914*, Clarendon Press, 1936
Farrer, J. A., *The Monarchy in Politics*, T. Fisher Unwin, 1917
Fitzroy, Sir Almeric, *Memoirs*, 2 vols., Hutchinson, 1925
Fulford, Roger, *Hanover to Windsor*, Batsford, 1960
Gladstone, Viscount, *After Thirty Years*, Macmillan, 1928
Gollin, Alfred, *Arthur Balfour and Imperial Preference*, A.
    Blond, 1965
Gore, John, *King George V: A Personal Memoir*, John Murray,
    1941
Guedalla, Philip (Editor), *The Queen and Mr Gladstone*,
    2 vols., Hodder & Stoughton, 1933
Gwynn, Steven, and Tuckwell, Gertrude, *Life of Sir Charles
    W. Dilke*, 2 vols., John Murray, 1918
Hardie, Frank, *The Political Influence of Queen Victoria,
    1861–1901*, 3rd ed., Frank Cass, 1963
Hardinge, Sir Arthur, *Life of 4th Earl of Carnarvon*, 3 vols.,
    O.U.P., 1925
Hardinge, Helen, *Loyal to Three Kings*, William Kimber, 1967
James, R. Rhodes, *Rosebery*, Weidenfeld & Nicolson, 1963
Jenkins, Roy, *Mr Balfour's Poodle*, Heinemann, 1954
Jenkins, Roy, *Dilke*, Collins, 1958
Jenkins, Roy, *Asquith*, Collins, 1964

Jennings, W. I., *Cabinet Government*, 3rd ed., Cambridge University Press, 1959

Keir, D. L., *Constitutional History of Modern Britain*, A. & C. Black, 1938

Kennedy, A. L., *Salisbury, 1830–1903*, John Murray, 1953

Lee, Sir Sidney, *King Edward VII:* Vol. 1, *From Birth to Accession*, Macmillan, 1925; Vol. 2, *The Reign*, Macmillan, 1927

The Letters of Queen Victoria, 1st series, 3 vols., 1837–61, editors: A. C. Benson and Lord Esher, John Murray, 1907; 2nd and 3rd series, 6 vols., 1862–1901, editor: G. E. Buckle, John Murray, 1926–32

Longford, Elizabeth, *Victoria, R.I.*, Weidenfeld & Nicolson, 1964

Lutyens, Mary (Editor), *Lady Lytton's Court Diary, 1895–1899*, Hart-Davis, 1961

McClintock, M. H., *The Queen Thanks Sir Howard*, John Murray, 1943

Mackintosh, J. P., *The British Cabinet*, Stevens, 1962

Magnus, Sir Philip, *Gladstone*, John Murray, 1934

Magnus, Sir Philip, *King Edward VII*, John Murray, 1964

Mallett, Victor, *Life with Queen Victoria*, John Murray, 1968

Monypenny, W. F., and Buckle, G. E., *Life of Disraeli*, 2nd ed., 2 vols., John Murray, 1929

Morley, Viscount, *Life of Gladstone*, 3 vols., Macmillan, 1903

Mowat, C. L., *Britain between the Wars, 1918–1940*, Methuen, 1955

Newton, Lord, *Lord Lansdowne*, Macmillan, 1929

Nicolson, Sir Harold, *King George V, His Life and Reign*, Constable, 1952

Ponsonby, Arthur, *Henry Ponsonby*, Macmillan, 1943

Ponsonby, Sir Frederick, *Sidelights on Queen Victoria*, Macmillan, 1930

Ponsonby, Sir Frederick, *Recollections of Three Reigns*, Eyre & Spottiswoode, 1931

Ponsonby, Magdalen, *Mary Ponsonby*, John Murray, 1927

Pope-Hennessy, James, *Lord Crewe*, Constable, 1955

Pope-Hennessy, James, *Queen Mary*, Allen & Unwin, 1959

Quarterly Review, April 1901, 'The Character of Queen Victoria'

Ramm, Agatha (Editor), *The Political Correspondence of Mr Gladstone and Lord Granville*: Vols. 1 and 2, 1868–76, Royal Historical Society, 1952; Vols. 3 and 4, 1876–86, Clarendon Press, 1962

St Aubyn, Giles, *The Royal George*, Constable, 1963

Strachey, Lytton, *Queen Victoria*, Chatto & Windus, 1921

Taylor, A. J. P., *Englishmen and Others*, Hamish Hamilton, 1936

Taylor, A. J. P., *English History, 1914–1945*, Clarendon Press, 1965

Weston, C. C., 'The Royal Mediation in 1884', *English Historical Review*, No. 323, Longman, April 1967

Wheeler-Bennett, Sir John, *King George VI, His Life and Reign*, Macmillan, 1958

Windsor, The Duke of, *A King's Story*, Cassell, 1951

Windsor, The Duke of, *Crown and People, 1902–1953*, Cassell, 1953

Woodward, Sir Llewellyn, *The Age of Reform, 1815–1870*, 2nd ed., Clarendon Press, 1962

Young, G. M., *Victorian England: Portrait of an Age*, o.u.p., 1936

Young, Kenneth, *Arthur James Balfour*, G. Bell, 1963

References

The nine volumes of *The Letters of Queen Victoria* are referred to as *L.*, followed by the volume number

When the name of author or editor appears without further explanation the relevant work is that listed in the Bibliography

CHAPTER ONE (pages 1–10)

1 Public Records Act, 1967
2 *English History, 1914–1945*, 612
3 Brett, I, 284, and II, 2 and 4–5
4 James, 381
5 Hardie, 16–23
6 Cf. Longford, 282
7 Blake, *Disraeli*, 434
8 Cf. G. M. Trevelyan, *British History in the Nineteenth Century* (Longmans, 1922), 339
9 Magnus, *Gladstone*, 169
10 Bagehot, 262. Cf. below, p. 57, for Disraeli's making of the same point
11 Guedalla, I, 29

12 Woodward, 189, n. 1
13 For a summary of Bagehot's assessment, and comments on it, see Hardie, 23–7
14 Quoted in full, Nicolson, 62–3
15 *Ibid.*, 226
16 Lord Riddell, *More Pages from My Diary* (Country Life Ltd., 1934), 218
17 Cf. Jenkins, *Mr Balfour's Poodle*, 1
18 Guedalla, *Palmerston* (Benn, 1926), 455
19 Magnus, *Gladstone*, 172
20 Blake, *Disraeli*, 435

CHAPTER TWO (pages 11–39)

1 Blake, *Disraeli*, 436. Cf. above, p. 7
2 Cf. Longford, 78
3 Ramm, I, 171; Gladstone to Granville, 3.xii.70
4 Monypenny and Buckle, II, 755; Disraeli to Lady Bradford, 5.v.74
5 Ramm, II, 264; Gladstone to Granville, 1.x.71
6 Magnus, *Gladstone*, 211. Cf. also 207 and 298

7 Cf. A. Ponsonby, 193; Ponsonby to Edward Hamilton, 16.xii.82
8 Monypenny and Buckle, II, 1406
9 A. Ponsonby, 161; memo. to Ponsonby, Nov. 1878
10 Gwynn and Tuckwell, I, 286. Cf. below, p. 23
11 A. Ponsonby, 191; Queen to Ponsonby, 21.v.82
12 *Ibid.*, 197; Queen to Ponsonby, 23.ix.85

13 *Ibid.*, 270
14 Cf. below, p. 52
15 Ramm, I, XIII
16 A. Ponsonby, 191 (27.v.82)
17 *Ibid.*, 192 (16.xii.82). Cf. Bernard Holland, *The Life of Spencer Compton, 8th Duke of Devonshire* (Longmans, 1911), II, 214
18 Magnus, *Gladstone*, 349
19 Holland, II, 172–3
20 Cf. James, 125
21 Cf. A. Ponsonby, 276
22 James, 192–3
23 F. Ponsonby, *Recollections*, 41
24 Cf. Hardie, 106–7
25 Cf. *ibid.*, 107–12
26 A. Ponsonby, 176–7
27 Cf. *ibid.*, 174–5
28 Cf. Guedalla, I, 48
29 Magnus, *Gladstone*, 207, and cf. above, p. 12
30 Ramm, I, 39 (24.vii.69)
31 See below, pp. 59–62
32 Longford, 468
33 Hardinge, III, 181
34 *Ibid.*, 200
35 A. Ponsonby, 202–6
36 Quoted Gladstone, 407, 1
37 Longford, 491
38 *L.*, VII, 102 (11.iv.86)
39 Longford, 485
40 Quoted, *ibid.*, 489
41 *Ibid.*, 489
42 *L.*, VII, 128
43 Guedalla, II, 462; telegram to Gladstone, 28.i.92
44 Gladstone, 340
45 Cf. Hardie, 177–8
46 Cf. J. L. Hammond, *Gladstone and the Irish Nation* (Longmans, 1938), 436
47 Cecil Woodham-Smith, *The Great Hunger* (Hamish Hamilton, 1962), 399
48 See below, p. 103
49 G. M. Young, 79, 1
50 Pope-Hennessy, *Lord Crewe*, 43
51 See below, pp. 138–41, 161–3
52 *L.*, VI, 47 (1878)
53 A. Ponsonby, 178; cf. *L.*, VIII, 452 (21.xi.94)
54 Cf. Hardie, 177–8
55 Roger Fulford (Editor), *Dearest Mama* (Evans, 1968), 168
56 Crewe, I, 437
57 See below, p. 23
58 Brett, I, 269 (15.xi.00), Journal
59 Mallett, 186; Marie to Victor Mallett, 15.ii.00
60 Cf. Longford, 244
61 *L.*, V, 162; Queen to Lord Halifax, 1.xi.71
62 *L.*, VII, 582 (20.iii.90)
63 Brett, I, 409; Esher to Edward VII, 21.v.03
64 Guedalla, II, 37
65 *L.*, VIII, 488; Queen to Sir Arthur Bigge, 23.iii.95
66 A. Ponsonby, 190; Queen to Ponsonby, 13.viii.81
67 Cf. above, p. 15, and below, pp. 43–4
68 *L.*, VIII, 442; Bigge to Ponsonby, 3.xi.94
69 *Ibid.*, 431 (25.x.94); cf. Hardie, 107–111
70 Longford, 414, quoting Queen's Journal, 13.vi.78. Cf. Guedalla, I, 341–2
71 *L.*, VIII, 414; Queen to Rosebery, 13.vii.94
72 *L.*, V, 131; Queen to Gladstone, 23.ix.71
73 *L.*, IX, 409; Queen to Salisbury, 20.x.99
74 Hardie, 137–8
75 Guedalla, II, 105; Queen to Gladstone, 20.vi.80. See also Hardie, 139
76 Magnus, *Edward VII*, 73–4
77 Longford, 536
78 A. Ponsonby, 280
79 Guedalla, I, 227; Queen to Gladstone, 6.v.70

80 Martin, *Queen Victoria as I Knew Her* (William Blackwood, 1908), 69–70; Queen to Sir Theodore Martin, 29.v.70

81 Mallett, 184; Marie Mallett's journal, 12.ii.00. Cf. Longford, 355

82 Guedalla, II, 152; Queen to Gladstone, 16.iv.81. Cf. A. Ponsonby, 48–9, and below, p. 67

83 A. Ponsonby, 49

84 Longford, 281

85 *Ibid.*, 554

86 A. L. Rowse, *The Question of the House of Lords* (Hogarth Press, 1934), 17. Cf. the entry under *Lords, House of*, in the index to Sir Robert Ensor's *England, 1870–1914*

87 Cf. above, p. 13

88 Gwynn and Tuckwell, I, 286. Cf. above, p. 13, and below, p. 46

89 Quoted by R. W. Seton-Watson, *Disraeli, Gladstone and The Eastern Question* (London, 1935), 221

90 Longford, 412

91 Magnus, *Edward VII*, 439

92 A. Ponsonby, 187

93 Cf. below, pp. 28–9

94 Monypenny and Buckle, II, 1303; Queen to Disraeli, 21.v.79

95 Blake, *Disraeli*, 674

96 A. J. Balfour, 113–14

97 Ramm, I, 94; Granville to Gladstone, 6.iii.70

98 *Ibid.*; Granville to Gladstone, 21.xi.69

99 *L.*, VI, 37–8; Queen to Disraeli, 28.vii.79

100 Cf. below, p. 53

101 Hardinge, II, 131

102 Longford, 400

103 Michael Holroyd, *Lytton Strachey* (Heinemann, 1967), I, 450, I

104 Mallett, 97; Marie Mallett to her husband, 12.xi.96

105 Cf. above, p. 11

106 Longford, 435

107 A. Ponsonby, 97

108 Fulford, 112–13

109 *L.*, VI, 378 (14.xii.82)

110 Cf. above, p. 23

111 *L.*, VI, 485 (15.iii.84)

112 *L.*, VI, 47; Queen to Lady Ely, 21.ix.79

113 Cf. above, p. 19

114 *L.*, VI, 447 (22.x.82)

115 Cf. Ensor, 192

116 *L.*, VI, 451 (30.x.83)

117 Monypenny and Buckle, II, 788–789 (24.xi.75)

118 *L.*, V, 428 (26.xi.75)

119 *L.*, IV, 243 (27.xi.64)

120 Cf. above, p. 7

121 A. Ponsonby, 171; to Lady Ponsonby, 20.x.79

122 Farrer, 304

123 *Ibid.*, 300

124 Cf. above, p. 12

125 *L.*, V, 504; Queen to Beaconsfield, 18.xii.76

126 *Ibid.*, 538 (4.vi.77)

127 Cf. A. Ponsonby, 156

128 Monypenny and Buckle, II, 979; Disraeli to Lady Bradford, 16.xii.76

129 A. Ponsonby, 170–1; to Lady Ponsonby, 20.x.79

130 *L.*, VI, 75 (8.iv.80)

131 Cf. above, p. 15

132 *L.*, VIII, 58 (14.xi.86)

133 Hardie, 75–7

134 Fitzroy, II, 656–7

135 F. Ponsonby, *Sidelights*, 144

136 Brett, I, 79; Journal, 6.i.80

137 Longford, 439

138 A. Ponsonby, 231

139 Cf. F. Ponsonby, *Recollections*, 43

140 *L.*, VI, 597 (5.ii.85)

141 Lutyens, 148

142 Cf. D. W. Brogan, *The Development of Modern France, 1870–1939* (H. Hamilton, Revised Edition, 1967), 334, 3

143 Cf. Hardie, 83

144 Martin, 89–90 (10.ii.74)

145 Monypenny and Buckle, II, 1399–1400 (9.iv.80)

146 *L.*, VI, 706 (3.xii.85)

147 Newton, 100

148 Longford, 518; to the Empress Frederick, 6.vii.92

149 *L.*, VIII, 545 (5.viii.95)

150 Strachey, 300

151 *L.*, V, 315 (11.xi.74)

152 A. Ponsonby, 182

153 Cf. above, p. 32

154 *L.*, VI, 73 (3.iv.80)

155 F. Ponsonby, *Sidelights*, 171 (15.vii.84)

156 *L.*, VI, 523 (25.vii.84)

157 *L.*, IV, 605 (9.vi.69); cf. below, p. 62

158 F. Ponsonby, *Sidelights*, 171 (15.vii.84)

159 *L.*, VI, 547 (7.x.84)

160 Cf. above, p. 32

161 A. Ponsonby, 201; Queen to Ponsonby, 19.xii.85

162 *L.*, VI, 712 (20.xii.85)

163 *Ibid.*, 714 (22.xii.85)

164 *L.*, VII, 23 (27.i.86). Cf. A. Ponsonby, 182

165 *L.*, VIII, 111 (25.iv.86)

166 Cf. *L.*, VII, 17 (24.i.86)

167 Longford, 70

168 See above, p. 33

169 A. Ponsonby, 172

170 *Ibid.*, 214–15

171 *Ibid.*, 221

172 *Ibid.*, 183; Queen to Ponsonby, 13.iii.80

173 Strachey, 267

CHAPTER THREE (pages 40–77)

1 Bagehot, 40

2 *Walter Bagehot* (Eyre & Spottiswoode, 1959), 65–6

3 F. G. Bettany, *Stewart Headlam* (John Murray, 1926), 84

4 Cf. below, p. 82

5 Cecil, III, 86. Cf. also Kingsley Martin, *Edinburgh Review*, April 1926, 383

6 Longford, 573

7 Cf. above, pp. 24–5

8 *L.*, IV, 186 (10.v.64)

9 *Ibid.*, 187 (12.v.64)

10 *Dearest Mama*, 339; Queen to Crown Princess of Russia, 31.v.64

11 *L.*, VIII, 297 (8.viii.93)

12 At Bradford (27.x.94)

13 *L.*, VIII, 492; Rosebery to Queen, 29.x.94

14 Cf. James, 361

15 Cf. Hardie, 108

16 Cf. below, pp. 48 and 51

17 *L.*, VIII, 442 (3.xi.94)

18 *Ibid.*, 440 (1.xi.94)

19 Askwith, *Lord James of Hereford* (Ernest Benn, 1930), 250

20 *L.*, IV, 505; Disraeli to Queen, 26.ii.68

21 *L.*, VI, 146–7; Disraeli to Queen, 23.ix.80

22 *Selected Speeches of Lord Beaconsfield*, II, 493 (3.iv.72)

23 Cf. above, p. 28

24 Bagehot, 67

25 A. Ponsonby, 237; Cromer to Ponsonby, 28.vi.92

26 Cf. above, p. 40

27 Cf. G. M. Young, 174

28 Cf. above, p. 13

29 Cf. above, p. 23

30 Gwynn and Tuckwell, I, 286

31 Guedalla, II, 130–1 (29.xii.80)

32 *Ibid.*, 132 (31.xii.80)

33 *Ibid.*, 161 (3.viii.81)

34 *Ibid.*, 43 (4.x.82)

35 See above, p. 31

36 *L.*, vi, 603; Ponsonby to Queen, 7.ii.85

37 Viscount Morley, *Recollections*, i, 278

38 A. Ponsonby, 191; Granville to Ponsonby, May, 1882

39 *L.*, vi, 619 (3.iii.85)

40 *L.*, vii, 23 (11.xi.86)

41 Cf. above, p. 31

42 Mackintosh, 238

43 Bagehot, 74

44 A. Ponsonby, 253

45 Gladstone, 141–2

46 Brett, i, 74; Journal, 19.ix.80

47 Ramm, iii, 311

48 Cf. above, p. 9

49 But cf. above, p. 49

50 *L.*, i, 276; Journal, 15.v.41

51 Sir Sidney Lee, *Queen Victoria* (Smith, Elder, 1904), 133–4

52 *L.*, ii, 91; Queen to Lord John Russell, 16.vii.46

53 F. Ponsonby, *Sidelights*, 184 (18.vii.64)

54 Cf. above, p. 43

55 *L.*, viii, 433 (27.x.94)

56 Cf. above, p. 43

57 *L.*, v, 379 (31.i.75)

58 *L.*, vi, 219 (15.v.81)

59 Magnus, *Gladstone*, 293

60 Cf. A. Ponsonby, 206–7

61 Cf. *ibid.*, 215–17

62 Cf. Hardie, 119–21

63 A. Ponsonby, 271

64 Cf. above, p. 25

65 *As We Were* (Longmans, 1930), 29

66 *L.*, vii, 615

67 See above, pp. 19–21

68 A. Ponsonby, 271

69 Herbert Morrison, *Government and Parliament* (o.u.p., 2nd edition, 1959), 81

70 *L.*, v, 348; Queen to Disraeli, 21.vii.74

71 F. Ponsonby, *Sidelights*, 184 (18.vii.74)

72 Cf. Longford, 305

73 A. Ponsonby, 217; Queen to Ponsonby, 10.viii.92

74 Bagehot, 67

75 See above, p. 46

76 A. Ponsonby, 80

77 See Hardie, 211–14, and F. Ponsonby, *Recollections*, 78–9

78 Cf. McClintock

79 Monypenny and Buckle, ii, 1022; Disraeli to Lady Bradford, June 1877

80 S. Childers, *Life of H. C. E. Childers* (John Murray, 1901), ii, 104

81 A. Ponsonby, 270; Harcourt to Ponsonby, 18.vi.82

82 Gladstone, 351–2

83 *Memories* (London, 1915), i, 183

84 Redesdale, *loc. cit.*

85 Bagehot, 30

86 Brett, i, 214; Journal, 16.v.98

87 *Ibid.*, 231; Esher to M. V. Brett, 15.v.99

88 Mallett, 5, 223

89 Fitzroy, i, 19

90 *L.*, ix, 604–12

91 Monypenny and Buckle, ii, 483–484

92 A. Ponsonby, 191; Queen to Ponsonby, 25.v.82

93 Jennings, 21, 340

94 F. Ponsonby, *Recollections*, 12

95 A. Ponsonby, 80

96 *Ibid.*, 297

97 Cf. above, p. 55

98 Brett, i, 187; Journal, 14.iii.95

99 Gladstone, 375

100 See above, p. 16

101 *L.*, vi, 561

102 Weston, 319

103 *Ibid.*, 296

104 Below, p. 109

105 *L.*, iv, 605 (9.vi.69)
106 See above, pp. 51–2
107 Cf. above, pp. 46–7
108 *L.*, vi, 76; Queen to Ponsonby, 8.iv.80
109 *L.*, vii, 279; Journal, 2.iii.87
110 *L.*, vi, 379; Gladstone to Queen, 14.vii.82
111 Guedalla, ii, 93; Queen to Gladstone, 30.iv.80
112 *L.*, viii, 529 (28.vi.95)
113 Jenkins, *Dilke*, 142
114 Kennedy, 157
115 Cf. above, p. 15
116 James, 187
117 Brett, i, 171
118 *L.*, vii, 42; Ponsonby to Queen, 3.ii.86
119 A. Ponsonby, 208
120 Cf. Hardie, 216–17
121 *L.*, vii, 95; Dilke to Granville, 2.v.80
122 *Ibid.*, 97; Dilke to Granville, 4.v.80
123 Guedalla, ii, 183 (26.iii.82)
124 *Ibid.*, ii, 220 (12.xii.82)
125 Jenkins, *Mr Balfour's Poodle*, 86–7
126 Guedalla, ii, 90; Queen to Gladstone, 27.iv.80
127 *Ibid.*, 225 (28.xii.82)
128 *Ibid.*, 226 (5.i.83)
129 Jenkins, *Mr Balfour's Poodle*, 154
130 Jenkins, *Dilke*, 20
131 H. Dalton, *Call Back Yesterday* (Frederick Muller, 1953), 15
132 *L.*, vii, 509; cipher telegram to Salisbury (9.vii.89)
133 *L.*, viii, 120; Queen to Ponsonby, 30.v.92
134 *Ibid.*, 138; Journal, 11.viii.92
135 *Ibid.*
136 *Ibid.*, 142; Ponsonby to Queen, 13.viii.92
137 A. L. Thorold, *The Life of Henry Labouchere* (Constable, 1913), 375

138 Cf. Jennings, 12–16
139 See above, pp. 23–4
140 See above, p. 49
141 A. Ponsonby, 254; Ponsonby to Gladstone, 13.vii.75
142 Cf. above, p. 22
143 Hardinge, iii, 103, 110
144 Cf. A. Ponsonby, 187
145 *The Letters of Disraeli to Lady Bradford and Lady Chesterfield*, edited by Lord Zetland (London, 1929), i, 129 (7.viii.74)
146 Cf. Farrer, 330
147 Jenkins, *Mr Balfour's Poodle*, 160
148 Cf. above, p. 22
149 Cecil, iii, 180
150 Sir Charles Mallett, *Herbert Gladstone: A Memoir* (Hutchinson, 1932), 97
151 Guedalla, ii, 9
152 Blake, *Disraeli*, 490
153 *Ibid.*, 278
154 Cf. Mackintosh, 123
155 Jennings, 372
156 Crewe, i, 165 (5.i.83), Rosebery's diary
157 A. Ponsonby, 257–8
158 Guedalla, ii, 67; Gladstone to Granville, 25.v.86
159 Gladstone, 352–3
160 *Eminent Victorians* (Phoenix Library edition), 265
161 Above, pp. 165–6
162 James, 365
163 Cf. Hammond, 329; Ramm, ii, 1 ff.; and A. Ponsonby, 208
164 *Gladstone* (London, 1933), 104
165 Gladstone, 114
166 A. Ponsonby, 166; to Lady Ponsonby, 30.vii.77
167 *Ibid.*, 164; to Lady Ponsonby, 16.viii.77
168 Monypenny and Buckle, ii, 754
169 Hardinge, ii, 356
170 Gladstone, 141
171 Cf., e.g. Guedalla, ii, 352

172 John Morley, *Walpole* (Macmillan, 1889), 157
173 Gladstone, 142
174 Hardinge, II, 372 (12.i.78)
175 See below, p. 84
176 Cf. above, p. 1
177 Cf. A. Ponsonby, 124
178 Longford, 375
179 Martin, 28
180 Monypenny and Buckle, II, 483
181 Ramm, II, 263; Gladstone to Granville, 29.ix.71
182 Bagehot, 53
183 See above, p. 66
184 Magnus, *Edward VII*, 3
185 Quoted Kingsley Martin, *The Crown and the Establishment* (Pelican edition, 1965), 46
186 A. V. Dicey, *Law of the Constitution* (Macmillan, 8th edition, 1927), 458
187 These lectures were published in *The Constitutional History of England* (Cambridge University Press, 1908). See p. 397
188 *Ibid.*, 401
189 Cf. above, p. 43
190 See above, pp. 23 and 46
191 Gwynn and Tuckwell, I, 286
192 Gladstone, XXVIII
193 Cf. Lee, I, 546
194 Gladstone, 335; memo. by Gladstone, 21.xii.71
195 A. Ponsonby, 190, 256; memo. by Ponsonby, 28.iii.81
196 M. Ponsonby, 68
197 Magnus, *Gladstone*, 427

CHAPTER FOUR (pages 78–115)

1 Cf. above, pp. 13, 23 and 46
2 Jenkins, *Mr Balfour's Poodle*, 143
3 Gwynn and Tuckwell, I, 500. Cf. Arthur Ponsonby's evaluation in *Henry Ponsonby*, 97
4 Below, p. 104
5 In Lord Edward Fitzmaurice's *Life of Lord Granville* (Longmans, 1905)
6 Fitzroy, I, 265
7 Gladstone, 141
8 F. Ponsonby, *Recollections*, 41
9 A. Ponsonby, 274
10 Gollin, 29, Knollys to Balfour, 22.x.02
11 *Ibid.*, 140–1
12 *Ibid.*, 159–60
13 *Ibid.*, 160
14 *Ibid.*, 163
15 *Ibid.*, 283
16 Cf. below, p. 94
17 Gollin, 178; King to Balfour, 1.x.03
18 Magnus, *Edward VII*, 294–5
19 *Ibid.*, 301–5
20 Fulford, 84
21 *Englishmen and Others*, 74
22 Lee, II, 43
23 *Ibid.*, 448
24 See below, pp. 118 and 132
25 Jenkins, *Dilke*, 144
26 Cf. James, 464
27 Mallett, 93–4; Marie Mallett to her husband, 28.x.96
28 Lee, I, 516
29 Magnus, *Edward VII*, 100
30 Cf. Brett, II, 460
31 Magnus, *Edward VII*, 147
32 Lee, II, 442
33 *Ibid.*, 78
34 James, 425
35 R. S. Churchill, *Winston S. Churchill*, II, 105
36 Cf. Fulford, 160; Gollin, 53; Lee, II, 448
37 Magnus, *Edward VII*, 349
38 Cf. R. S. Churchill, *Winston S. Churchill*, II, 107
39 *Ibid.*, 185
40 Lee, II, 482

41 James, 464, and Magnus, *Edward VII*, 421
42 James, 464
43 Magnus, *Edward VII*, 412
44 *Ibid.*, 421
45 Pope-Hennessy, *Lord Crewe*, 72-3; Knollys to Lord Crewe, 1.viii.09
46 Magnus, *Edward VII*, 430-1
47 Lee, 11, 475
48 *Ibid.*, 653
49 *Ibid.*, 712
50 Pope-Hennessy, *Lord Crewe*, 116, and Gore, 252
51 R. S. Churchill, *Winston S. Churchill*, 11, 327
52 Official information
53 Cf. above, p. 15
54 Pope-Hennessy, *Lord Crewe*, 72, 75
55 Magnus, *Edward VII*, 72
56 Lee, 1, 518
57 *Ibid.*, 199
58 See above, p. 11 and pp. 25-6
59 Magnus, *Edward VII*, 152
60 *Ibid.*, 174
61 *Ibid.*, 216
62 Crewe, 1, 204
63 Magnus, *Edward VII*, 247
64 *Ibid.*, 192
65 *Ibid.*, 190
66 Ramm, iv, 452; Gladstone to Granville, 11.vi.86
67 Magnus, *Edward VII*, 447
68 *Ibid.*, 352
69 Jenkins, *Asquith*, 235
70 Magnus, *Edward VII*, 353
71 Cf. Brett, 11, 228
72 Magnus, *Edward VII*, 355
73 Pope-Hennessy, *Lord Crewe*, 155
74 R. S. Churchill, *Winston S. Churchill*, 11, 107-8
75 Lee, 11, 665
76 *Ibid.*, 468, 652
77 Magnus, *Edward VII*, 350
78 *Ibid.*, 443
79 *Ibid.*, 425

80 *Ibid.*, 425-6. Cf. Brett, 11, 372
81 Magnus, *Edward VII*, 249
82 Lee, 11, 467
83 E. L. Woodward, *Great Britain and the German Navy* (o.u.p., 1935), 125
84 Magnus, *Edward VII*, 390
85 Magnus, *Gladstone*, 378
86 Lee, 11, 173. But cf. above, p. 79
87 Fitzroy, 1, 146, and Brett, 11, 1-2
88 Lee, 11, 173-4, 178; Gollin, 82-3
89 Lee, 11, 180
90 *Ibid.*, 478
91 Cf. above, p. 57
92 Fitzroy, 1, 247
93 Cf. Lee, 11, 4 and 36
94 Magnus, *Edward VII*, 280
95 K. Young, 227
96 Brett, 11, 107
97 Magnus, *Edward VII*, 283
98 Fitzroy, 1, 265
99 Brett, 11, 97
100 *Ibid.*, 265
101 Cf. below, p. 93
102 See above, p. 57
103 Cf. F. Ponsonby, *Recollections*, 102
104 Magnus, *Edward VII*, 283-4
105 Cf. *ibid.*, 280
106 Cf. above, p. 106
107 Cf. below, p. 100
108 Cf. Ensor, 569
109 Cf. Magnus, *Edward VII*, 390
110 Cf. Asquith, 11, 93
111 Magnus, *Edward VII*, 214
112 Asquith, 82
113 Cf. Ramm, 11, 306, 342
114 Jenkins, *Dilke*, 143
115 Magnus, *Edward VII*, 237
116 Cf. Ramm, 11, 289; Granville to Gladstone, 8.xii.71
117 A. Ponsonby, 102
118 Ramm, iv, 370; Granville to Gladstone, 12.vi.85
119 F. Ponsonby, *Recollections*, 273
120 Ramm, 1, 160; Granville to Gladstone, 18.xi.70

121 Magnus, *Edward VII*, 205. Cf. A. Ponsonby, 110–12; Sir Arthur Ellis to Sir Henry Ponsonby, 19.iv.89
122 Magnus, *Edward VII*, 299–300
123 *Ibid.*, 429
124 *Ibid.*, 335–6
125 Lee, II, 230. Cf. R. B. Haldane, *Autobiography* (Hodder & Stoughton, 1931), 207–8
126 K. Young, 197; Balfour to Lady Elcho, 10.ii.01
127 F. Ponsonby, *Recollections*, 275. Cf. Lee, II, 37, 455
128 Magnus, *Edward VII*, 322
129 Pope-Hennessy, *Lord Crewe*, 70–2
130 Above, p. 19
131 Magnus, *Edward VII*, 323
132 *Ibid.*
133 Lee, II, 93
134 *Ibid.*, 201
135 Fitzroy, I, 159
136 Cf. above, p. 81
137 Magnus, *Edward VII*, 278
138 *Ibid.*, 330
139 *Ibid.*, 331
140 *Ibid.*
141 *Ibid.*, 334
142 *Ibid.*, 333
143 *Ibid.*, 285
144 *Ibid.*, 284
145 *Ibid.*, 325
146 Quoted, *ibid.*, 284
147 Quoted, *ibid.*, 295
148 *Ibid.*
149 Quoted, *ibid.*, 296
150 *Ibid.*, 327
151 Cf. above, p. 20
152 Haldane, *Autobiography*, 142–3
153 Magnus, *Edward VII*, 347
154 Cf. Brett, II, 325
155 Magnus, *Edward VII*, 383, 387. Cf. Brett, II, 280
156 Cf. *ibid.*, 267
157 Magnus, *Edward VII*, 385
158 *Ibid.*, 402
159 Lee, II, 507
160 Magnus, *Edward VII*, 387
161 Cf. *ibid.*, xiii, 277
162 *Ibid.*, 358, 367; Lee, II, 99
163 Magnus, *Edward VII*, 366
164 Cf. *ibid.*, 373, and F. Ponsonby, *Recollections*, 129
165 Magnus, *Edward VII*, 375
166 *Ibid.*, 376
167 Brett, II, 210
168 *The World Crisis* (abridged and revised edition, 1931), 65
169 Magnus, *Edward VII*, 324
170 *Ibid.*
171 Cf. Brett, II, 460
172 Cf. above, p. 98
173 Magnus, *Edward VII*, 277
174 Brett, II, 322
175 Lee, II, 516, 539, 547
176 Brett, II, 322
177 Magnus, *Edward VII*, 408
178 *Ibid.*, 398
179 See above, p. 92
180 Quoted, Magnus, *Edward VII*, 410
181 *Ibid.*
182 *Ibid.*, 277
183 Jenkins, *Asquith*, 327
184 Sir Harold Nicolson, *Lord Carnock* (Constable, 1930), 275
185 Magnus, *Edward VII*, 395
186 Newton, 293; Balfour to Lansdowne, 11.i.15
187 Magnus, *Edward VII*, 336
188 Newton, 342
189 F. Ponsonby, *Recollections*, 173
190 Cf. Michael Balfour, 245
191 Lee, II, 223
192 Newton, 275–6
193 Magnus, *Edward VII*, 311
194 F. Ponsonby, *Recollections*, 170
195 Newton, 278
196 *Hanover to Windsor*, 161–2
197 Cf. Lee, I, 36
198 *Ibid.*, 780–4
199 Cf. above, p. 78
200 Lee, I, 246

201 *Ibid.*, 259
202 Magnus, *Edward VII*, 155
203 *Ibid.*
204 Jenkins, *Dilke*, 144
205 Magnus, *Edward VII*, 204
206 F. Ponsonby, *Recollections*, 182
207 Cf. Lytton Strachey in the *Daily Mail* (11.x.27), 10
208 Lutyens, 80
209 Cf. Magnus, *Edward VII*, 94, and Ensor, 568
210 A. G. Gardiner, *Life of Sir William Harcourt* (Constable, 1923), II, 336
211 Magnus, *Edward VII*, 361
212 *Ibid.*
213 *Ibid.*, 404
214 Ensor, 207
215 Quoted, Magnus, *Edward VII*, 395
216 See J. Holland Rose, *Origins of the War* (o.u.p., 1914), 62
217 Newton, 293
218 Lee, II, 675
219 Magnus, *Edward VII*, 315
220 Lee, II, 646 and 649
221 Ensor, 569. Cf. Michael Balfour, 308, 349, 351, 355
222 Nicolson, *Carnock*, 274. But cf. Magnus, *Edward VII*, 408
223 Cf. Fulford, 162
224 Magnus, *Edward VII*, 309, 352. Cf. R. S. Churchill, *Winston S. Churchill*, II, 217–19
225 Cf. above, p. 93, and Fulford, 162, 1
226 See above, p. 39

227 Cf. Fulford, 37
228 Cf. Magnus, *Edward VII*, 354, 356
229 Lee, II, 460–3
230 *Ibid.*, 460
231 Hardie, 58–60
232 Jenkins, *Mr Balfour's Poodle*, 25
233 Lee, II, 658–9
234 Jenkins, *Mr Balfour's Poodle*, 37
235 Newton, 368–9; memo. by Lansdowne, 12.x.08
236 Magnus, *Edward VII*, 434
237 Brett, II, 373
238 *Ibid.*, 404
239 Lee, II, 665
240 Jenkins, *Mr Balfour's Poodle*, 37, 59
241 Magnus, *Edward VII*, 437, and Jenkins, *Asquith*, 200–1
242 Brett, II, 411
243 Jenkins, *Asquith*, 203
244 *Ibid.*, 202
245 Given in Jenkins, *Asquith*, 539–542
246 Magnus, *Edward VII*, 453
247 Cf. Brett, III, 155
248 Jenkins, *Asquith*, 202–3
249 Brett, II, 424
250 Jenkins, *Asquith*, 207; cf. *Mr Balfour's Poodle*, 80–1
251 Jenkins, *Asquith*, 231
252 R. S. Churchill, *Winston S. Churchill*, II, 347
253 Jenkins, *Asquith*, 211
254 Lytton Strachey, in the *Daily Mail*, 11.x.27, 10
255 *Fifty Years of Parliament*, II, 87

CHAPTER FIVE (pages 116–169)

1 R. S. Churchill, *Winston S. Churchill*, II, 343
2 Cf. Nicolson, 233, 251, 253, 415; Brett, III, 131, 162; Viscount Templewood, *Nine Troubled Years* (Collins, 1954), 159–60
3 Margot Asquith, quoted Jenkins, *Mr Balfour's Poodle*, 123
4 Mallett, xxi
5 Nicolson, 138–9
6 Brett, III, 57
7 Jenkins, *Mr Balfour's Poodle*, 168

8 Nicolson, 149
9 Jenkins, *Mr Balfour's Poodle*, 100
10 See above, p. 114
11 A. Ponsonby, 103; Knollys to Ponsonby, 8.xii.72
12 Nicolson, 133
13 Cf. below, p. 160
14 Nicolson, 134
15 *Ibid.*, 134
16 *Ibid.*, 130
17 *Ibid.*, 136
18 Asquith, II, 109
19 Violet Bonham-Carter, *Winston Churchill as I Knew Him* (Eyre & Spottiswoode and Collins, 1965), 202
20 Brett, III, 43
21 Cf. above, pp. 73–4
22 Nicolson, 137
23 Brett, III, 65
24 W. S. Churchill, 262
25 Gore, 412
26 Jenkins, *Asquith*, 221
27 Nicolson, 137–8
28 Gore, 254
29 Nicolson, 139
30 Jenkins, *Mr Balfour's Poodle*, 168
31 Nicolson, 138
32 W. S. Churchill, 262
33 Magnus, *Edward VII*, 460
34 Official information
35 Brett, II, 458
36 Nicolson, 129
37 Cf. F. Ponsonby, *Recollections*, 102–3
38 Magnus, *Edward VII*, 460
39 Nicolson, 135
40 *Ibid.*, 149
41 R. S. Churchill, *Lord Derby*, 127
42 Official information
43 Magnus, *Edward VII*, 460. Cf. Brett, III, 145
44 Nicolson, 130
45 See above, p. 112
46 Jenkins, *Mr Balfour's Poodle*, 145
47 Nicolson, 162
48 See above, p. 120
49 Pope-Hennessy, *Lord Crewe*, 124; Crewe to Hardinge
50 Cf. Newton, 424
51 See Dugdale, II, 67; Balfour to Long, September 1911, and cf. Brett, III, 43–4
52 Jenkins, *Mr Balfour's Poodle*, 132. Cf. Brett, III, 40, 43, and Newton, 408
53 *Chapters of Autobiography*, 179
54 Newton, 410
55 Jenkins, *Asquith*, 229
56 Nicolson, 154
57 *Ibid.*
58 *Ibid.*, 155
59 Jenkins, *Asquith*, 235
60 *Ibid.*, 231
61 Jenkins, *Mr Balfour's Poodle*, 166
62 Nicolson, 149
63 *Ibid.*, 219
64 *Ibid.*, 117, 156
65 *Ibid.*, 200
66 *Ibid.*
67 Brett, III, 117
68 Chamberlain, 486–7
69 Cf. above, p. 118
70 Nicolson, 201
71 *Ibid.*
72 Dugdale, II, 100–1
73 Cf. F. Ponsonby, *Recollections*, 289
74 Extensively quoted in Nicolson, 234, n. 1
75 Blake, 229
76 Nicolson, 201
77 *Ibid.*, 222. Cf. Blake, 154–5
78 Quoted in full by Nicolson, 223–224
79 Quoted in full by Jenkins, *Asquith*, 541–9
80 *Ibid.*, 234
81 *Ibid.*, 236
82 *Ibid.*, 545
83 Cf. above, p. 132
84 Nicolson, 223
85 *Ibid.*, 225
86 Bell, 721

87 Quoted in full, Nicolson, 225–9
88 Brett, III, 152
89 Bell, 721
90 For this interview, see Nicolson, 233–4
91 *Ibid.*, 232
92 For the King's attitude to Asquith, see Nicolson, 229; Jenkins, *Asquith*, 454; Brett, III, 170. For his attitude to Bonar Law, see Nicolson, *loc. cit.*; Jenkins, *Asquith*, 296, 455
93 Cf. Blake, 134
94 Cf. Fitzroy, I, 457–8
95 Jenkins, *Asquith*, 286, 1
96 *Ibid.*
97 Brett, III, 161
98 *Ibid.*, 162
99 Nicolson, 235
100 *Ibid.*, 233
101 Cf. Brett, III, 147, and Jenkins, *Asquith*, 302
102 Jenkins, *Asquith*, 315
103 Ensor, 454
104 Blake, 135, 137
105 Bell, 729
106 For the text of his speech, see Nicolson, 242, 2
107 Jenkins, *Asquith*, 319, and Bonham-Carter, 301
108 Cf. Jenkins, *Asquith*, 321
109 Nicolson, 243
110 Jenkins, *Asquith*, 321; cf. above, pp. 138–9
111 Lord Ullswater, *A Speaker's Commentaries* (Edwin Arnold, 1925), II, 164
112 See above, p. 133
113 Nicolson, 248
114 For examples, *ibid.*, 255
115 Below, p. 181
116 *Great Contemporaries*, 261
117 Nicolson, 197
118 Cf. below, p. 181
119 Lord David Cecil, *Max* (Constable, 1964), 331
120 *Ibid.*, 435

121 Reprinted in *Englishmen and Others*, 70–5
122 Nicolson, 212
123 *Ibid.*, 255
124 *Ibid.*, 317
125 *Ibid.*, 272
126 *Ibid.*, 347
127 *Ibid.*, 348
128 Mackintosh, 576
129 Nicolson, 319–20
130 *Ibid.*, 408–9
131 Jenkins, *Asquith*, 483
132 Nicolson, 331
133 Jenkins, *Asquith*, 481
134 *Ibid.*, 505
135 Nicolson, 264, 1
136 *Ibid.*, 264
137 Magnus, *Edward VII*, 372. Cf. Brett, II, 220
138 Brett, II, 220, 224
139 Nicolson, 251–2
140 Magnus, *Edward VII*, 426
141 Nicolson, 504
142 *Ibid.*, 507
143 F. Ponsonby, *Recollections*, 282
144 Cf. W. S. Churchill, 261, and Brett, II, 433
145 Jenkins, *Asquith*, 282
146 *Ibid.*, 296
147 Nicolson, 389
148 *Ibid.*, 492
149 *Ibid.*, 432
150 *Ibid.*, 340
151 *Ibid.*, 389
152 *Ibid.*, 492
153 *Memories* (Collins, 1951), 107–8
154 Nicolson, 121–2
155 Brett, IV, 296; to Thomas Jones, 9.x.24
156 Nicolson, 510
157 Jenkins, *Asquith*, 235, n. 1
158 Nicolson, 383. Cf. Taylor, *English History, 1914–45*, 208–9
159 *Ibid.*, 382, 1, and 434
160 *Ibid.*, 384
161 R. S. Churchill, *Lord Derby*, 550
162 Nicolson, 400, 1

163 *Ibid.*, 400
164 *Ibid.*, 384
165 *Ibid.*, 389. Cf. above, pp. 146–7
166 *Memoirs*, 343–4
167 Nicolson, 447
168 *Retrospect*, 168
169 Templewood, *Nine Troubled Years*, 18
170 Nicolson, 448
171 *Ibid.*, 449
172 *Ibid.*, 454
173 *Ibid.*, 461
174 Bassett, 128
175 Nicolson, 461
176 Bassett, 130
177 Nicolson, 464
178 *Memoirs*, 221–2
179 *Government and Parliament*, 77–8
180 Nicolson, 493
181 Cf. Taylor, *Englishmen and Others*, 72
182 Nicolson, 506
183 Jenkins, *Asquith*, 401
184 A. J. P. Taylor, 'Politics in The First World War' (Raleigh Lecture on History for 1959, reprinted from the *Proceedings of the British Academy*, in *Politics in War-Time*) (Hamish Hamilton, 1964), 11–44
185 Brett, II, 251. For Joseph Chamberlain's views on the point, see R. S. Churchill, *Winston S. Churchill*, II, 28
186 Nicolson, 260–1
187 Cf. Brett, III, 235, 247
188 Nicolson, 266–7, and Jenkins, *Asquith*, 342–3
189 Nicolson, 268–9
190 Duff Cooper, *Haig* (Faber and Faber, 1935), 104
191 Nicolson, 288
192 *War Memories*, IV, 2274; Popular Edition (Odhams Press, 1938), 1371
193 Brett, IV, 58

194 *World Crisis*, IV, 386
195 Nicolson, 303–4
196 Lee, II, 80
197 Nicolson, 303–4
198 *Ibid.*, 305–6
199 *Ibid.*, 319
200 *Ibid.*, 321
201 *Ibid.*
202 Cf. Brett, III, 311
203 Nicolson, 66–8. Cf. Magnus, *Edward VII*, 292
204 Brett, III, 17
205 Nicolson, 141, 218, 474
206 *Ibid.*, 267–8
207 *Ibid.*, 474
208 Magnus, *Edward VII*, 397
209 *Ibid.*, 292
210 *War Memoirs*, I
211 II, 162–3
212 Nicolson, 252. Cf. below, p. 166
213 The Duke of Windsor, *Crown and People*, 30
214 Nicolson, 413
215 *Ibid.*, 175
216 Cf. above, p. 56
217 Nicolson, 175
218 *Ibid.*
219 *Ibid.*, 181
220 *Ibid.*, 176
221 *Ibid.*, 371
222 *Hanover to Windsor*, 87
223 Above, p. 102
224 Brett, I, 161; Journal, 28.viii.92
225 Cf. Nicolson, 121, 157
226 See above, p. 102
227 See above, p. 127
228 Nicolson, 133
229 *Ibid.*, 153
230 Cf. above, pp. 132, 139
231 *Memories and Reflections*, II, 109
232 Nicolson, 289–91
233 *Ibid.*, 465–6
234 *Ibid.*, 403, 413
235 *Ibid.*, 418
236 Cf. above, p. 144
237 Nicolson, 418–19. Cf. Taylor, *English History*, 247

238 F. Ponsonby, *Recollections*, 62
239 Brett, I, 258; Esher to M. V. Brett, I.iii.00
240 Nicolson, 57
241 *Ibid.*, 148
242 *Ibid.*, 353
243 Cf. Mowat, 84
244 Nicolson, 354
245 Fitzroy, II, 719
246 Taylor, *English History*, 157
247 Fitzroy, II, 719
248 Nicolson, 358
249 *Ibid.*, 359
250 Martin, v, 418–26. Cf. 'How the Prince Consort Saved the United States' by Sir John Wheeler-Bennett, in *A Wreath to Clio* (Macmillan, 1967), 110–27
251 Jenkins, *Mr Balfour's Poodle*, 133
252 Cf. above, p. 54
253 Cf. above, p. 109
254 See below, p. 172
255 *Hanover to Windsor*, 185
256 *Ibid.*
257 *Ibid.*, 184
258 *Ibid.*, 187
259 Cf. above, p. 143
260 Cf. Magnus, *Edward VII*, 237
261 Nicolson, 385

262 *Ibid.*, 162
263 *Ibid.*, 317
264 *Ibid.*, 342
265 H. R. Winkler, *Great Britain in The Twentieth Century* (American Historical Association, 1960)
266 Cf. W. S. Churchill, 259
267 *Ibid.*, 260
268 See above, p. 128
269 Cf. above, pp. 155–6; and compare K. Martin, *The Crown and the Establishment*, 95–101
270 F. Ponsonby, *Recollections*, 285
271 Nicolson, 477–82
272 *English History, 1914–1945*, 473
273 *Ibid.*, 403
274 Lord Birkenhead, *Halifax* (Hamish Hamilton, 1965), 171
275 Nicolson, 384–5
276 Cf. above, p. 64
277 Cf. above, pp. 83–4
278 Raymond Postgate, *Life of George Lansbury* (Longmans, 1951), 225
279 *Ibid.*, 151–2
280 Cf. above, p. 90
281 Nicolson, 202–3
282 *Ibid.*, 360
283 *Ibid.*, 311
284 Cf. above, pp. 144, 161

CHAPTER SIX (pages 170–186)

1 *A King's Story*, 310–11
2 Cf. above, p. 158
3 *A King's Story*, 296
4 *The Crown and the Establishment*, 105
5 *A King's Story*, 257
6 Hugh Dalton, *The Fateful Years* (Frederick Muller, 1957)
7 Thomas Jones, *A Diary with Letters, 1931–50* (O.U.P., 1954), 303; diary, 11.i.37
8 Birkenhead, 159
9 Cf. Jones, *A Diary*, 228, and *A King's Story*, 311

10 *Ibid.*, 377
11 *Ibid.*, 341, 1
12 *Cabinet Government*, 335
13 Dalton, *Fateful Years*, 113; Dalton to G. F. Hudson, 11.xii.36
14 *A King's Story*, 366
15 *Ibid.*, 324
16 *Ibid.*, 351–2
17 *Ibid.*, 324
18 *Ibid.*, 352
19 Cf. Birkenhead, 138
20 *The Abdication of King Edward VIII* (Hamish Hamilton, 1966), 79

21 G. M. Young, *Stanley Baldwin* (Rupert Hart-Davis, 1952), 241
22 Private notes of Sir Edward Peacock, quoted Birkenhead, 144
23 Private notes of Sir Edward Peacock, quoted Birkenhead, 147
24 See above, p. 171
25 *A King's Story*, 257
26 *Crown and Parliament*, 41
27 *A King's Story*, 260
28 *Ibid.*
29 *Ibid.*
30 Quoted Wheeler-Bennett, 154 and Nicolson, 366 (27.iv.23)
31 R. J. Minney, *The Private Papers of Hore-Belisha* (Collins, 1960), 238; diary, 16.ix.39
32 Cf. Wheeler-Bennett, 300
33 See above, pp. 174-5
34 Cf. Taylor, *Politics in War-Time*, 204
35 Wheeler-Bennett, 710
36 *Ibid.*, 293-4
37 Alexander, Grand Duke of Russia, *Once a Grand Duke*, quoted R. K. Massie, *Nicholas and Alexandra* (Gollancz, 1968), 41
38 Wheeler-Bennett, 348
39 *Ibid.*, 359
40 *Ibid.*, 361-2
41 *Ibid.*, 402
42 *Ibid.*, 403
43 *Ibid.*, 362, 1
44 *Ibid.*, 392
45 *Ibid.*, 389
46 *Ibid.*, 392
47 Lord Moran, *Winston Churchill: The Struggle for Survival* (Constable, 1966), 14
48 Wheeler-Bennett, 419-20
49 *Ibid.*, 419
50 *Ibid.*, 424
51 Cf. above, pp. 101-2
52 Wheeler-Bennett, 422
53 *Ibid.*, 490-1
54 *Ibid.*, 454-5
55 *Ibid.*, 459-60
56 *Ibid.*, 482-4
57 *Ibid.*, 493
58 *Ibid.*, 494-6
59 *Ibid.*, 496-7
60 *Ibid.*, 506
61 *Ibid.*
62 See above, pp. 141-2
63 Nicolson, 249
64 Wheeler-Bennett, 415
65 *Ibid.*, 438
66 *Ibid.*, 595
67 *Ibid.*, 601-6
68 *Ibid.*, 439-40
69 Birkenhead, 454
70 Taylor, *English History*, 473
71 Dalton, *Fateful Years*, 306-7, 309
72 Wheeler-Bennett, 447
73 *Ibid.*, 536
74 *Ibid.*
75 *Ibid.*, 537
76 *Ibid.*, 364
77 Beaverbrook, *Abdication*, 109
78 Lord Attlee, on BBC TV (16.x.64). Cf. Wheeler-Bennett, 638
79 *Ibid.*, 664-5
80 *Ibid.*, 652
81 *Ibid.*
82 Cf. above, p. 147
83 Wheeler-Bennett, 653
84 *Ibid.*
85 *Ibid.*, 650, 706
86 *Ibid.*, 653
87 *Ibid.*, 650
88 *Ibid.*, 649
89 Cf. above, pp. 167-8
90 Wheeler-Bennett, 336
91 *Ibid.*, 681
92 *Ibid.*, 703
93 *Ibid.*, 706
94 See above, p. 183
95 Wheeler-Bennett, 700-2
96 Cf. above, p. 177
97 Wheeler-Bennett, 630

Index